# This Present Darkness

# This Present Darkness

Meet Me on the Battlefield

KRISTEN WELCH

*Foreword by Abraham Ruelas*

WIPF & STOCK · Eugene, Oregon

THIS PRESENT DARKNESS
Meet Me on the Battlefield

Copyright © 2021 Kristen Welch. All rights reserved. Except for brief quotations in critical publications or reviews, no part of this book may be reproduced in any manner without prior written permission from the publisher. Write: Permissions, Wipf and Stock Publishers, 199 W. 8th Ave., Suite 3, Eugene, OR 97401.

Wipf & Stock
An Imprint of Wipf and Stock Publishers
199 W. 8th Ave., Suite 3
Eugene, OR 97401

www.wipfandstock.com

PAPERBACK ISBN: 978-1-7252-9296-3
HARDCOVER ISBN: 978-1-7252-9297-0
EBOOK ISBN: 978-1-7252-9298-7

08/17/21

For my beloved father, Norman Dale Scott

"For once you have fallen low. Let us see in the future how high you can rise."

Sherlock Holmes from "The Adventure of the Three Students" by Arthur Conan Doyle

Holmes is often recognized for his contributions to the birth of forensic science. What he is less known for, but what you can find in most stories with him in it, is evidence of his forgiving spirit and his relentless faith that even if you have made a mistake, in the future you can do better. He was one of my father's favorite fictional characters, and, like Holmes, his faith in the potential of others was generous and inspiring.

# Contents

| | | |
|---|---|---|
| Foreword by Abraham Ruelas | | ix |
| Preface | | xi |
| Acknowledgments | | xxi |
| Introduction | | xxiii |
| 1 | Mystics, Mothers in Israel, Exhorters, and Laborers in Christ<br>Women Preachers, First-Wave Feminism, and the Right to Speak | 1 |
| 2 | The Role of Education in First- and Second-Wave Feminism<br>Bluestockings, Literary Societies, and the Transition from "Butterflies to Eagles" | 33 |
| 3 | "What Shall I Say with Regard to Daughters?"<br>Politics and Feminism | 54 |
| 4 | The Ultimate Feminist DIY Project<br>Constructing Realities in the Age of the Cyborg | 78 |
| 5 | "She Gets Up While It Is Still Night"<br>Theology and Feminism | 102 |
| 6 | Tallyho on all the Ballyhoo!<br>The Anti-Feminists and the Treachery of Visual Culture | 133 |
| 7 | Making Decisions about the Future<br>Defining Yourself, Choosing a Program, Entering the Profession | 150 |
| Appendix A | | 163 |
| Appendix B | | 174 |

| | |
|---|---:|
| Appendix C | 180 |
| Appendix D | 195 |
| Appendix E | 204 |
| Appendix F | 211 |
| Appendix G | 217 |
| Bibliography | 223 |

# Foreword

In a meeting over coffee at a Society for Pentecostal Studies conference, Professor Kristen Welch approached me with an idea: "Let's write a book together." Since we share a passion for writing about women in ministry and education leadership, this made great sense. The result was *The Role of Female Seminaries on the Road to Social Justice*, a co-authored book published by Wipf and Stock in 2015.

In working with Professor Welch, I found her to be a tireless and meticulous researcher and an excellent writer. In reading her current work, *This Present Darkness: Meet Me on the Battlefield*, I encounter the same level of intensity in her research about feminism, women's rights efforts, and their interactions with the Christianity she holds dear to her heart.

Intellectual exchange is at the heart of the academy, which students experience in institutions known as colleges and universities. The balance of power in the intellectual exchange between professor and student tends to be weighted in favor of the professor because firstly, the professor tends to be more knowledgeable in the topic at hand; and secondly, the professor holds the position of authority. Given that professors are human, there can be a tendency for a professor to hold onto a particular perspective to the detriment of healthy intellectual exchange.

In writing this book, Kristen Welch aims to empower students with a well-formed and balanced view of feminism: its main ideas, its transitions over time, and key individuals in the movement. A central goal in writing this book is, in her words, "to undermine the authoritarianism so often encountered on campus," thus enhancing the possibility of the intellectual exchange so valued on college and university campuses. Students who read this book are armed with knowledge about the progression of feminist thought, from the early conceptualizations of equality of the sexes, through the various waves of feminism to postfeminist perspectives. Sensitive to the sometimes-racial exclusivity of feminist perspectives, Professor Welch gives a voice to women of color and their unique expression of feminist ideals.

Professor Welch also pays tribute to the role of women in ministry and educational leadership who have advanced the idea of female equality. While many times their work was in the pulpit and in faith-based schools, by embracing their equality before God, these women advanced the struggle to achieve recognition of women's equality in society. Faith-based women contributed significantly toward expanding educational opportunities for women, especially when in United States history this was, for the most part, a gender-segregated endeavor, both in terms of the goals of education for men and women and the institutions of higher education available to men and women.

Professor Welch does not shy away from feminist critique of the Bible or of Christianity but walks the reader through these objections and provides both her own responses as well as those of fellow Christian scholars. In these sections of the book, she walks us through counter-analyses of Scriptural passages such as Proverbs 31 and then explores how theological reflection has developed through its encounter with the different waves of feminism.

Reading this book will give the reader an understanding that feminism is very nuanced and not a monolithic train of thought. The reader will also gain a sense of appreciation for the contributions of Christian women toward the achievement of feminist goals. At the same time, the ways in which feminist and Christian thought both align and diverge are clearly explained. And, for those readers who seek to gain an even deeper understanding of feminism, Professor Welch provides a wealth of resources beyond this book to explore.

In writing this book, Professor Welch has made a great contribution toward student empowerment as they engage in intellectual exchange with their professor in discussions about feminism. At the same time, anyone reading this book comes away with a deeper understanding of the richness of feminist thought and its intersection with the Christian concept of gender equality.

Abraham Ruelas
Adjunct Professor of Communication
Fuller Theological Seminary
Author, *Women and the Landscape of Higher Education:
Wesleyan Holiness and Pentecostal Founders*
Wipf and Stock, 2010

# Preface

"For we do not wrestle against flesh and blood, but against the rulers, against the authorities, against the cosmic powers over *this present darkness*, against the spiritual forces of evil in the heavenly places." (Eph 6:12 ESV; italics added)

"Unto the upright there arises light in the darkness."—Ps 112:4, NKJV

Make no mistake. The book you are holding in your hands has been written by a Christian author. I grew up in the International Pentecostal Holiness Church before becoming a part of an array of Assemblies of God churches since middle school. The purpose of this book is not to make you a Pentecostal, however. Nor is it to convince you to support women preachers, the subject of my dissertation and first two books. It is to help you answer the question: What is feminism and what does it have to do with Christians? Whether or not you accept or reject feminism, you may wish to explain your position and the reasons for it, particularly if you are a college student, since "just because" doesn't cut it in grad school—nor do half-baked summaries of what you think all feminists represent politically or spiritually.

When my students want to write about feminism or to use it as a lens of analysis, I ask them to name which feminist theory they will be using. This usually stumps them. I then ask: How many types of feminist theories are there? They usually respond with some sort of answer about how they simply wish to talk about the fight for equality for women within one context or another—sometimes the workplace, sometimes the classroom, sometimes in politics, sometimes in church. This is common. The first peer-reviewed journal article I published spoke about the way some used the term "feminist" to limit or to destroy the work of women in the church. The use of the term was based on a lack of real information as well as a malicious desire to curb the ambitions of women—the same belief that these people all know exactly who feminists are and what they believe, even though there is a great deal to be learned about a range of theories that are still growing and deepening in complexity. It is also a result of fundamentalists who want women like Beth Moore, an immensely popular Christian teacher, to "go home."[1] Why? Because they believe they have accurately defined a "woman's place." You might assume the battle over women's rights is limited to religious contexts. It would be one sort of battle if sexism really were limited to the church, but instead we find it in the workplace, in our neighborhoods, in our communities, in politics, and just about anywhere people congregate and try to work together, including our own homes.

Whatever the context may be, there's a great deal of passion over a term few have ever been able to really understand. There is also a great deal of missing history when it comes to how women have gained an equal footing in social, religious, and political contexts. How so? It is missing because it is so very complex and because it draws upon so many different historical events and movements. In some cases, it is missing because it was removed, diminished, or denigrated. It was largely the work of Second Wave Feminists who put women into the history books. Before these scholars at the university began to research and recover the works of women, we got the story of how America came to be mostly at the hands of men alone. We overlooked women writers, philosophers, and leaders. We allowed people to be deleted from church histories as various denominational sects became mainstream. It is through the work of both Christian and non-Christian scholars today that the history of women preachers is being recovered. The history of women in other disciplines is also an ongoing work of recovery.

My PhD in Rhetoric, Composition, and the Teaching of English gives me a certain perspective on the topic of feminism. Since it's only been in the last few years you could earn a PhD in women's and gender studies, and since many of those programs are interdisciplinary with courses taken in a variety of disciplines meshed into one program, my perspective is that of a person interested in feminism as a form of rhetoric. In my opinion, rhetoric is a means of creating knowledge; that is, I think it is epistemic. These arguments, which are created out of discourse and within communities of discourse, reveal the role of persuasion in creating knowledge. The discourses at work to create knowledge also show how values and beliefs are challenged in the process. Such challenges may cause the audience to critically reflect

1. Lee, "John MacArthur."

on their own ideologies and the contexts that inform those ideologies. Rhetoric is the study of power with language as the central, but not the only, text. Other texts would include visuals (art, photography, architecture, styles of dress, etc.), body language, music, and the effects of kairos.[2]

This all means I am invested in this interdisciplinary area of study that overlapped with my own doctoral program, dissertation, and first three books, and, of course, this book as well. Since feminists use language to claim power and to enact social change, the way these claims are constructed and received is fascinating to me as a scholar of rhetoric and composition. I would like to help my readers understand some of the most prominent positions feminists take (and have taken) and what the relationships are between feminism and Christian women, as many of us who are scholars and Christians also consider ourselves to actively support women's rights, even if we don't use the term "feminist" to describe it. In fact, many Christian women refused to adopt the term long before "postfeminism" became a way to describe supporting equality but not using the term to do so.

And why not? One example comes from the women's marches which were reported on by *The New York Times* in 2017. These marches happened in several major cities and drew "hundreds of thousands of women."[3] Attendees wore pink hats and boasted an array of speakers who were—it seemed to me—deliberately vulgar. The march was a bid for attention and for political action. In my opinion, Trump and his disgusting remarks about groping women were merely a trigger for a long-simmering need to vocalize discontent with women's position at work, in politics, and in other places. It was an attempt to unify a group that is perhaps better defined by difference. And would Christian women want to stand among the women marching on Washington? To wear the hat? To hear the bombastic language pouring from the podium? Apparently so. But when pro-life women's groups attempted to join the list of partners with other leaders of the march, they were removed from a list that included about four hundred groups.[4] So whether you are an aspiring feminist or not, you may wish to be able to argue for your beliefs on this matter with a deeper understanding about what is at stake and just who is trying to control the narrative. Some have found hope in the new Vice President, Kamala Harris. Yet although there is now a woman in the White House, this in no way solves a problem or unifies us. When politics enter the picture, unity is difficult to achieve.

2. Kairos means something like "at the opportune time." Good timing is a basic way of understanding it. So when someone tries to persuade you, doing so at the right time is effective. Doing so at the wrong time often means failure.

3. Hartocollis and Alcindor, "Women's March."

4. Bernstein, "More Pro-Life."

To begin, let me list some different types of feminism for you. *In Feminist Thought: A More Comprehensive Introduction* by Rosemary Tong and Tina Fernandes Botts, the chapters are devoted to a category of feminism and then the most prominent subcategories. It is divided into the following chapters:

- Liberal Feminism
- Radical Feminism
- Marxist and Socialist Feminisms
- Women of Color Feminism(s) in the United States
- Women of Color Feminism(s) on the World Stage: Global, Postcolonial, and Transnational Feminisms
- Psychoanalytic Feminism
- Care-Focused Feminism
- Ecofeminism
- Existentialist, Poststructuralist, and Postmodern Feminisms
- Third Wave and Queer Feminisms

Specifically, it is important to discuss Transnational Feminisms—Kimberlé Crenshaw's theory of intersectionality which demonstrates how overlapping systems might create oppression for women because of their race, social or economic status, political beliefs, and other factors—and finally, standpoint theory. All of these things help us understand why there are so many different iterations of feminism, and these theories will be explained in the book. There are also definitions in the glossary at the back of the book.

To the list above, we might also add the following categories of feminism:

- Anarchist
- Black and Womanist
- French
- Multiracial
- Separatist and Lesbian
- Third-World
- Transfeminism
- I-Feminism

Students might ask: Why are there so many? How do I make sense of these? How do I find a complete list of feminist theories? In addition to these theories, a great deal of fourth-wave feminism is tied to technology and an array of groups and scholars have emerged to discuss the relationships between the two. At the end of this book is a list of the most prominent theories along with succinct definitions. Major issues tied to each wave are included. A list of feminist writers is included, and a timeline is provided to help students orient themselves in the story of how women won equal rights in this country.

It might be helpful to point out that feminist thought and history are typically divided into three waves: the first wave includes the seventeenth to nineteenth centuries with roots in earlier times, the second wave is roughly around the 1960s and '70s, and the third wave started sometime in the 1980s or '90s. Some say we are now in the "postfeminist" wave; others say we are in the fourth wave. It's all up for debate. The first three categories, however, are particularly useful for situating feminist ideas as they have emerged as a result of the concerns associated with each era, and I will return to these categories many times in this book.

These lists are not a complete set of secular feminist theories, but they also do not include theological feminisms. One of those is known as "biblical feminism," which emerged during the second wave. The Evangelical Women's Caucus was formed in 1975 and was active until it embraced homosexuality.[5] So in the 1980s, the Christians for Biblical Equality (CBE) was formed.[6] In 1990, Gretchen Gaebelein Hull, who is one of the founders of CBE, defined biblical feminism in contrast to secular feminism as follows:

> Secular feminism centers around competing for equal rights; biblical feminism centers around creating equal opportunities to serve. The secular feminist says, "I am entitled to compete on an equal basis with men." The biblical feminist says, "I seek the freedom to follow Christ as he calls me to use my gifts in God's service."[7]

Furthermore:

> Biblical feminists believe that Scripture affirms the worth and value of men and women equally—and that all who have accepted Christ's offer of new life should have equal opportunity to serve God. They take seriously Paul's statement that "there is

---

5. Deasy, "Women," 279.
6. Deasy, "Women," 279.
7. Hull, "Christian Response."

neither male nor female, for we are all one in Christ Jesus" (Gal. 3:28). Biblical feminists advocate partnership, not competition; mutual submission, not dominion by one sex over the other; the priesthood of all believers, not a male hierarchy.[8]

But as you may suspect, the ties between feminism and religion are not all that simple. The field of feminist theology, or the methods used to interpret and apply Scripture in analysis or practice or for other purposes, points toward several key issues that concern women who do not accept a second-class status in the home or church. These key questions revolve around women's leadership:

- Can women be pastors? Or leaders, but in a lesser capacity?
- What does the Bible say about hierarchy and how is that contextualized properly?
- How did Christ treat women? What was Christ's view of women and what was his practice?
- Is God male or female?
- Did women bring evil into the world as told in Genesis, or were both responsible? Should we take Lillith more seriously? Lillith, by the way, was the rumored first wife of Adam in the Garden of Eden and is known as the world's "first feminist," according to the New World Encyclopedia. She refused to submit to Adam and is associated either with lustfulness and leading men astray or with harming children.[9] The folklore associated with her describes her as a "night demon."
- Should women be silent in the church?
- Should wives submit to their husbands without question?

However, the relationship between feminism and theology is much more complex than these questions imply. Feminist theologians focus on different things that might include one or more of these areas:

- Exegesis (i.e., how you interpret Scripture) and hermeneutics (i.e., "the branch of knowledge that deals with interpretation, especially of the Bible or literary texts")[10]
- History and tradition
- The doctrine of God (Who is he? Or is it she?)

8. Hull, "Christian Response."
9. "Lilith."
10. "Hermeneutics."

- Creation and eschatology (i.e., the doctrine of "death, judgement, and the final destiny of the soul and humankind")[11]
- Theological anthropology (or a focus on confronting stereotypes used to define women's nature)
- Christology
- Ecclesiology (i.e., the study of churches)
- Marriage and sacraments
- Ethics and morals
- Spirituality[12]

It is no wonder that those who are new to understanding and defining feminism can become quickly overwhelmed. It is also no secret that it will not take long before a conservative Christian finds a plethora of ideas that are deeply repulsive in both secular and theological feminist theories: ideas that support pornography, beliefs that advocate for all forms of sexuality including incest, arguments for the defense of abortion, advice for the practice of goddess worship, the composition of alternative creation stories—the list goes on and on.

So why do so many Christians either claim to be feminists or, at the very least, claim to hold a strong belief in the equality of men and women? How do we reconcile all of these divergent strands of historically and culturally situated thought with Christianity?

Oh, but there's another problem. To further complicate matters, how can we speak of Christianity as though the term represented one set of beliefs? When Dr. Vinson Synan wrote *The Century of the Holy Spirit: 100 Years of Pentecostal and Charismatic Renewal*, he included a picture of a tree with many, many branches to represent and name all of the offshoots of Pentecostal denominations, and Pentecostalism is just one of many different types of Protestant religions: Protestant religions that have formed and fallen apart over the years; Protestant religions that have a history of their own that is often contradictory and complex. And then there are the Catholics. They are part of an ongoing narrative that changes over time and in different places. Reducing the term "Christian" down to one set of ideas is ludicrous when we bring the term into relationship with real people in lived contexts and experiences that have changed over time.

Then there is Christianity as it is experienced in the U.S. and there is Christianity as it emerges in divergent experiences and religions across the

---

11. "Eschatology."
12. "Feminist Theology."

globe. There is Christianity as it is practiced today and there is Christianity as it has been practiced in different ways and in different places since the life of Christ. And what about before Christ? How does that relate to Christianity?

The term *Christian* means a follower of Christ. But how that is established in theology and praxis is a subject that has enough books to fill a library. The history of Christianity itself might fill another library.

To further complicate matters, women who are theologians often take a serious departure from Christianity. One example is the very influential Mary Daly. In the late '90s, her exclusion of all men from her upper-level classes at Boston College resulted in her "leave of absence" from the institution, or "retirement."[13] She renounced Christianity and came out as a lesbian in the 1970s[14] but held onto her place at Boston College for over thirty years until she began excluding men from her classes. She decided to sue for her right to teach, but she was still not allowed to return. Instead, she reached a settlement out of court.[15] Another example is Rosemary Radford Ruether, who tried to rewrite Christian tradition and tell creation narratives from a feminine perspective in *Sexism and God-Talk*; it was a radical departure that went much further than just finding a place for equality in Scripture. Both women were in the Catholic tradition, but today, the scope of liberals within Christianity has widened to include more than just vocal scholars such as these, but pastors and congregants who follow a political agenda completely comfortable with liberal values from an array of religious standpoints. The Pew Research Center includes Lutheran, Episcopalian, Presbyterian, Unitarian, and others in the list of liberal churches, with their position on homosexuality as the dividing line these days.[16]

It is easy to be overwhelmed by all of this. This book aims to explain what feminism and Christianity, broadly speaking, have to do with each other. The purpose is to simplify and to educate. When you are finished reading this book, you will be able to articulate a historically and biblically based perspective on equality and women that you may not have been able to articulate before. You will have an idea of which branches of feminist thought you might wish to devote some of your time and research to exploring (if any). When you encounter feminist strands of thought in college classes or in conversations with others, you will be able to articulate your position or at least be able to figure out what you need to research further

13. "Mary Daly, Quite Contrary."
14. "Mary Daly, Profile."
15. "Mary Daly, Controversial Feminist."
16. Masci and Lipka, "Where Christian Churches."

in order to do so. You will encounter strands of feminist thought in all sorts of classes as it is relates to many different fields of study: history, theology, literature, sociology, psychology, leadership, STEM, business, and on and on. In fact, many of the women's and gender studies programs in the U.S. are interdisciplinary, so even majoring in this area means you have to branch out into more than one discipline.

This book is meant to undermine the authoritarianism so often encountered on campus. Professors sometimes only offer the information and scholarship that supports views they hold dear. They have years of education and long years of experience that an undergraduate and (many) graduates are no match for in the classroom. This book is meant to put the student in charge; it is meant to help you create a position that is negotiated instead of one that is forced upon you. However, whether you are a college student or not, this book is worth the time to read. It will change the way you see our American history. It will change the way you read and interpret the Bible.

In the end, you are free to accept or to reject the idea of women's right to equality. However, if you read this book, you will no longer be free to remain uninformed.

Therefore, if you are brave enough, I invite you to meet me on the battlefield.

# Acknowledgments

Thanks go out to my husband, Jerry, for his encouragement and support. Jerry never doubts that I am going to do what I set out to do—not now, with years behind us filled with our accomplishments, or twenty-eight years ago when we were starting out, young and unproven in the hardships of this world. I am also grateful to my mother, LaDonna Scott, who has offered her encouragement and her belief in me at crucial times along the way. My daughter, Anna Nicole Johnson, is one of those young women who brings her enthusiasm and bright spirit into every communication, and I am so grateful for her kind words as I worked on this book. My son, Jadon Lynn Welch, has reminded me of my obligation to finish the book, checking in periodically to see if I was still working on things. I appreciate his gentle reminders along the way. Also, thanks to Abe Ruelas, who gave his feedback on the draft as well as writing the foreword. I am grateful for the readers who gave me feedback on earlier drafts, which include Laura Beth Vardaro, Becky Gualtiere, my dear friend Meredith Roberts, Daniel Isgrigg, Doris Wilson, and Olivia Brandt. Finally, thanks to my friend Ron Hyde, who offered suggestions for images to include on the cover.

# Introduction

This book is designed for college students who wish to know more about feminist history and theories, as well as the other theories that feed into both. I've grown tired of hearing about anyone being "woke" or having his or her "consciousness raised." I think that describing an adoption of "feminist" beliefs and couching it in terms of a religious conversion is wrong. Feminism is nothing more or less than a belief that men and women are equal and should have access to equal social, political, legal, educational, occupational, and spiritual rights. Yet in the year 2021, the term is synonymous with left-wing ideology and there doesn't seem to be much room for anyone else. The implication is that a belief in equality somehow indicates a belief in a range of political views we might associate with liberals. It's not always true, though. In fact, the truth about feminism is complicated enough to warrant the publication of this book.

One reason I wrote this book for college students is that in colleges and universities, professors and students love to explore the theories that make up the vast and divergent collection of theories tied to the broad historical categories of first-, second-, and third-wave feminism. They love to explore the current movement, which some label as the fourth wave and others as postfeminism. However, as learners typically new to these histories and theories, students are at a distinct disadvantage, and sometimes the authoritarianism tied to the absorption of book knowledge (not wisdom, not biblical knowledge) and to the position of professor with all its connotations leads those new to feminism in directions that aren't good for them to go. If presented with the false either/or position of being a feminist or not being a feminist, students might not have enough information about feminism to carefully negotiate their own position.

Another reason I wrote this book is that a few years back, I spent a day in a workshop on feminism at my field's biggest conference, the Conference on College Composition and Communication. Next to me sat a woman with a faint, but growing, mustache. But, as odd as it is that the image of that slender woman is still stuck in my mind, it was the speaker who has weighed heavily on my heart all these years. She spoke glowingly of her realization that she was feminist, but she also shared that she was on anti-depressants and had taken a job in another state, leaving her young son behind with an ex-husband. Her smiling, confident endorsement of what she thought freedom was—now that she was a feminist, that is—was sadly ironic in light of these details she shared. She had made big decisions about her career and her family because of feminism. It had clearly not benefitted her. In fact, I think it may have broken her heart.

Put this in contrast with a young woman I wrote about for a speech I gave at the Centennial Celebration of the International Pentecostal Holiness Church in 2011. In that speech, I spoke on women, and I talked about unity. At the end, I shared a memory with my audience. I had been to a church meeting somewhere in South Carolina, and the current bishop was speaking. I do not remember what he said. What I do recall is a young woman, baby on her hip, praying for one and then another afterwards. She made me cry; her image is still there inside of me, pressed on my heart. She taught me so much. She taught me that in prayer there is unity. One does not act as master over another. In prayer there is humility. One does not capitalize on any element of status or superiority. In prayer there is healing and there is hope. One does not look to cut others down or blame others when things go wrong. In prayer, families come together and mothers hold tightly to their children, no matter what the trends in society may be. In prayer there is purest form of love that exists because God is in prayer, Christ is in it, and the Holy Spirit, our great comforter, is in prayer.

To sum things up, I am writing this book because I want Christian college students to have a way to understand and to thereby control their response to feminist thought. It is incredibly important to know history, and the range of theories can be useful to many students. However, it is by no means a unified group of theories or a unified group of women. The waves are descriptive, but the dates associated with them shift depending on who you are reading. Also, contemporary scholars too often ignore the role Christians have played in winning equal rights for women. Feminism has room for the most conservative of women and the most liberal. However, the textbooks on feminist methodologies, the feminist anthologies, and the resources for feminist thought tend to separate Christian and non-Christians.

The truth is richer and more complex than the oversimplification that one group has nothing to do with the other.

Furthermore, the use of ideas such as postmodernism, social constructionism, and the like should not hold power over a student simply because they sound complex (and they are) or simply because they are built on erudite theories written by gifted, but sometimes misguided, scholars that academics tend to worship as they breathlessly speak names like Foucault, Bourdieu, Althusser, Derrida, and so on. The ideas offered in a university should be held at arm's length, put into context, analyzed, and reflected upon before a negotiated, partial, and careful adoption of new beliefs might be internalized by a student. For the Christian student, I would add that part of the critical thinking process should include putting these ideas into prayer.

And what does God have to do with theories created by feminists? Everything, for I have often allowed God to lead me in my studies. I don't fear reading texts I don't agree with. After all, God exposes the weaknesses in them when I allow him to show me. There is nothing too difficult for our Creator, the living God we serve. There is no theory he can't untangle. In fact, such an idea is laughable. He is above and beyond anything we can create in our universities or write in our books, and he will illuminate what you need when you need it if you work hard, pray, and dedicate yourself fully to your studies. He will also inspire you.

Let me tell you how he inspired me. When I was in the middle of earning my doctorate, I went home and went up to my grandfather's old office. He was a Pentecostal preacher, and he loved to read. I knelt and saw a book he had collected that had been written by a woman preacher. All of a sudden I could feel his presence, which is just the way laughter feels. I still remember the way the sunlight warmed that room. I remember that moment as though no time had passed at all. In that moment, I knew I was to do this work. I wrote my dissertation on Pentecostal women preachers from Oklahoma. I used that to create my first book. In my second book, I included interviews from Pentecostal women preachers living on the East Coast. In my third book, co-authored with Dr. Abraham Ruelas, I explored the role education played in obtaining social justice for women. And now this book, my fourth, begins with a Scripture my mother told me was given to her when she was worried about me many years ago. God is in this. And in my heart, there is no label more important to me than that of *Christian*.

Let me lay out a few basics for you in this introduction so you have the big picture as you read the chapters to come. Here, I would like to give you an overview of first, second-, and third-wave feminism. I would like to share the goals of each wave. I would like to tell you of the shift away from Christian involvement in obtaining rights for women, and how it has returned in the voices of women such as Lisa Bevere, who has a radically different message expressed in books like *Fight Like a Girl: The Power of Being a Woman, Lioness Arising: Wake Up and Change Your World. Girls with Swords: Why Women Need to Fight Spiritual Battles*, and so many other books that speak to women as Christians, not as political activists.

I would also like to show you I create, discover, validate, and analyze knowledge as a Christian so you can consider your own process.

1. In 1 Cor 2, Paul tells his reader that he did not bring "human wisdom" or "persuasive words" to them (i.e., the hallmarks of rhetoric which many scholars believe Paul had received training in). "Faith should not be in the wisdom of men but in the power of God" (1 Cor 2:5 NKJV). "Call to Me, and I will answer you, and show you great and mighty things, which you do not know" (Jer 33:3 NKJV). So I look first to God.

2. There are at least two levels of knowledge: human and divine. Human knowledge is limited, fragmented, and in need of the divine. "For now we see in a mirror dimly, but then face to face. Now I know in part, but then I shall know just as I am known" (1 Cor 13:12 NKJV). My conclusion is that I understand that even in my best efforts, I will not know everything in the end.

3. When investigating a theory I think is accurate, it could be a tool I use for analysis, but it could also shape my ideology. If you find yourself in this position, spend time with the theory. Put it into prayer. Put it into biblical context, especially in terms of Christ. Remember that he went further than the law and addressed the condition of the heart. Theories have the power to change hearts. They are beliefs, observations, discoveries, and insights. What they are not is scientific facts, such as we see and verify in the natural world, although some scholars treat theory as though it were fact.

4. Human knowledge and wisdom are built on constructed truths that are relative to a time and place. For the Christian, the truth is found in the living person of Christ. We can look at his self-description in John 14:6 to see. This profound shift in the location and source of truth means everything.

5. We need the Holy Spirit to help reveal the truths of Scripture to us. I'm always suspicious of the interpretation of Scripture by a non-Christian. What could they possibly know that is valuable to me at all when it comes to the Bible? Ephesians 1:17: "I keep asking that the God of

our Lord Jesus Christ, the glorious Father, may give you the Spirit of wisdom and revelation, so that you may know him better" (NKJV).

6. Never elevate a human theory to god-like status. Also, keep people off of pedestals no matter their position, their title, their list of publications, their list of accomplishments, and so on. Everything and everyone is flawed in some way.

7. College programs, especially in grad school, are often tight-knit communities. Rise above relationships as you shape your views. Let influence from the Bible, from Christ, and from prayer come first. Make choices; do not indulge yourself in groupthink and relinquish your grip on your own perspective. Of course, be kind to all around you as your work will be flawed too, especially if you are majoring in the humanities, social sciences, or theology, since these are places of deep, intellectual exploration instead of areas of study where the objects of study are concrete more than they are abstract.

So what defines first-wave feminism? To begin, when was the term *feminism* first used? According to the *Stanford Encyclopedia of Philosophy*, it changed from meaning "qualities of females" to a belief in and an advocacy for the equality of the sexes.[17] This happened after the First International Women's Conference in Paris in 1892. However, the reach of first-wave feminism goes back much further than 1892. In fact, first-wave feminism in America is traced back to eighteenth-century America and the letters of Abigail Adams to her husband and spans all the way up to the early parts of the twentieth century.

While the political thought associated with key feminists is discussed in chapter 3, we can trace feminist thought back further than the eighteenthth century in western culture. As I explain in chapter 2, which focuses on education as a means of advancing the cause of social justice and equality for women, women such as Christine de Pizan, for example, were writing in the fifteenth century and arguing for a woman's right to get a full education. But it stretches back even further than that. For example, the exploration of women preachers in chapter 1 brings us back to the earliest "mothers in Israel" in the Old Testament, who were leaders and warriors, to the prophetess Anna mentioned in the New Testament and the many women who were sharing the gospel in the early church. After them came the female mystics who circumvented patriarchal structures to claim authority by saying they had heard directly from God.

---

17. "Feminist Philosophy."

Women preachers in what would be the United States shook up restrictions on women's speaking publicly in the era of first-wave feminism, and many who served in other political or educational capacities would argue for the right of women to preach, such as in Frances Willard's *Woman in the Pulpit*, because they knew the power of creating a woman's ethos or credibility based on divine approval, which undermined the false notion that women speaking publicly were "promiscuous" or "manly." The revivals of the First and Second Great Awakenings cannot be understated in terms of influence which moved away from credibility built on degrees and moved it to common people who had been inspired by God. The Quakers, even as far back as Margaret Fell's "Women's Speaking Justified"—published in England in 1666—were enormously influential, as they allowed women to speak in church and used the Bible to build a case for that right.

Interestingly enough, Pentecostal theologians such as Estrelda Alexander, who researches African-American Pentecostals and includes a study of women preachers, and Kimberly Ervin Alexander, who researches (mostly white) Church of God women preachers, show us that the debate over women preachers brings us full circle in today's wave of feminism, although many disagree over whether we are even in a wave or have moved past feminism altogether. As feminist theologians, these two scholars put a discussion of women preachers into relationship with a belief in women's equality, but in an entirely different way than women did in the nineteenth century in America. Yet the relationship between women's rights and biblical interpretation is still there and—at the center?—women preachers.

In Appendix A is a list of the concerns associated with first-wave feminism. The problems stemmed from the fact that laws prevented women from having their testimony count in court, from retaining custody of their children after divorce—even in abusive relationships—from having a right to their own wages, and from really having a say over their own bodies after marriage, which resulted in abuse and rape in some cases. Most of the time, a woman could not own property in her own name.[18] Worst of all, American women lived in a society where they had no political power, since they could not vote.

Other problems were that women did not have access to the same educational opportunities that men had access to. Nor did women have work opportunities outside of the home that did not include manual labor, such as cleaning. Many women had no choice but to work and were subjected to manual labor such as cleaning, laundry, cooking, and caring for other people's children.

---

18. "Women and the Law."

But by the end of the nineteenth century, the coverture laws that so limited women were overturned and by 1920, women were granted the right to vote at the federal level. Second-wave feminism describes a period of time where women became concerned with many different things. I would say most people place this in the 1960s and 1970s. The National Organization for Women (NOW), which formed in 1966, had Betty Friedan as the first president.[19] Echoing Seneca Falls, this group wrote a Bill of Rights in 1967 which included demands to:

1. Pass the Equal Rights Amendment.[20]
2. Give women equal employment opportunities.
3. Protect women's jobs after having a baby.
4. Let working parents deduct child-care expenses from their taxes.
5. Establish public childcare facilities.
6. Give women the right to obtain an equal education.
7. Reform welfare programs to help women who need job training, housing, and family allowances.
8. Stop limiting women's contraceptive choices.

In addition, the goals of second-wave feminists, which are laid out in detail in Appendix A, were to make a place for women in the university. Today, women's studies programs, journals, conferences, and publications are all a result of the efforts of women who started to study women in the archives, recovering a forgotten or diminished history of their involvement in so many facets of life and culture. They also took the battle to the mind. Sexism in the workplace was one area of focus, but so were mindsets women had that limited their potential.

Second-wave feminists went further, though. They began to embrace all forms of sexuality and to consider gender to be a fluid construct. They fought for contraceptives and the right to an abortion. For some, it meant redefining God or re-examining Scripture with a new interpretation. Finally, they, like first-wave feminists, sought political power, but on an entirely different level. Educated and powerful, they formed organizations that inspired change.

Yet second-wave feminists also realized that feminism had largely been focused on the needs of white, middle-class women. A bridge into third-wave feminism was the Combahee River Collective statement published

19. Tong and Botts, *Feminist Thought*, 23.
20. Tong and Botts, *Feminist Thought*, 24.

in 1977.[21] They added a focus on race, class, and sexuality. Furthermore, transnational feminism emerges out of the third wave in the work of those who wish to obtain different types of social justice in different countries and cultures. It's less a unified theory than it is the idea that work is needed by those who hope to win rights for women, particularly outside of the United States. Chapter 4 discusses many of the building blocks that make up third-wave feminism—in particular, identity politics—and includes a discussion of transnational feminism.

Feminist theologians are the main topic of chapter 5 and they occupy an entirely different area than that of women preachers. Theologians typically hold at least a master's degree—if not a doctorate—if they are working in a university. I did not include the voices of amateur theologians or pastors in this chapter (except for my own amateur voice!). Picking up the strands of third-wave feminism, they address issues with race, class, and identity, but they focus most heavily on how the Bible is interpreted and then applied to our social structures in and out of the church. For example, liberation theology (a term coined by Gustavo Gutierrez in 1968) embraces the connection between theology, experience, and praxis, and reconstructionist theology pays attention to the experience "of patriarchy and androcentrism"; brings "these experiences into dialogue with a feminist reading of the Bible and/or other Christian texts"; and develops "strategies for transformative action or praxis that are liberating."[22] Keep in mind that theologians may or may not be Christians. For example, Mary Daly renounced Christianity but continued her work as a theologian at a university.

Fourth-wave feminism, or post-feminism, is not quite as easy to explain. Perhaps it is too recent to define more clearly than to say that technology has changed everything about the way we communicate, the way we form communities and alliances, and the way we support some and destroy others in our society. Chapter 6 explores anti-feminists and visual culture and explains the role of social media in shaping feminist thought both now and in the past. However, chapter 4 does cover feminists such as Donna Haraway in what might now be considered outdated definitions of the *cyborg*.

The conclusion ties things together into a definition of feminism I have articulated. In short, the main effect of feminist thought is to interrupt a narrative that excludes, reduces, or imprisons women in a physical, mental, or intellectual sense. The conclusion also offers you, as a student, advice on choosing a graduate school program and in choosing where you might

---

21. Combahee River Collective, "A Black Feminist Statement," cited in Freedman, *Essential Feminist Reader*, 325.

22. Clifford, *Introducing Feminist Theology*, 34–35.

teach should you earn a doctorate. This is based on my personal experience; programs change so often that it is difficult to come up with a list of programs. Also, women's studies programs are often interdisciplinary, but they are sometimes housed in one discipline or another.

This book also offers you some tools. For example, Appendix A reiterates the concerns of first-, second-, and third-wave feminists I have also shared with you here, but in much more detail. Appendix B offers you selected key terms in feminist thought. Appendix C has a glossary of the main feminist theories, although I could not possibly hope to list them all. Many dictionaries of feminist theories or feminist theologies are readily available and quite affordable if you want something more comprehensive.

Appendix D offers you a list of selected readings authored by feminists in the hope of pointing you toward the most widely read, although I am sure others will disagree about what I chose to include or not include. Appendix E is a detailed timeline of major events in feminist history. Appendix F is where I suggest how to analyze a theory and its source. Following that is some guidance on how to use feminism as a lens for literary criticism (since I am an English professor).

To conclude, the goal of this book is not to "convert" you to feminism. It is not to get you to agree with my religious doctrines, including the support of women preachers, although that is near to my heart and has been the subject of my research for many years. It is not to get you to adopt a particular view of what equality means either. The goal of this book is to offer you a way to understand and engage with a complex narrative. Since history is simply the best story-telling efforts of those who uncover facts, some histories ignore the people who do not seem important to them. So women get left out. Women preachers are ignored. Some liberal groups turn a blind eye. It depends on who is relating a particular bit of history and for what purpose.

In summary, this book attempts to offer you a version of history that will help you see where the struggle for women's rights and the work of Christians overlaps. Not all of the Christians will be perfect models for you to follow. Again, my aim is to tell the truth. My aim is to give you power over this part of American history which is replete with diverse and often contradictory groups and theories. My aim is to put you in the position to make your own decisions about feminism, about the equality of women, and about what Christianity does or does not have to do with women's rights. As an educator, my goal is to inspire critical thinking (analysis, reflection, negotiation). It is not to create a following of people who simply replicate my views. So please read this book with an open mind and work out where you stand.

# 1

## Mystics, Mothers in Israel, Exhorters, and Laborers in Christ

*Women Preachers, First-Wave Feminism, and the Right to Speak*

The Battlefield: Conservative Christian culture in America and biblical interpretations that limited women, particularly in the eighteenth and nineteenth centuries.

The Opponents: Men and women who had accepted the idea that women as speakers (or as published authors) indicated that they were "promiscuous," "manly," and "immodest" versus women determined to speak and to publish for political reasons and for the purpose of preaching, exhorting, and joyfully speaking for God.

*Guiding questions for chapter 1:*

1. How did a woman's ethos, as determined by her and co-created by an audience of listeners or readers, limit or empower her in the eighteenth and nineteenth centuries in America?

2. How did Christian women, such as Quakers and participants in the revivals of the two Great Awakenings, move authority away from

college-educated men and into the hands of the common people, including women?

3. How did women preachers, who presented themselves as pure and called by God in a time where female public speakers were denigrated with epithets like "promiscuous," undermine the prejudices the public (both men and women) held against women speaking in public?

4. How is the work of women preachers ironic? Given that many did not claim equality with men and used alternate names to sidestep the issue (Mothers in Israel, exhorters, prophetesses, etc.), did they help advance women's right to speak publicly even though they clearly did not intend to do so? And what about the women preachers who were far outside of mainstream Christianity? Should we recognize the work of women whose work misled other Christians because they held great influence over some?

5. Why did so many women argue for a woman's right to speak by basing it on a long list of biblical figures? Why did so many argue for a woman's right to preach when they themselves were not preachers nor did they intend to be? What is the significance of the debate over a woman's right to speak in terms of Christian exegesis done by amateurs and not by educated theologians?

First-wave feminists included women preachers and Christian leaders who forged a path for the right to speak in public, although their contributions were ironic since these women claimed to be speaking for God and did not claim to fight for women's equality. Yet they still eroded the patriarchal constructs that were in place to silence women. Without the right to speak publicly, feminists' other social, educational, and political reform initiatives could not have been achieved. While most of the prominent leaders in social movements, such as the Woman's Christian Temperance Union, were Christians, it is in the role of women preachers that we see how women undermined the cultural prejudices that tried to silence them and undermine their authority and ethos in a more pervasive and influential way, because their numbers were greater and they validated their work through spiritual—not human, social, or even educational—credentials.

What we have in the nineteenth century is a clash of cultural waves at the climax of the long story of limitations on women. These included social and legal restrictions on women as well as religiously-justified restrictions on women that supported the social and legal restrictions. In the middle of these competing waves is ethos, or a woman's perceived integrity, ability, and credibility. Denied an equal education, her ethos could not draw on that. Denied experience in occupational fields that went beyond manual labor, she could not draw on that aspect of ethos or credibility-making. Denied leadership roles, she could not draw on that. But it is this last area—the one that put her as the most important and powerful sort of leader in a society largely influenced by religious ideals, even if not necessarily full of true Christians—that toppled barriers to the others. As soon as women began to speak in church; as soon as the Great Awakenings allowed the uneducated but "called" to speak to the congregation; as soon as women began to hold the position of preacher—whether they were in the pulpit or denied that social space—women whose ethos drew on a "call" from God to preach, an inspiration of the Holy Spirit to speak, an encounter with Christ to minister now drew on a pure ethos of God-ordained integrity instead of the moral weakness associated with Eve.

Their credibility was shored up by the congregation's beliefs in the practices of free worship and speaking for both men and women that was no longer jealously owned by a few, educated men. Their ability became evident as they emerged as charismatic leaders without the benefit of training or denominational support, at least in most cases. Women preachers effectively undermined everything women were supposed to be—emotional rather than reasonable, of weak moral fiber, "promiscuous" as speakers—through both practice as speakers, in the content of what they said, and in written texts they published in the emerging printing industry that told the stories of their lives and their encounters with God. While a few secular women argued for equality, their impact was less than that of Christian women because Christianity mattered to Americans of the nineteenth century. Living in a post-Christian society today does not change this fact.

*Ethos* is a Greek term that refers to a speaker's or writer's credibility, communication of goodwill to the audience, and expertise through education or experience. It is at the center of how women have been denied their rights because it is a central point that others have used to undermine the credibility of women. It is one of the three main pillars of appeal, with logos (appeals to logic and reason) and pathos (appeals to emotions) as the other two. A fourth factor, kairos, refers to the timing of a persuasive speech or text and how that relates to its effectiveness. Aristotle (Plato's student who was, in turn, Socrates's student) defined these three appeals, namely ethos, pathos, and logos. James May breaks ethos down further as (1) that which exhibits intelligence, goodwill, *arête* (excellence), and virtue, (2) the character of the audience, and (3) the creation of the speaker's character in the speech and/or the creation of the defendant's character in his speech.[1] In

---

1. May, "Ethos," 2–3

Aristotle's *Rhetoric*, one of the earliest attempts to describe the nature and practice of rhetoric, we see that rhetoric is dependent upon both audience and speaker, and how it changes according to its context. He saw rhetoric as a *dynameis* used to see the available means of persuasion in each case. So ethos, as a central part of any communication, is something that is dynamic and co-created with an audience.

In the United States, a woman's credibility and expertise were under constant attack, and sometimes still are. In the ideas associated with the "Goodwife" in colonial America, women were suspected of being immoral based on Eve's actions in the Garden of Eden. Since it was a woman who was deceived, logic dictated that women could not be trusted. Since a woman's one act of leadership in the garden led to the fall of mankind, her leadership was inherently flawed and by extension, so was the leadership of all women. In the era of the "ideal woman," primarily during the nineteenth century, women were accused of being illogical. All sorts of "scientific" reasons, such as having a period or a uterus, were claimed as the cause for a woman's illogical behavior or reasoning. However, even in ancient Greece, these arguments were offered with women characterized as being little more than an imperfect copy of a man. In the time of Republican motherhood women were inhibited by their lack of education and appropriate experience from doing any sort of work outside the home and from doing many types of intellectual work. Ironically, the ideals of Republican motherhood were used to bargain for an education for women which, by the end of the nineteenth century, was equal to that offered to men in some places, but when they gained the education and experience they needed to do anything outside of the domestic sphere, they still had to face the effects of sexism because the assumption remained—despite their education and all of the evidence to the contrary—that they were incapable and not equal to men, especially intellectually. Often, men were associated with reason and women were associated with emotion throughout the arguments made for and against women's equality. What is important is that when women preachers spoke, if the audience attributed them that right—that authority—then the audience was changed and their prejudices against women speaking were weakened. Anytime a woman preacher gained a following, she undermined the prejudice against women speaking publicly to some extent.

The point of all this is to say that women who spoke publicly had to form some sort of ethos that gave them the credibility needed to do so successfully. Ironically, while women struggled to speak publicly on matters of social and political interest and concern, women preachers were able to do so in a way that undermined the idea that they were "promiscuous" for speaking to a "mixed" audience—that is, an audience consisting of both men and women—by presenting themselves as "pure" and as humbly speaking for God. At times, they did so by voicing their unworthiness. While this further complicates things, the irony of having power as a public speaker who casts his or her ethos as being unworthy to speak is firmly grounded in Scripture. It is a way that weakness is interpreted as strength.

How so? The short answer: Paul. He, more than any other biblical writer, defines the practice of Christianity for many Christian denominations. Paul was a masterful practitioner of a type of written rhetoric which was often autobiographical. Paul persuaded through charismatic speaking and writing. He presented himself paradoxically as weak, but the events of his life as well as his personal impact provided evidence to the contrary. He claimed direct divine knowledge from God. He claimed direct divine knowledge from God. Later, Americans would interpret this to mean that they did not need an education to hear from God or to speak for God.

Paul's goal was to convert the reader, not to venerate himself. The women preachers of the early United States were much the same. We see a reflection of Paul's paradoxical construction of ethos in the way women preachers denied their power and then proceeded to exercise it, and in how they claimed to be weak as speakers and intellectuals and then produced speeches and written texts that clearly defied such descriptions.

For those who are less familiar with Paul, he is the master of paradox in his description of himself and builds his ethos upon this paradoxical construction. He establishes his ethos as a true Christian minister by characterizing Christian ministers in general in 2 Cor 6:3–7 as "steadfast" in spite of great difficulties, as "innocent" in behavior but strong in their "grasp of truth," as patient and "kind" through "gifts of the Holy Spirit," and as full of "unaffected love" and the "power of God." He then artfully outlines the paradoxical description of the Christian minister, cleverly turning him into the image of a spiritual warrior:

> We wield the weapons of righteousness in right hand and left. Honour and dishonour, praise and blame, are alike our lot: we are the impostors who speak the truth, the unknown men whom all men know; dying we still live on; disciplined by suffering, we are not done to death; in our sorrows we have always cause for joy; poor ourselves, we bring wealth to many; penniless, we own the world. (2 Cor 6:7–10 REB)

Paul is a powerful writer, and since his letters were dictated because of his poor eyesight, he must have been an intelligent speaker who drew upon a different kind of charisma than what people were used to seeing in the courts or political venues. Evidence of the paradox of a timid speaker with strong, intelligent ideas is in the following verses: "I, Paul, appeal to you by the gentleness and magnanimity of Christ—I who am so timid (you say) when face to face with you, so courageous when I am away from you" (2 Cor 10:1 REB). And in 2 Cor 10:10: "'His letters [Paul is repeating what he has heard others say about himself],' so it is said, 'are weighty and powerful; but when he is present his is unimpressive, and as a speaker he is beneath contempt'" (REB). In response Paul writes, "I may be no speaker, but knowledge I do have; at all times we have made known to you the full truth" (2 Cor 11:6 REB).

Like Paul, the women preachers seem to deny their strength, abilities, and even their education when constructing an ethos, but then provide a multitude of evidence that communicates they have the authority and knowledge needed to speak, even if they do not point this out or they deny it. So what conclusions can we draw? Ethos, for the Pauline orator, is built through intimacy with God and humility, not through education, expertise, or rhetorical technique in speaking—although Paul was most definitely educated. The knowledge that is valued is that of God's wisdom, and the preacher's job is to communicate that knowledge to others. The preacher shares "God's hidden wisdom" as it is "revealed" through the Spirit because the "spirit explores everything, even the depths of God's own nature" (1 Cor 2:7–10 REB). Therefore, the preacher interprets "spiritual truths to those who have the Spirit" and speaks "of these gifts of God in words taught us not by our human wisdom but by the Spirit" (1 Cor 2:13 REB). The "debator," as a representative of those rhetoricians with secular educations, is described as one who is full of worldly knowledge and expertise (1 Cor 1:20 REB). The impetus to put "worldly" wisdom to the side in favor of spiritual sources of wisdom was a central tenet of participants in the First and the Second Great Awakenings, which included women preachers. Later, the practice of denying women a college degree that would, to some degree, legitimize their role as preachers was undermined by the pentecostal practice of relying upon baptism in the Holy Spirit as the only needed credential for ministry. Paul claimed his knowledge and insights came directly from God; it was logical for other Christians to make a similar claim.

*The Lord announces the word, / and the women who proclaim it are a mighty throng.—Ps 68:11, NIV*

In colonial and then in post-Revolutionary War America, women preachers, exhorters, "female laborers in Christ," and "Mothers in Israel" acted under an authority higher than that of men, like the women of the early church and the mystics. Women achieved equality by shifting their source of authority from men to God. Just how significant an achievement this was for colonial women is revealed in Thomas Jefferson's letter to his daughter. Written in 1790 when she married, he makes it clear that for a woman, God and personal ambitions are second to the concerns of men: "The happiness of your life now depends on the continuing to please a single person. To this all other objects must be secondary."[2] Also, in 1789, Elizabeth Foote Washington wrote: "One of my first resolutions I made after marriage was never to hold disputes with my husband . . . for it is their [women's] business to give up to their husbands."[3] In her opinion, this was God's plan from the beginning, from the Garden of Eden where Eve was made servant to Adam after the fall.

These two women show how women believed subordination to their husbands was the "right" thing to do as late as the eighteenth century. Indeed, most colonials viewed the patriarchal structure as simply following God's plan. Yet Mary Beth Norton, author of *Liberty's Daughters: The Revolutionary Experience of American Women, 1750-1800*, also writes that "the pervasive acceptance of female subordination in the secular realm did not necessarily imply a secondary status in religion."[4] Women preachers are one of the most notable groups of women who stepped outside of patriarchal boundaries.

But how can this be? Biblical passages dictate that women are to "learn in silence" and to not "teach or to have authority over a man" (1 Tim 2:12; 1 Cor 14:33 NIV). When women such as the seventeenth-century English Quaker Margaret Fell Fox argued for a woman's right to speak, they built it on many Old and New Testament examples of women who were speaking and leading and who were clearly doing so within the contexts of God's will. These arguments are repeated in women's arguments for equality in great detail in the nineteenth century and by many women in the twentieth and twenty-first centuries as well.

So the very foundation of a woman's right to speak had to be, and was, found in the hermeneutics that justified it. Those who have studied female mystics in Western history, such as Joan of Arc, Beatrice of Nazareth, Teresa of Avila, and many others, note that the first lever that moved the foot of subjugation off of the necks of women was that these women bypassed human, imperfect, male authority to heed the voice of a perfect God made of spirit, not flesh. Subjugation to imperfect men was in no way parallel to the relationship they experienced with a God who made them in his perfect image in the moment of creation. Before the curse, Adam and Eve were clearly equal, but differently gifted, partners—although I must make

---

2. Norton, *Liberty's Daughters*, 61.
3. Norton, *Liberty's Daughters*, 62–63.
4. Norton, *Liberty's Daughters*, 125.

it clear here that I am not making an argument for complementarity but for equality because complementarianism denies the fact that we are born with unique gifts that might be considered more "feminine" or "masculine" depending on the cultural norms in place at the time. Sin made men and women adversaries. It was not God's plan that women were to suffer; it was the consequence of disobedience.

Many also point to the many women who preached in the early church. Preceding these women is Anna, the temple prophetess, who held Christ as a baby (Luke 2:36–38). According to "Women Church Leaders in the New Testament," the list of these women in the first years of Christianity include Philip's daughters (Acts 21:9), Priscilla (Acts 18:26; Rom 16:3–5; etc.), Phoebe (Rom 16:1–2), Junia (Rom 16:7), possibly Chloe (1 Cor 1:11), Euodia and Syntyche (Phil 4:2–3), Nympha (Col 4:15), Apphia (Phlm 2), "the chosen lady" (2 John 1), "the chosen sister" (2 John 13), and probably Lydia (Acts 16:40).[5]

The story of American women preachers begins with a Puritan in the seventeenth century named Anne Hutchinson. It is a very American story of success and of resistance, as Hutchinson was the first to resist patriarchal rule. Oddly enough, it was because of her success as a Bible teacher that she landed in court. Obviously, being a successful Bible teacher is not committing a crime. The fact is that Puritans were intolerant of any who did not follow their beliefs, and they had the legal power to force others to submit. In early America, government and religion were closely tied together, with those occupying Virginia (which refers to the entire eastern seaboard in the early seventeenth century as colonists first arrived) required to attend church, pay taxes to support the church, and contribute to the financial support of ministers.[6] Persecution and imprisonment of dissenters was common and serious enough that it inspired Thomas Jefferson's "Virginia Statute for Establishing Religious Freedom" which was drafted in 1777, introduced to the legislature in 1779, and passed in 1786.[7] This also led to the First Amendment.

Later known for their part in the Salem Witch Trials, the early Puritans held power in Massachusetts in the early 1600s. When Anne Hutchinson and her family arrived by ship from England to join a Puritan colony in the Massachusetts Bay in 1634, merely a handful of decades after the first settlers had come to Jamestown in 1607, she was expected to conform to Puritan mandates.[8] The idea of America at the time had utopian overtones:

5. Mowczko, "Women Church Leaders."
6. "Thomas Jefferson."
7. "Thomas Jefferson and the Virginia Statute."
8. Lindley, *You Have Stept,*, 1.

"Founded in 1630, Massachusetts was to be a godly experiment, a 'city on a hill' whose example of the right ordering of society under God would shine back to the same England that had persecuted the Puritans," according to Susan Lindley, author of *"You Have Stept Out of Your Place": A History of Women and Religion in America*. Gail Collins, author of *America's Women: 400 Years of Dolls, Drudges, Helpmates, and Heroines*, agrees with this perspective. Collins notes that "the church was everything in early New England, the organizing principle around which the government, the community, and individual households revolved."[9]

Soon after she arrived, Hutchinson began holding well-attended weekly meetings at her house. In a colony of only about a thousand people, this well-spoken woman drew Puritans to her by preaching a gospel of grace.[10] Her popularity is best summed up in a quote by a newcomer named Edward Johnson, who said that Hutchinson "[preached] better Gospell than any of your black-coates that have been at the Ninneversity." However, Hutchinson's teachings and overt opposition to women teaching in general resulted in the enmity of the Puritan governor, John Winthrop.[11]

Part of Winthrop's dislike for Hutchinson was clearly a result of the fact that she had the rare gift of an education. Her father had been a clergyman in England and had educated her well beyond the levels other women could obtain, encouraging her to engage in theological debates with him.[12] With such popularity and with the confidence born of a good education, she would have been hard to stop in Winthrop's Puritan colony. She stayed out of reach for a long time. Her undoing was her challenge to Puritan authorities based on what she was teaching and the fact that she was a woman who taught both men and women. This resulted in the authorities pushing John Cotton, Anne's mentor and supporter, into agreeing she had to be "brought under control."[13] They went so far as to pass a "series of resolutions aimed at curbing dissidence, including a direct condemnation of the meetings at the Hutchinson home."

Prejudice against her is reflected in the words of the minister, Hugh Peters, in a statement made to Hutchinson: "You have stept out of your place, you have rather bine a Husband than a Wife and a preacher than a Hearer; and a Magistrate than a Subject."[14] Her main accuser was the gov-

---

9. Collins, *America's Women*, 28.
10. Collins, *America's Women*, 29.
11. Lindley, *"You Have Stept,"*, 2–3.
12. Collins, *America's Women*, 28.
13. Collins, *America's Women*, 29.
14. Lindley, *"You Have Stept,"*, 3.

ernor, though. We can assume he was a prideful sort of man from the fact that Winthrop's wife often expressed the fear that "she was not worthy of him."[15] Her subservience is sharply contrasted with Hutchinson's education and eloquence and an ethos built on her intelligence rather than capitulation to social mores.

Both Winthrop's power and his revulsion to women who attempted to argue with his theology are evident in his opening statement at Hutchinson's trial held in 1637. Winthrop said that Hutchinson acted in a way "not fitting for [her] sex" by holding meetings at her house, and that she had been brought to trial to "reduce" her.[16] After a theological debate in which he tried to fault Anne for preaching a doctrine of grace instead of "works"—to which she offered a strong defense—he shifted the discourse and demonstrated his power, taunting her by saying, "Daniel was delivered by a miracle; do you think to be deliver'd so too?"[17] Indeed, there was no rescue for Hutchinson; she was soon defeated in Winthrop's court. At the end of the trial, she was imprisoned and later banished to Rhode Island.[18]

What is significant here is that an educated woman speaking about God led to one of the first documented clashes between men and women in America that was focused on a woman speaking publicly and on matters of faith and religion. A woman wanting to speak about religion clearly threatened the social hierarchy the Puritans wished to maintain. Hutchinson's great success undermined the patriarchal norms that were supposed to keep her in her place. Yet she went unchallenged for a time because she was speaking for God, not for herself.

The next woman to defy the Puritans was one of Hutchinson's supporters, a woman named Mary Dyer. She left the church after Hutchinson's banishment and moved to Rhode Island along with her husband, William Dyer. "In the 1650s they returned to England, where Mary Dyer joined the Society of Friends or Quakers," Lindley writes, and "upon returning to New England, she felt called to witness to her former Puritan neighbors in Boston."[19]

By that time, the Puritans banished any Quakers who came to Massachusetts and even passed a law in 1658 allowing them to enforce the death penalty for any Quakers who would not stay out. Mary Dyer, banished in both 1638 and in 1657, came back in 1659 to visit two Quakers who had been imprisoned in Boston and ended up being banished yet a third time.

15. Collins, *400 Years*, 29.
16. "Transcript of the Trial."
17. "Transcript of the Trial."
18. Lindley, *"You Have Stept,"* 5.
19. Lindley, *"You Have Stept,"* 8.

In that same year of 1659 she returned, however, and was "literally on the scaffold" when given a reprieve and then banished yet again. She still came back in 1660 and was executed for her persistence. By this time, even her husband "questioned her sanity," but Lindley writes that "Mary Dyer knew quite clearly what her protest was and why she had to make it." In a letter to the General Court of Boston she claimed to "be following God's will and call" by protesting the treatment of Quakers in Massachusetts.[20]

We can comfortably characterize Dyer not only as a "martyr to religious liberty," as Lindley does, but also as a martyr for women's rights, creating an ethos built on fervent belief and determination, not one of a woman easily deterred by challenges. Notice that Dyer justified herself by appealing to the authority of God over that of men. She, like so many others who have been grouped into first-wave feminism, was willing to face any challenge in the face of injustice. And she was courageous enough to pay for her beliefs with her own life. In her final letter, Dyer compares herself to Esther who had to reveal to her husband, the king, that she was a Jew after Mordecai had manipulated him into issuing a decree to kill all of the Jews. The Puritans were likewise murdering the Quakers under the guise of law. At the end of Dyer's letter, she warned the Puritans that they would reap what they had sown.

In 1666, just a few years after the execution of Mary Dyer, a Quaker named Margaret Fell Fox published "Women's Speaking Justified, Proved, and Allowed by Scriptures" in England. Quakers, who allowed women to speak in their services, played a big role in women's liberation in the United States. When Quakers came to America in the 1620s and '30s and challenged religious authorities of the time with radical practices that allowed women to speak, they loosened the deep roots of prejudice that labeled women as "manly" or "promiscuous" for speaking publicly—labels that were commonly voiced for centuries—by replacing the negative stereotype with the idea of a woman literally speaking for God and being the voice of God.

When Fox wrote her famous tract, she began by referencing a scripture in John where women were the first to preach the resurrection of Christ and followed that with discussing the prophecy of Joel and a selection of other scriptures. In her first line, she specifically stated that she was writing to those who objected to women speaking in the church and then she pointed out how in the Garden of Eden both men and women were made in God's image. Silencing women is a form of subjugation that Fell saw as part of the curse in Genesis. After the fall, Fox argued, according to Scripture, if women did not speak, the seed of the serpent would. She went through a multitude of Old and New Testament examples of women speaking for and

---

20. Lindley, *"You Have Stept,"*, 8.

doing work for God, and then she confronted the Pauline scriptures that call for silence. She wrote:

> And what is all this to such as have the Power and Spirit of the Lord Jesus poured upon them, and have the Message of the Lord Jesus given unto them? Must not they speak the Word of the Lord because of these undecent and unreverent Women that the Apostle speaks of, and to, in these two Scriptures? And how are the men of this Generation blinded, that bring these Scriptures, and pervert the Apostles Words, and corrupt his intent in speaking of them? And by these Scriptures, endeavour to stop the Message and Word of the Lord God in Women, by contemning and despising of them. If the Apostle would have had Womens speaking stopt, and did not allow of them, why did he entreat his true Yoak-Fellow to help those Women who laboured with him in the Gospel? Phil. 4. 3. And why did the Apostles joyn together in Prayer and Supplication with the Women, and Mary the Mother of Jesus, and with his Brethren, Acts 1. 14. If they had not allowed, and had union and fellowship with the Spirit of God, wherever it was, revealed in Women as well as others? But all this opposing and gainsaying of Womens Speaking, hath risen out of the bottomless Pit, and spirit of Darkness that hath spoken for these many hundred years together in this night of Apostacy, since the Revelations have ceased and been hid, and so that spirit hath limited and bound all up within its bond and compass, and so would suffer none to speak, but such as that spirit of Darkness, approved of, Man or Woman.[21]

In her closing lines, she refers to those who would stop women from speaking as "ministers of Darkness."[22]

Her argument fails in some aspects because her rhetorical strategy of admitting to weakness in one area in order to claim indisputable strength in another seems to undermine the larger argument for a woman's right to speak publicly. For example, although Fox argues for spiritual equality, she does not argue that women are just as strong as men physically or intellectually. She admits to weakness in order to provide scriptures that say God is perfected in weakness and that he uses the intellectually weak to confound the wise. In short, she reaffirms the erroneous belief in the intellectual inferiority of women, and while she focuses on an interpretation of Scripture that will further her argument, it comes at a price. It is an imperfect imitation

---

21. Fell, "Women's Speaking Justified," 680.
22. Fell, "Women's Speaking Justified," 684.

of the apostle Paul's practice of obtaining authority through submission, of claiming weakness in a show of strength.

It is because of these types of ironies that religious arguments that have furthered the cause of social justice and equality for women have been discounted and sometimes ignored. This was a defense of preaching that was written to those who opposed it, not to Quakers who not only allowed women to speak freely in their meetings but also to hold "women's meetings in both England and America" where they developed "administrative skills" and took leadership roles.[23] Even so, Quaker women were considered such a threat to male authority by the Puritans that in 1656 the Quakers Mary Fisher and Ann Austin had their books burned in Boston and were "met with physical humiliation, punishment, and deportation" to Barbados.[24] Also threatening to the social order was the fact that almost half of the Quaker missionaries were women, giving them formal roles as speakers for Christ.[25] Finally, as those deeply familiar with Scripture, they could craft arguments for their own defense based on the Bible. The reason these women appealed to the Bible in their arguments and the reason they recounted their relationship with God was because this was an appeal to the highest authorities—the Word and God. They created an ethos out of their "call" to share the gospel with others which superseded that imposed by men and women in colonial America. Thus, the roots of first-wave feminism that call for a woman to speak publicly are found in the context of deep religious faith.

Women preachers were a phenomenon that characterized the practices of certain sects outside of mainstream Protestant religions. They certainly were not endorsed by Catholics. Yet it was not without struggle that other sects, such as Methodism, allowed women to speak. The Protestant John Wesley, the founder of Methodism, originally opposed women preaching but later changed his mind.[26] In fact his mother, Susanna Anneseley Wesley (1699–1742), shared "popular family devotions" with her community of believers.[27] When John was asked why he allowed women to preach, he replied: "Because God owns them in the saving of souls, and who am I to withstand God?"[28]

What is most fascinating about women preachers is how they shook up societal norms. Catherine Brekus, professor of the History of Religion

23. Lindley, "You Have Stept," 11–12.
24. Lindley, "You Have Stept,", 10.
25. Lindley, "You Have Stept,", 10.
26. Brekus, *Strangers and Pilgrims*, 133.
27. Hyatt, "Spirit-Filled Women," 236.
28. Brekus, *Strangers and Pilgrims*, 133.

in America at Harvard Divinity School, explains that women who were participants in the revivals in the First Great Awakening in the 1740s and '50s claimed a right to speak because they were so caught up in God. In conjunction with the move from an intellectual experience of religion to revivals among diverse groups, including Moravians, Methodists, Calvinists, Dutch Reformed (1720s), Puritans, and Baptists (1760s)—which were characterized by "charismatic preaching, emotional outbursts, public conversions, and heated debates among the standing clergy"—women found a place to speak in religious gatherings.[29] Nineteenth-century women made their voices heard by praying out loud, testifying, and doing both along with reciting scriptures when they were exhorting. Speaking aloud in church subverted any battle over who got to occupy the pulpit because women exercised their voices in these other ways.[30] Brekus points out that many women who spoke in church did so from the pew, not the pulpit, but the Methodists in the North did both.[31]

Often known as "Sisters in Christ" or "Mothers in Israel," Methodist women from the North were especially active as itinerant preachers.[32] Slaves were able to claim the authority to preach as well by claiming direct revelation from God.[33] Although considered a sect instead of an established denomination, the Methodists in total had about a half a million members by 1830, and their numbers speak of widespread influence. It is important to note that the term "mother in Israel" does not refer to a kindly, gentle mother nurturing all around her, which, based on the name, might be the assumed center of "ethos" by someone unfamiliar with the Bible. However, in Judges chapter 4, Deborah leads the battle against Israel's enemies, resulting in forty years of peace. In her victory song, she does two things of significance. She sings about how her people suffered because of their enemies: "Villagers in Israel would not fight; / they held back until I, Deborah, arose, / until I arose, a mother in Israel" (Judg 5:7 NIV). She also celebrates Jael, a woman who drove a tent peg through the temple of the enemies' leader, Sisera (Judg 4:17-24). So, by the work and strength of these two warrior women, the Israelites obtained peace, both "mothers in Israel." Another example of a "mother in Israel" is in 2 Samuel. As the Israelites laid siege to the cities of Abel and Beth Maachah, "a wise woman cried out from the city" (2 Sam 20:16 NIV). She asked to speak to Joab, the leader, and when he came, she

---

29. Brekus, *Strangers and Pilgrims*, 33–34.
30. Brekus, *Strangers and Pilgrims*, 127–28.
31. Brekus, *Strangers and Pilgrims*, 132.
32. Brekus, *Strangers and Pilgrims*, 131.
33. Brekus, *Strangers and Pilgrims*, 130.

reasoned with him. "You seek to destroy a city and a mother in Israel," she said (2 Sam 20:19 NIV). He responded that he just wanted the head of his enemy. "So the woman said to Joab, 'Watch, his head will be thrown to you over the wall'" (2 Sam 20:21 NIV). These women, these "mothers in Israel," were deadly. So as part of the ethos of women preaching in early America, for those familiar with the Bible the connotation was one of serious warfare, of good versus evil.

The "mother in Israel" ethos lay outside of the stereotypical positions in place in American culture, even though they were also based on religious perspectives. Positive changes in culture occurred because of the influence of women preaching, but also because of the influence of a shift in the definition of the ideal woman. Women were no longer defined by the stereotype of the colonial "Goodwife," who was more prone to evil and lust than men, but were now viewed as "Republican mothers," who were assumed to be more virtuous.[34] As I explain in *The Role of Female Seminaries on the Road to Social Justice for Women*:

> The transition from colonial "Good Wife" to "Republican Motherhood" and later to the 19th century "True Woman" was characterized by descriptions of how woman's moral character and influence were perceived. "For the Puritan Good Wife," a woman was to exhibit wisdom in a religious sense, but for the "Republican Mother," a woman was to exhibit wisdom in a political sense. Historian Susan Lindley quotes Linda Kerber as saying, "Motherhood was discussed almost as if it were a fourth branch of government, a device that ensured social control in the gentlest possible way." Yet, it would be a mistake to separate the religious disposition of the Good Wife from that of the Republican Mother. While varying amounts of attention were given to a woman's function, Lindley writes that "we must be careful not to separate too sharply 'political' and 'religious' spheres or functions." Also, although religion was an obvious type of social control, a sincerely felt relationship with God was often the pathway to spiritual peace and freedom within any social or political context. However, a crucial component for women's social emancipation came from women working to subvert the religious structures that tried to prohibit equality— not by turning away from God—but by providing an exegetical perspective that allowed for new hermeneutics to reveal that the Bible was not meant to limit but to liberate.[35]

---

34. Brekus, *Strangers and Pilgrims*, 146–47.
35. Welch and Ruelas, *Role of Female Seminaries*, 16–17.

Part of what gave women preachers a credible ethos was what the audience accepted as valid for their credentials to speak and to teach others. Brekus writes that "by emphasizing religious experience over education," participants in these sects "helped to break down the boundaries separating laity from clergy."[36] This echoes the earlier discussion in this chapter where I shared how the apostle Paul emphasized inspiration and revelation from God and argued that it superseded worldly knowledge and credentials. Charismatic worship and the right to speak characterized religious groups anywhere that women were allowed to speak in religious settings in the eighteenth and nineteenth centuries, but this also characterized the Pentecostals of the twentieth century, with the addition of a person obtaining greater levels of credibility when she spoke in tongues. It is ironic that Paul was the root of the religious fervor that allowed women the right to speak when he so clearly denied them that right in Scripture.

Even the traditional place of the preacher in the pulpit was shaken by American women and men. For example, the New Light clergy of the nineteenth century got out of the pulpit and mixed among the congregation while preaching;[37] something similar to the preaching style of Pentecostals from the twentieth century up until now. This movement out of the pulpit moved the space a speaker could occupy, allowing for more voices and for more participation from women who felt that by speaking from the pew, they were not challenging male authority. Brekus points out that in early America, many women who spoke in church did so from the pew, not the pulpit, but the Methodists in the North did both.[38]

There were many women preachers in the eighteenth and nineteenth centuries in America. Most of these women preached the Bible with great integrity and effectiveness. These include:

- Sarah Wright Townsend (Separate Baptist), 1759
- Margaret Meuse Clay (Separate exhorter), n.d.
- Mrs. Cook (African Methodist exhorter), 1811
- Zilpha Elaw (African Methodist), 1827
- Rachel Evans (African Methodist), n. d.
- Julia A. J. Foote (African Methodist), 1845
- Polly Hatheway (Congregational exhorter), 1812

---

36. Brekus, *Strangers and Pilgrims*, 37.
37. Brekus, *Strangers and Pilgrims*, 37.
38. Brekus, *Strangers and Pilgrims*, 132.

- Laura Smith Haviland (Wesleyan Methodist), 1844
- Elleanor Knight (Christian Connection), 1824
- Jarena Lee (African Methodist), 1819
- Harriet Livermore (nondenominational), 1822
- Sarah Orne (Methodist), 1839
- Sojourner Truth (nondenominational), 1845[39]

This is a small slice of a list provided by Catherine Brekus in an appendix to *Female Preaching in America*. Some of the Wesleyan/Holiness women preachers Susie Stanley lists in *Holy Boldness* include

- Mary Lee Cagle, b. 1864
- Sarah A. Cooke, b. 1827
- Mary A. Ettinger Glaser, b. 1836
- Lucy Drake Osborn, b. 1844
- Phoebe Palmer, b. 1807
- Amanda Smith, b. 1837
- Hannah Whitall Smith, b. 1832
- Alma White, b. 1862[40]

A couple of the more interesting and influential ones will illustrate how these women shattered cultural norms. When we look back at figures such as the seventeenth-century Protestant preacher and prophet Bathsheba Kingsley, who claimed to have direct communication with God and who would accost people wherever she went, talking about their wickedness and the horrible judgments that were to follow if they did not change,[41] then we must remember that all of these women, whether they gained acceptance or inspired resistance, drew attention to the absurdity of trying to force women to be silent through social pressure. Bathsheba was beaten by her husband and reprimanded by the great revival leader Jonathan Edwards but still refused to be silenced, even traveling as an itinerant preacher for a while.[42] She, like others, refused to allow resistance to silence her.

---

39. Brekus, *Strangers and Pilgrims*, 342–46.
40. Stanley, *Holy Boldness*, xiv–xxiv.
41. Brekus, *Strangers and Pilgrims*, 25.
42. Brekus, *Strangers and Pilgrims*, 23–26.

Not all women preachers held to solid doctrinal beliefs and practices; in fact, some were "mythmakers," but they still eroded the foundation of prejudice against women through their influence.

*Preach the word; be prepared in season and out of season; correct, rebuke and encourage—with great patience and careful instruction. For the time will come when people will not put up with sound doctrine. Instead, to suit their own desires, they will gather around them a great number of teachers to say what their itching ears want to hear. They will turn their ears away from the truth and turn aside to myths.—2 Tim 4:2–3, NIV*

One of the most interesting female preachers and "mythmakers" was the eighteenth-century "Public Universal Friend," or Jemima Wilkinson. While many American women preachers held to traditional interpretations of the Bible, she was one of those who had an unusual experience that attracted an audience to her. An ethos does not have to be built on the truth in order to be a magnet for followers. Wilkinson claimed to be a prophet and to communicate directly with God.[43] According to the *Encyclopædia Britannica*, she was born on November 29, 1752 in Rhode Island. After she became ill, she returned in October of 1776, claiming to have died and coming as the "Publick Universal Friend." This so inspired her followers that they "declared her a messiah," although she never claimed to be one.[44] She grew up as a Quaker, but after attending some meetings that were inspired by George Whitefield's revivals, she was dismissed from a Friends meeting in August of 1776. After getting sick and then claiming to have died and returned, she would only answer to the title of Publick Universal Friend or P.U.F. and referred to herself using male pronouns. Some members of her sect began a settlement near Seneca Lake in New York in 1788, and she joined them in 1790. By then, they had 260 people. She moved a few miles away in 1794 with her most devoted followers. Things eventually fell apart because of conflicts.[45] Brekus notes that Wilkinson preached conventional sermons but had many followers until her death. One story that reveals her popularity was that in 1782 she was invited to preach at the Methodist Episcopal Church in Philadelphia. The church was so overrun with listeners that many

---

43. Brekus, *Strangers and Pilgrims*, 82.
44. "Jemima Wilkinson."
45. "Jemima Wilkinson."

didn't even get to see her, but she reportedly refused to serve as entertainment and called her auditors to repentance.[46]

*Now the Spirit expressly states that in later times some will abandon the faith to follow deceitful spirits and the teachings of demons, influenced by the hypocrisy of liars, whose consciences are seared with a hot iron. They will prohibit marriage and require abstinence from certain foods that God has created to be received with thanksgiving by those who believe and know the truth.—1 Tim 4:1–3, NIV*

Although an unusual woman, as a precursor for women's rights P.U.F. had certainly been successful in demonstrating that a woman could be as effective a leader as a man, even to the point of extreme devotion—as her followers showed, even if there were serious flaws in her identity. Like P.U.F., there was another interesting religious leader in her time known as Ann Lee or Mother Ann who was doctrinally unsound but enormously popular. Born in England in 1736, she brought the Shaker sect from England to the American colonies.[47] Uneducated and from a working-class family, she worked in a textile mill in her younger years. She was 22 when she joined the Shakers, who were known for the "shaking and dancing that characterized their worship."[48] "The Shakers had a habit of interrupting local congregations by bursting into their services, railing against the church, and accusing married couples of whoredom."[49]

When Lee married, it became an unhappy union and led to her doctrine of celibacy later on.[50] She ended up giving birth to four children, all of whom died young. While imprisoned by English authorities in 1770, Lee had a vision that showed her how lust interfered with the work of Christ. It was during this lengthy incarceration in 1770 that Lee saw the "grand vision of the very transgression of the first man and woman in the Garden of Eden, the cause wherein all mankind was lost and separated from God."[51] It was further revealed to her that she was the female successor to Jesus and the incarnation of the second coming of Christ. From then on, she referred to herself as Mother Ann. Ann Lee emerged from this experience with the

---

46. Brekus, *Strangers and Pilgrims*, 81.
47. "Ann Lee."
48. "Ann Lee."
49. "Women in Religion."
50. "Women in Religion."
51. "Ann Lee."

status of a martyr within the society and the undisputed new leader of the sect. As Mother Ann, she boldly proclaimed her gospel at every opportunity: life with God begins by confession and is perfected by denial of the lusts of the flesh through celibacy."[52]

Ann chose to immigrate to America in 1774 with her husband and eight of her followers. Within two years, her husband left her and never returned. She and her followers were pretty successful drawing in converts, but their efforts often resulted in violent reactions, such as a time they were horsewhipped. Ann herself was "shamefully and cruelly abused" in one incident and never fully recovered.[53] "In spite of her convictions concerning celibacy, which doomed the Shakers to eventual extinction," Ann Lee was in many ways a progressive eighteenth-century woman who made a significant impact on her world.[54] She was a pioneer for justice and equality. She taught by example the equality of the sexes, economic justice, religious tolerance, and true democracy.

The Shakers in America lived a communal life based on common ownership of property and goods, celibate purity, and confession of sins. As a forerunner of women's rights, Ann Lee shows the power of charisma when overcoming limitations due to a lack of education or privilege. Like Jemima Wilkinson, she achieved godlike status among her followers, elevating her ethos to a place beyond criticism for her true followers. Of course, this may say more about the age than the woman, but it again shows the way religious groups provided indisputable proof that a woman could lead and could lead effectively, even to the point of being equated with God. Also, the idea that education was not needed as a qualification for a preacher was based in part on the realization that the early church in the New Testament was led by uneducated disciples called by Christ, as well as the scriptures attributed to the apostle Paul. Brekus notes the irony of how women preachers were often called "manly" for being able to expound the Scriptures better than their male counterparts at times, even without the benefit of an education.[55] It demonstrates the reluctance the community had in letting go of beliefs that supported women's intellectual inferiority, even in light of evidence that contradicted these beliefs.

The nineteenth century witnessed African American women speaking, often in the role of preachers, so their contributions to women's rights is even more significant as they had to overcome two major challenges: gender

---

52. "Women in Religion."
53. "Women in Religion."
54. "Women in Religion."
55. Brekus, *Strangers and Pilgrims*, 202.

and race. Zilpha Elaw was one of them. According to Hilary Ritchie, Zilpha was born in 1790 in Pennsylvania and went to live with a Quaker family after her parents died when she was twelve.[56] Jonette O'Kelly Miller describes a vision Zilpha had: "One day while milking a cow, Zilpha saw Jesus walking toward her. He appeared to say, 'Thy prayer is accepted; I own thy name.' Zilpha first thought she was seeing things; but when the cow looked in the same direction, bent its front legs and lowered its head to the ground, she knew the Lord had come to answer her prayer."[57]

Miller also recounts what is known as a "call story":

> In 1819, Zilpha was afflicted with an illness that lasted two years. One night as she lay on her sickbed, she received an angelic visitation and was told she would live and attend another camp meeting, where the Lord would reveal her life's purpose.
>
> One year and four months later, the promise was fulfilled. At a camp meeting in Burlington, she heard someone say, "Go outside of the tent while I speak with thee."
>
> As soon as she stepped outside the tent, she was led to exhort all those who stood near. Then she heard a voice say, "Now thou knowest the will of God concerning thee; thou must preach the gospel; and thou must travel far and wide." From then on, she submitted wholly to her divine commission.[58]

Later, she opened a school for Black girls, but then felt she should return to preaching. She preached between 1827 and 1840 as an itinerant preacher and then left for England in 1840. As Susie Stanley points out in *Holy Boldness: Women Preachers' Autobiographies and the Sanctified Self*, Elaw spoke out against racism. She characterized racist Americans as those who "readily sacrifice their intelligence to their prejudices."[59] Thus, her construction of ethos required much more than an acceptance of her calling.

In *Words of Fire: Anthology of African-American Feminist Thought*, several women preachers are listed in chapter one, including Maria Miller Stewart, Sojourner Truth, and Julia A. J. Foote. These women not only spoke, but both Stewart and Foote published their works. Truth dictated her stories. As one can imagine, Black women had a much different path into the ministry than white women. This resulted in a different vision of their role as equals in society, thereby creating an ethos of strength and fortitude that went far beyond their white contemporaries. Their inclusion in

---

56. Ritchie, "Zilpha Elaw."
57. Miller, "Zilpha Elaw."
58. Miller, "Zilpha Elaw."
59. Stanley, *Holy Boldness*, 13.

an anthology of feminist thought demonstrates an acknowledgement that religious rhetoric has contributed to the story of how women gained greater levels of equality in American society.

African Americans came to Christianity by a different route than other Americans. Anne Clifford explains that "at the turn of the eighteenth century a group of Anglican missionaries, known as the Society for the Propagation of the Gospel, came to the colonies with a special mission: preach Christianity to African slaves."[60] This is significant because the constant influx of slaves meant that African traditions were continuously revived. These traditions allowed women to be "diviners, herbalists, prophetesses, sages, and priests." In fact, for Africans, "to live was to participate in a religious drama," Clifford writes. Thus when the revivals of the Great Awakening in the 1740s came about, many African slaves were caught up in the movement and "by the mid 1750s, hundreds of slaves worshipped in Southern churches."[61] Both Moses, who led the Hebrews out of slavery, and Jesus, who stood up for the poor and downtrodden, were central to their faith.

By the time of the Second Great Awakening in the 1800s, more Black women than men attended church, but there were many new Black churches, allowing Blacks to obtain leadership roles.[62] Also, Northern preachers carried the message of abolitionism to Southerners. Maria Stewart and Sojourner Truth were preachers and abolitionists. After the Civil War, African American missionaries from the North came to covert those in the South, founding the African Methodist Episcopal Church in 1787 and the African Methodist Episcopal Zion Church in 1796.[63] As a result, Black women rejected the "true womanhood" ideals of white culture and embraced a vision of themselves as "ministers in their homes" with a "greater call to prophesy and evangelize."[64] It is easy to see a sharp contrast between the confidence that Sojourner Truth expresses in her speech "Ain't I a Woman?" and the more traditional sermons of white women preachers. Truth's challenging words included the following: "Look at my arm! I have plowed and planted and gathered into barns and no man could head me" and "Where did your Christ come from? From God and a woman!"[65]

Women preachers played a central role in gaining women the right to speak publicly, but so did the women who argued for their right to preach

---

60. Clifford, *Feminist Theology*, 156.
61. Clifford, Feminist Theology, 147
62. Clifford, *Feminist Theology*, 157.
63. Clifford, *Feminist Theology*, 159.
64. Clifford, *Feminist Theology*, 160.
65. Clifford, *Feminist Theology*, 158.

even though they were not preachers themselves. Two of note were Phoebe Palmer, who wrote *Tongue of Fire on the Daughters of the Lord*, and Frances Willard—best known for her leadership of the Women's Christian Temperance Union—who wrote *Woman in the Pulpit*. As is easy to see, defenses of a woman's right to preach had distinct political overtones in the context of the nineteenth century. The two were often intimately connected because to win the right to preach meant to win the right to speak publicly. The right to speak publicly meant women were able to grasp cultural and political power, as Willard did as the head of the WCTU.

In yet another category there were those women who blended their call to preach with politics. One of the most well-known preachers of the nineteenth century, who was the subject of the poem "Snow Bound" by John G. Whittier, was Harriet Livermore.

Born in 1788 in New Hampshire, Harriet had the rare gift of an education. Never tying herself to a single denomination, she concentrated on her goal to "restore the apostolic simplicity of the primitive church." She followed no creed except what she deemed "biblical truths" taken from the New Testament.[66] She became an itinerant preacher in 1821. A letter from 1827 describes her as eloquent:

> Her language was correct, persuasive, and judging by my own feelings, the profound attention and sympathy of the audience, extremely eloquent. Many wept even to sobbing . . . Judging, as I said, by my own feelings . . . I should say she is the most eloquent preacher I have listened to since the days of Mr. Waddell. But no language can do justice to the pathos of her singing. For when she closed by singing a hymn that might with propriety be termed a prayer . . . her voice was so melodious, and her face beamed with such heavenly goodness as to resemble a transfiguration, and you were compelled to accord them all to her.[67]

In 1827 Livermore preached in the House Chamber of Congress and returned several times in the 1830s. In spite of her popularity and these accomplishments, she was also known for having a temper, and she was thought to be mad by those who knew her. She traveled to Jerusalem ten times before she ran out of money and tried to evangelize the Native Americans in Kansas because she thought they were the lost tribes of Israel. She never married and narrowly avoided a pauper's burial because a friend donated her own plot for her burial.[68] Thus, her ethos was strengthened by

66. "Livermore, Harriet."
67. "Livermore, Harriet."
68. "Livermore, Harriet."

her ability to speak to Congress but was subsequently undermined by her flawed beliefs about Israel.

Those women preachers who have been lost to historical memory were no doubt inspired by those speaking publicly and took it upon themselves to enjoy the same privilege. However, the rise toward equality is not a steady or constant thread in the story. In fact, the practice of allowing women to speak rose and fell in waves. Since "Protestant revivalists" of the Second Great Awakening (1790–1840) "were suspicious of elite education and rejected traditional patterns of priestly authority," women became "female laborers" or preachers although still bowed to male authority. However, "as Protestantism became more institutionalized," these women were no longer allowed to speak or preach as leaders. It was a cycle repeated in different Protestant denominations at different times, but towards the end of the nineteenth century, it was clear that women had significantly eroded the barriers that denied them a voice. Today, especially within Pentecostal denominations, women have permanently gained the right to preach. Women in the social sphere no longer derive a benefit from these women, but the history is clear. When America was new, women speaking as preachers helped to change commonly held beliefs in colonial America that linked the act of women speaking publicly to the idea that they were being immodest, a belief that persisted into the nineteenth century.[69]

Another part of what eroded the barriers to women speaking was an increase in the population. Brekus points out that the population of America exploded during 1800 and 1820 when it went from 5.3 million to 9.6 million and again between 1820 and 1840 when it reached about 17 million.[70] The larger population, which included many immigrants, would obviously make it harder for any particular religion and its institutions to try to control Americans to the level experienced in the colonies before the Revolutionary War. As a result, in the final decades of the nineteenth century "female preaching finally gained acceptance beyond the Quakers, Universal Friends, and Shakers."[71]

In addition to the role women preachers played in opening the doors for a woman to speak publicly as a pure servant of God instead of as a "promiscuous" woman stepping out of her place in society, it was in the eighteenth and nineteenth centuries that the printing press really allowed women to have another "voice" as authors. They could publish autobiographies, doctrine, sermons, and other texts, as well as fiction and didactic

---

69. Zikmund, "Women Leaders," 288–89.
70. Brekus, *Strangers and Pilgrims*, 121.
71. Brekus, *Strangers and Pilgrims*, 119.

books. This extended their voice far beyond those in their presence and became a powerful impetus for women's leadership in reform movements that impacted prisons, prostitutes, education, abolitionism, insane asylums, temperance, and other areas. They used their voice to preach through the text, expounding on religious matters and shaping public opinions. As is noted by Mary Kelley, author of *Learning to Stand and Speak*:

> Between the American Revolution and the Civil War, women in the North and the South emerged as leaders in the nation's lively trade in texts. The number of genres in which they wrote expanded rapidly, as did the role they took in shaping a distinctively American literature. In the novels, histories, poems, and biographies they published and the magazines they edited, these women contributed to national discourses on religious doctrine and denominationalism, on politics and political parties, on women and domesticity, and on the nation and its potential as the world's redeemer. By the 1840s and the 1850s, the most successful of these writers and editors could expect to make a livelihood with their pen.[72]

The proliferation of women's writing in the nineteenth century also created an opportunity for women to be editors. Kelley focuses on Sarah Josepha Hale, editor of the *Lady's Book*, which was later renamed *Godey's Lady's Book*.[73] Although it is widely known that Hale spent forty years editing the most popular woman's magazine in its time, it is not widely known that she published *Woman's Record; or, Sketches of All Distinguished Women, from "the Beginning" till A.D. 1850*, which contained the biographies of sixteen hundred women.[74] She excluded African Americans and working-class women, but she did include some of the founders of female seminaries and academies. Clearly, women were using all opportunities to circumvent silence, in public or in the church, and in many cases they spoke as Christians and to an imagined audience of Christians. An ethos fashioned as a writer was much different than one as a speaker, and in many ways it was even more powerful since the influence was multiplied with having more readers and not being tied to time or to place, as it was with a speaker.

Publications by women preachers published in the nineteenth century include:

---

72. Kelley, *Learning to Stand*, 10.
73. Kelley, *Learning to Stand*, 7.
74. Kelley, *Learning to Stand*, 9–10.

- Ann Lee (1736–84): *Testimonies of the Life, Character, Revelations and Doctrines of Our Ever Blessed Mother Ann Lee, and the Elders with Her: Through Whom the Word of Eternal Life Was Opened in This Day of Christ's Second Coming by Rufus Bishop, Seth Youngs Wells, Shakers* (1816)

- Mary Dyer (1611–60): *A Remonstrance against the Testimony and Application of Mary Dyer: Requesting Legislative Interference against the United Society Commonly Called Shakers: Together with Some Affidavits and Certificates Showing the Falsity of Her Statements* (1818)

- Jemima Wilkinson (1752–1819): *Some Considerations, Propounded to the Several Sorts and Sects of Professors of This Age: On the Following Important Subjects. I. The Jew Outward, Being a Glass for the Professors of This Age; with a Postscript to the Same Subject. Ii. A Warning, in the Bonds of Love, to the Rulers, Teachers, and People of This Nation, Concerning Their Church and Ministry. Iii. An Advertisement to the Powers and People of This Nation. Iv. An Answer to That Common Objection against the United Friends, That They Condemn All but Themselves. : To Which Is Added, an Exhortation to the United Friends, Everywhere Scattered Abroad. Printed by Bennett Wheeler* (1779)

- Jemima Wilkinson (1752–1819): *A Wonderful Dream* (1810)

- Harriet Livermore (1788–1868): *Scriptural Evidence in Favor of Female Testimony in Meetings for the Worship of God* (1824)

- Nancy Towle (1796–1876): *Vicissitudes Illustrated, in the Experience of Nancy Towle, in Europe and America* (1833)

- Elleanor Knight: *A Narrative of the Christian Experience, Life, and Adventures, Trials and Labours of Elleanor Knight: To Which Is Added a Few Remarks and Verses* (1839)

- Sarah Edwards (1724–68): "Narrative" from the *Works of Jonathan Edwards* (1839)

- Laura Smith Haviland: *A Woman's Life Work: Labors and Experiences of Laura Smith Haviland* (1889)

I separated out the publication by African American women preachers for the purpose of showing just how prevalent their publications were in a time that presented added challenges to them due to racism. A few of these are:

- Zilpha Elaw (1790–1846): *Memoirs of the Life, Religious Experience, Ministerial Travels and Labours of Mrs. Zilpha Elaw, an American Female of Colour* (1845)

- Jarena Lee (1783–1864): *Religious Experience and Journal of Mrs. Jarena Lee, Giving an Account of Her Call to Preach the Gospel, Revised and Corrected from the Original Manuscript Written by Herself. Published for the Author* (1849)
- Amanda Smith (1837–1915): *An Autobiography: The Story of the Lord's Dealings with Mrs. Amanda Smith, the Colored Evangelist* (1893)
- Julia Foote (1823–1900): *A Brand Plucked from the Fire: An Autobiographical Sketch* (1886)
- Maria Miller Stewart, "Religion and the Pure Principles of Morality" (1831)

These lists are woefully short and only offer a fraction of what was being published at the time. Yet it does allow you to see the variety of these pieces. As voices in the continued cultural battle over who would define Christianity and according to what principles, these writings demonstrate a rejection of silence and are a type of resistance, particularly for African American women who refused the limitations placed on them by a deeply racist society which still allowed slavery until the Emancipation Proclamation of 1863. These works also show how eager women were to have a voice in American society and to reach their audience.

Ironically, because of the tyranny of some religious sects, the First Amendment passed in 1791 and broke the connections between church and state that allowed some to use the courts to enforce their religious doctrines. Yet as we can see, the influence and power of religion in shaping American life remained in place. Again, women preachers made important contributions to the goals of first-wave feminism by providing women with opportunities to speak publicly and in print. If their influence had not been important, then the desire to expunge them from the denominational histories of the 1830s and '40s would not have been necessary, as Catherine Brekus notes.[75] This historical desire to ignore or to remove women from the records is now counterbalanced by the new narratives that highlight women's history, and it is what drives many scholars into archival work.

Thus, despite the prevalence of women speaking, preaching, and publishing in the nineteenth century, their history was largely lost. In fact, it was the work of second-wave feminists who made it their goal to recover the lost histories. For example, Alice Kessler-Harris, Professor of American History at Columbus University, points out that it was in the 1960s that female historians began to see that women had been left out of history.[76] She

---

75. Brekus, *Strangers and Pilgrims*, 297.
76. Kessler-Harris and Juravich, "Seeking Women's Rights."

estimates that less than 10 percent of graduate students were women at the time. She was part of a group that created journals, conferences, and other opportunities for women to share their research as they began to recover women's histories. They celebrated women publishing books on women's history. But again, it was a work of recovery. This is why so few know of the history of women preachers. Male church historians expelled them from their records, and it has been the work of twenty- and twenty-first-century scholars to recover them.

To sum up, driven by a desire to speak for God, women preachers ignored, redefined, stretched, or confronted the biblical and social mores that sought to keep them silent and to undermine their work, drawing on examples from both the Old and New Testaments that presented women as leaders, warriors, prophets, and instruments of God. Although many contemporary Christian women do not claim to be feminists (and the term was not even in use until the early twentieth century, according to Nancy Cott),[77] those who have worked to recover women's history have been able to frame the divergent experiences of these women with a common theme: they all spoke publicly and they would not remain silent. When the women of the Seneca Falls Convention—which marks the official beginning of women's rights in the US—met in 1848, they were not the first to stand and speak for something they believed in.

Again, it is important to note that women preachers drew on a spiritually-defined ethos, or claim to credibility, that secular women did not. This ethos often included a "call story," which meant the women felt they had spoken directly to God or to Christ and had been given the directive to preach. It included claims to an "anointing" or evidence that a member of the Trinity was speaking through them to the congregation. For Pentecostals in the twentieth century and beyond, it included a claim that one had spoken in "tongues" and it often meant a demonstration of that gift in teaching or preaching. To speak in tongues is to speak in other languages or unknown languages, just as the disciples did in Acts 2 when the early Christians were sent the Holy Spirit. A woman, Agnes Ozman LaBerge, is known as the first to receive tongues as a sign of the baptism of the Holy Spirit in 1901.[78] This became accepted as a part of Pentecostal practices in its various forms. The irony of a Christian ethos is that the less a woman is full of herself, the more she is respected as a vessel of God. Even so, nineteenth-century and early twentieth-century women rejected the call so often and so regularly that

---

77. Cott, *Grounding of Modern Feminism*, 13.
78. "Agnes N. Ozman."

scholar Harvey Cox labeled it the "call-refusal motif," but ultimately, some women embraced the call to preach.[79]

*The Lord announces the word, / and the women who proclaim it are a mighty throng.—Ps 68:11 NIV*

While the call-refusal stories have largely disappeared, women preachers have only multiplied in number and in influence. Popular women preachers of today include Lisa Bevere, Priscilla Shirer, Beth Moore, Paula White, Victoria Osteen, Joyce Meyer, Lysa Terkeurst, and many others. To say that these women have nothing to do with women's claims to be equal and authoritative is to overlook a part of history scholars are hard at work trying to recover from the archives. Yet none of these women would claim to be feminists.

In conclusion, contemporary women preachers demonstrate that women have shifted away from the ironic position of having to symbolically bow to societal pressure while still taking their place in the pulpit. They have now shifted to holding unapologetic positions as caring leaders who work hard to inspire a congregation and lead them in the right direction. Of course, these positions of power are mostly in secular contexts. In *What Women Want: Pentecostal Ministers Speak for Themselves*, Kimberly Ervin Alexander and James P. Bowers point out that in the Church of God, many still believe that "a radical feminist agenda is being pushed by a few women" and that "women seeking equality as ministers undermine marriage and family," two myths that they specifically refute with the facts.[80] And what are the facts? The facts are that they interviewed "726 credentialed Pentecostal women ministers in the COG [Church of God] from across the United States" and found they were "mostly white," "politically conservative," "married," "middle-aged," and educated with either a bachelor's or a master's degree. The typical female minister's "views on the role of women do not vary appreciatively from the male ministers given her predominant affirmation that 'men are the scripturally designated priests of the home.'"[81] As I argued in my first published article on women preachers, the term "feminist" is used to attempt to destroy the careers of women in the church.[82] Alexander and Bowers observed that same factor at work, claiming that "this vitriolic language is intended to paint a picture of women as dangerous to the cherished

---

79. Cox, *Fire from Heaven*, 130–32.
80. Alexander and Bowers, *What Women Want*, 33, 25.
81. Alexander and Bowers, *What Women Want*, 87–88.
82. Welch, "Post-1960s Pentecostalism."

conservative identity" of many women preachers.[83] These accusations create "an external culture war that promotes male dominance as the lynchpin to marital, familial, and church health."[84] Published in 2018, the work of these scholars clearly illustrate that a woman's ethos is still at the heart of debates over her right to be considered equal, especially when it comes to her taking the position in a church as a pastor.

Again, at the heart of public speaking or writing (a form of speaking publicly as well) is a person's ethos. What makes one credible is tied to one's audience. It is co-created with them, and so to look at these texts and these stories in retrospect is to see both the speaker and the audience, meeting in shared worlds created through effective communication, through salient rhetorics. Estrelda Y. Alexander published the *Black Fire Reader: A Documentary Resource on African American Pentecostalism* in 2013 and illustrates the way that race has played a role in shaping arguments over a woman's right to preach. She offers an anthology of excerpts from African Americans who share opinions on many aspects of Pentecostalism and devotes an entire chapter to women which begins with a poem titled "Women's Rights."[85] In chapter three of her book, she includes a history that many ignored or dismissed for many years: Pentecostalism in America was birthed out of the Azusa Street Revivals, which were led by African Americans William Seymour, Lucy Farrow, and Jennie Evans Seymour. Although it is not until third-wave feminism that African Americans start demanding a seat at the table in secular feminist groups, Alexander charts a history that goes back much deeper and that illustrates the profound influence African Americans have had on American religion, especially within Pentecostalism.

Finally, I and many other scholars have worked hard to collect archival information and to conduct interviews with twentieth- and twenty-first-century women preachers. Knowing that ethos is a multi-layered, living sort of thing prone to definition and re-definition, it is easy to see how credibility might ebb and flow based on the status of women in a particular denominational, social, or spiritual structure in effect at any given time. However, while non-Christians view their identity and lifework in terms of a calling they find within themselves, Christians view their identity and lifework in terms of a calling that comes from outside of themselves and through God, one that resonates with what is inside of themselves. While a particular woman's ethos may be attacked through her own faults; through rumors, insinuations, lies, and partial truths; through her own blind spots,

---

83. Alexander and Bowers, *What Women Want*, 92.
84. Alexander and Bowers, *What Women Want*, 92.
85. Alexander, *Black Fire Reader*, 158.

misguided ambition, and all of the things that make us fully human, women preachers still have a voice today. It is not one that tries to mimic a man's voice, but rather it is a unique voice, all their own. I invite you to read the interviews I collected in *"Women with the Good News": The Rhetorical Heritage of Pentecostal Holiness Women Preachers*, published by the Centre for Pentecostal Theology Press in 2010, or *Deep Roots: Defining the Sacred Through the Voices of Pentecostal Holiness Women Preachers*, which came out in 2013 and is available through Kindle Publishing. These interviews will help you understand the great leaps in ethos that differentiate women of today from those of the nineteenth century.

So what should you take away from this discussion?

- Women who wanted the right to speak publicly or to publish written work under their own names and not with a pseudonym, like it or not, were indebted to women speaking for God.
- Women preachers—"exhorters," "laborers for Christ," "mothers in Israel"—often did not wish to challenge the social norm and only spoke in religious contexts because they felt compelled to do so. Their examples and influence had the ironic effect of opening doors for secular women to speak. It is ironic because the women who argued for the right to preach often did not carry that into an argument for a woman's right to speak publicly outside of religious gatherings.
- The limits on the rights of women in the eighteenth and nineteenth centuries in America were real and had serious consequences.
- Women found a voice through publishing, and many of these texts were religiously based arguments for a woman's right to speak or to preach that were inscribed into their autobiographies, sermons, and other genres.
- Christian women circumvented male systems of authority when they claimed to be called to preach by God and used their calling to undermine the illusion that a woman had a "place" that limited her.
- African American women were able to speak, but they did so from even more tenuous, dangerous positions as they preached or argued against slavery, and they also used the printing press to disseminate their doctrines and their stories, helping to undermine some of the racism in America.
- Social norms were enforced by both men and women, but the Bible was a recognized source of authority and therefore the most important text for defending women's rights in eighteenth- and nineteenth-century

America because the country was deeply influenced by Christianity. Different sects created social norms based on prevailing interpretations of Scripture.

- Scriptures that call for women to be silent and submit to men are contradicted by scriptures that advise women to cover their heads when they prophesy, define Christians as equal in Christ, and claim that women will prophesy in the "last days." This was a powerful tool for undermining the belief that women should not be able to speak publicly in church or in society.

- Contemporary women preachers can be analyzed in terms of ethos, the heart of authority for anyone. The role of ethos in claiming authority is central to understanding the effectiveness of women preachers and how they continue to exert influence by heeding the call to preach.

# 2

# The Role of Education in First- and Second-Wave Feminism

*Bluestockings, Literary Societies, and the Transition from "Butterflies to Eagles"*

The Battlefield: Texts and sermons that argued women were not physically capable of being educated on the same level as men, undergirded by the belief that women belonged in the home and should not pursue a career or intellectual or political work beyond that sphere.

The Opponents: "Scientists," philosophers, preachers, and men and women who believed women were not rational creatures, who thought women were physically incapable of learning, and who thought the purpose of women's lives was limited to raising a family and pleasing a husband versus men and women who argued that women were capable and had a right to be educated (for the purpose of being better Republican mothers or becoming teachers until married—and later, for the purpose of pursing a profession).

*Guiding questions for chapter 2:*

1. Why did men and women wish to limit educational opportunities for women? Why did early female seminaries and academies originally

only educate women in music, languages, and subjects like needlework or painting?
2. What types of cultural resistance sought to undermine an educated woman's ethos, or credibility?
3. How were the arguments designed to gain support for opening female seminaries and academies an ironic combination of reasons for offering women an equal education and reasons that supported cultural norms that limited their opportunities?
4. How did highly educated second-wave feminists use their positions as university professors to make a place for recovering the lost or ignored history of women in the United States? How did they create a place for scholarship on women to be included in the university?
5. In what ways were female seminaries and academies distinctly tied to Christian values and openly born out of the marriage between Christianity and education? What role did the idea of "missionary educators" play in opening the door for women who wanted to teach? How did these women, like women preachers, shift the ethos of a woman away from insulting "science" that claimed women were intellectually inferior toward a recognition of their ability to learn and teach?
6. How did women's public oral exams help shape a changing ethos of women by honoring their knowledge?
7. How did the printing press create a way for women to have public voices they could claim as their own without apology? How did the proliferation of women's magazines, such as *Godey's Lady's Book*—run by a female editor with articles written by both men and women—help change the public's views on women in America?

"Bluestockings" became an insult meant to define arrogant, boring women who used their education in an unflattering way. What's unflattering? Well, in the eighteenth century—and in the century that followed—"unflattering" was used to describe education or intelligence that was unapologetically on display. This only applied to women. Men were free—much more so than women—to flaunt their accomplishments and to display their knowledge without constraint.

Originally, the term *bluestockings* referred to a specific group of middle-rank eighteenth-century women who met to discuss their "scholarly accomplishments," which included "educational treatises," writings on Shakespeare, translations of the Greek playwright Epictetus, poetry, and an eight-volume *History of England*, according to *Women's Worlds: The*

*McGraw-Hill Anthology of Women's Writing*.[1] These women included Elizabeth Vesy (1715–1791), Frances Glanville Boscawen (1719–1805), Hester Mulso Chapone (1727–1801), Mary Granville Delaney (1700–1788), Elizabeth Montague (1720–1800)—known as "Queen of the Blues"—Elizabeth Carter (1716–1806), and Catherine Macaulay (1731–1791)—the author of a set of eight volumes of history—among others.[2]

The group was named when Benjamin Stillingfleet wore a pair of "blue worsted stockings" to one of their gatherings; he was too poor to afford the fashionable black silk stockings in fashion. The name was used as an insult to attack British women who were "proud of their accomplishments, despite growing prejudice against 'learned ladies.'" The term was carried into late eighteenth- and nineteenth-century American society and applied to women when others wished them to hide their education and intelligence to better fit into society.[3]

Denying women or other groups of people an education was a way to control and to limit them. Ridiculing others for obtaining an education was simply a result of the desire to maintain that control. In fact, this is the centerpiece of John Stuart Mills's (1806–1873) *The Subjection of Women*, where Mills argued that women had been enslaved to men through a lack of access to education because "the masters of women wanted more than simple obedience, and they turned the whole force of education to effect their purposes."[4] In other words, education made women less subservient.

The history of men's resistance to educating women stretches back to ancient Greece, as Gary Clabaugh explains in an article titled "A History of Male Attitudes Towards Educating Women," where he traces this attitude from antiquity to modern times. The belief that women could not go beyond their feelings and thus were biologically incapable of being educated; a professed desire to maintain a patriarchal social order; and the idea that women were imperfect versions of men (and men were imperfect versions of God)—these objections were almost without exception later imported into Christianity, its doctrines, and its practices, along with the idea that women could not be trusted because of their role in the fall of mankind in the Garden of Eden. Yet as Christianity developed, Catholics allowed women to serve in monasteries and have access to education, as mystics promoted a positive view of women. This positive view was often grounded in an adoration of the Virgin Mary, and as Martin Luther (1463–1546)—who

---

1. Warhol-Down, *Women's Worlds*, 285–86.
2. Warhol-Down, *Women's Worlds*, 285–86
3. Warhol-Down, *Women's Worlds*, 286.
4. Mill, *Subjection of Women*, 27.

did not see women as anything more than a way to obtain "solace" and "bear children"—argued, in the desire for women to be educated so they could read the Bible.[5] The push for women to have basic literacy in order to read the Bible gave them access to a very limited, basic education in the centuries that followed.

In light of the open resistance to women's education espoused by many, including great thinkers such as Socrates, Aristotle, Pythagoras, Livy, Seneca, Juvenal, Goethe, Nietzsche, Tolstoy, and so many others, the importance of education in the battle for women's rights is clear. Withholding knowledge was a way to subjugate women and support the illusion that men were more capable of intellectual endeavors than women.

It is significant that *The Essential Feminist Reader*, edited by Estelle Freedman, begins with an excerpt from Christine de Pizan's *The Book of the City of Ladies*, which was published in France in 1405. The excerpt opens with these lines: "One day as I was sitting alone in my study surrounded by books on all kinds of subjects, devoting myself to literary studies, my usual habit, my mind dwelt at length on the weighty opinions of various authors whom I had studied for a long time."[6] Clearly, Pizan was an educated woman, rare for her time. She gives the reader an image of herself with a backdrop of books, engaged in learning. By doing so, she defines herself. She undermines the attack on a woman's ethos that labeled the woman as uneducated or incapable.

Pizan goes on to explore why, in the books they wrote, men so often characterized women as frail and less intellectually capable, and then she pretends to have a conversation with Lady Reason, who assures her:

> My daughter, since I told you before, you know quite well that the opposite of their opinion is true . . . if it were customary to send daughters to school like sons, and if they were then taught the natural sciences, they would learn as thoroughly and understand the subtleties of all the arts and science as well as the sons.[7]

When feminists of today trace their roots, they trace it to a woman arguing for other women to be educated because they are (and were) just as capable of men—if given a chance. However, it is important to point out that the roots of arguments for women's education are almost always situated within Christian thought and doctrines. The relationship between women's

---

5. Clabaugh, "History," 176.

6. Christine de Pizan, *The Book of the City of Ladies*, quoted in Freedman, *Essential Feminist Reader*, 4.

7. Christine de Pizan, *The Book of the City of Ladies*, quoted in Freedman, *Essential Feminist Reader*, 6.

liberation and Christianity is as undeniable in arguments for female education as it was with public speaking. Yet this avenue was also full of irony and frustration, with advocates for women's education often bowing to patriarchal structures as they tried to justify a place within the male-dominated society that would allow them to be educated.

Another often-anthologized text is by the Mexican nun Sor Juana Inés de la Cruz, who wrote "La Respuesta" in 1691. It was a response to the publication of Sor Juana's theological criticism of a famous sermon, a document that was published without her permission along with a letter from her bishop praising her for her "brilliance," but also asking her to refrain from "secular study and writing of any kind," and especially to avoid the "masculine field of theology."[8]

In her reply, Sor Juana followed the same pattern Margaret Fell Fox used in 1666 by listing all of the biblical women who had acted as leaders. She also put her knowledge on display by drawing on other examples of women who lead, such as the Sibyls, Minerva ("daughter of great Jupiter and mistress of all the wisdom of Athens, adored as goddess of the sciences"), Polla Argentaria, Arete, Nicostrate ("inventor of Latin letters and most erudite in the Greek"), and the list goes on and on.[9]

Like Pizan, she also began by presenting herself as an educated woman. In her first few lines, she wrote: "I study because I must."[10] Then, after communicating the breadth of her knowledge by establishing a long line of brave, educated, and wise women who had come before her, she argues that it is foolish for "malicious" souls—hinting broadly at her bishop—to try to interpret Scripture.[11] "It is like putting a sword in the hands of a madman," she wrote, "though the sword be the noblest of instruments for defense," because "in his hands it becomes his own death and that of many others."[12] The reason for attacking her bishop's interpretation of Scripture is obvious. He was using it to justify his attempt to silence her.

The whole of her letter is a defense of a woman's right to learn and to use her knowledge as she wishes. In it, Sor Juana confronts the Pauline scriptures from 1 Timothy that say a woman should learn in silence and should not teach or take authority over a man, arguing that these are words fit for Paul's time, not hers. She wrote, "There can be no doubt that in order to understand many passages [of Scripture], one must know a great deal

8. Bizzell and Herzberg, "Sor Juana," 781.
9. Bizzell and Herzberg, "Sor Juana," 784.
10. Bizzel and Herzberg, "Sor Juana," 784.
11. Bizzell and Herzberg, "Sor Juana," 785.
12. Bizzel and Herzberg, "Sor Juana," 785.

of the history, customs, rituals, proverbs, and even the habits of speech of the times in which they were written, in order to know what is indicated and what is alluded to be certain sayings in divine letters."[13] By drawing out these contexts, she emphasizes that none of us actually reads something "literally" outside of our culture and experience. This is a point lost on some Christian fundamentalists today.

Both Pizan and Sor Juana were fighting to defend what they knew to be of such great value: an education. Mary Astell would ask for the same thing in *A Serious Proposal to the Ladies*, published in England in 1694. Like the other two women writing in the seventeenth century, Astell wrote from a Christian perspective and suggested that a monastery—to be referred to as a "Religious Retirement"—be built for women.[14] This would help them to be "kept out of the road Of Sin" to enjoy a "*contemplative* Life." She argues that women should be educated so they wouldn't be misled. "For since GOD has given Women as well as Men intelligent Souls, why should they be forbidden to improve them?" she asks. Astell says she does not mean to go against the Pauline scriptures calling for women to not teach or usurp authority, but she sees no reason that they can't be educated so they can "form in our own minds a true Idea of Christianity."[15]

Mary Wollstonecraft would naturally be next, as she argued for women's education as well as women's rights, but I'm going to come back to her in the next chapter when I discuss politics.

Another milestone on the fight for a woman's education is Judith Sargent Murray, who wrote *On the Equality of the Sexes* in 1791 and published it about a year ahead of Mary Wollstonecraft's more famous text. In it, she too addresses the scriptural and cultural ties that bind, but she also writes:

> And if we are allowed an equality of acquirements, let serious studies equally employ our minds, and we will bid our souls arise to equal strengths. We will meet upon even ground, the despot man; we will rush with alacrity to the combat, and, crowned by success, we shall then answer the exalted expectations, which are formed. Though sensibility, soft compassion, and gentle commiseration, are inmates in the female bosom, yet against every deep laid art, altogether fearless of the event, we will set them in array; for assuredly the wreath of victory will encircle the spotless brow. If we meet an equal, a sensible friend,

---

13. Bizzel and Herzberg, "Sor Juana," 787.

14. Mary Astell, *A Serious Proposal to the Ladies*, quoted in Freedman, *Essential Feminist Reader*, 21.

15. Mary Astell, *A Serious Proposal to the Ladies*, quoted in Freedman, *Essential Feminist Reader*, 22.

we will reward him with the hand of amity, and through life we will be assiduous to promote his happiness; but from every deep laid scheme, for our ruin, retiring into ourselves, amid the flowery paths of science, we will indulge in all the refined and sentimental pleasures of contemplation: And should it still be urged, that the studies thus insisted upon would interfere with our more peculiar department, I must further reply, that early hours, and close application, will do wonders; and to her who is from the first dawn of reason taught to fill up time rationally, both the requisites will be easy.[16]

In another influential piece which was written in 1799, Hannah More wrote "Strictures on the Modern System of Female Education" and argued against the ridicule of women. She also argued for valuing their influence. In the eighteenth and nineteenth centuries, influence was touted as the best, most preferable way a woman could obtain and exercise power. Obviously, the problem with influence is that it indicates that a person does not actually have power but has to inspire another to take action. So influence could result in action—but only through the hands of another. A second-place prize, to be sure, if it's all you have to enact change.

She advocated for a woman to be educated by writing that she imagined "a country where our sex enjoys the blessings of liberal instruction, of reasonable laws, of a pure religion, and all of the endearing pleasures of an equal, social, virtuous, and delightful intercourse."[17] Like others of her time, she argued that as mothers, women would use their education for raising and educating their children."To you also is consigned the mighty privilege of forming the hearts and minds of your infant sons," she says to encourage her readers to pursue an education.[18]

The history of women's education in the United States demonstrates how the long battle for an education, which led to equal opportunities for employment, was finally won. In what would become America, the first school to educate young women was established by the Ursuline Sisters in New Orleans in 1727.[19] "Ursuline" refers to a Roman Catholic religious order of women that was "dedicated exclusively for the education of girls."[20] It was founded in 1535 in Brescia, Italy by St. Angela Merici. Ursula was a fourth-century martyr and St. Angela founded the order after having a vision.

16. Murray, *On the Equality*.
17. Warhol-Down, *Women's Worlds*, 296–97.
18. Warhol-Down, *Women's Worlds*, 306.
19. Welch and Ruelas, *Role of Female Seminaries*, 47.
20. "Ursuline."

The next school opened in 1742 and was called the Bethlehem Female Seminary.[21] It was in Pennsylvania. Several opened after that, with Sarah Pierce's Litchfield Academy opening in 1792. The Quakers and the Moravians were responsible for opening many of the schools available to women in the eighteenth and nineteenth centuries.

The timeline of the schools that opened in the eighteenth and nineteenth centuries as listed in *The Role of Female Seminaries on the Road to Social Justice for Women* includes:

1784, Bingham's School for Girls, Boston, Massachusetts

1807, Ann Smith Academy, Lexington, Virginia

1812, Friends' Academy, New Bedford, Massachusetts (remember that "Friends" refers to Quakers)

1813, Maryville Female Academy, Tennessee

1818, Madame Perdreville's school for girls, Missouri

1819, Brainerd Mission, Chattanooga, Tennessee—a school for Cherokees

1821, Troy Female Seminary, New York

1823, Hartford Female Seminary, Connecticut

1827, Shelby Female Academy, Lexington, Kentucky (First Lady Mary Todd Lincoln attended between 1827 and 1837)

1828, Ipswich Female Seminary, Massachusetts

1830, Sims Female Academy, Alabama

1832, Wheelock Academy, Oklahoma—a school for the Choctaws

1833, Chillicothe Female Seminary, Ohio (First Lady Lucy Ware Webb Hayes attended from 1837 to 1844)

1835, Forsyth Female Academy, Georgia

1837, Mount Holyoke Female Seminary, South Hadley, Massachusetts

1839, Farmville Female Seminary, Virginia (now Longwood University)

1843, Geauga Seminary, Chester, Ohio (First Lady Lucretia Rudolph attended from 1847 to 1849)

1846, Cherokee National Female Seminary, Oklahoma

1848, Oak Ridge Mission, Oklahoma—for the Seminoles.

---

21. Welch and Ruelas, *Role of Female Seminaries*, 47.

1849, Springfield Female Seminary, Ohio (First Lady Caroline Levinia Scott Harrison graduated in 1853)

1852, The Bloomfield Academy for Chickasaw Females, Oklahoma

1880, Sasakwa Female Academy, Oklahoma—for the Seminoles

1891, Mekasukey Academy, Oklahoma—for the Seminoles[22]

This is a severely reduced list, as the number of female seminaries and academies opening in the US is in the hundreds and, as scholar Thomas Woody noted, many would often only open for a short time before closing.[23] Woody conducted extensive archival research on women's education and published a two-volume series called *A History of Women's Education in the United States* in 1929 (I was only able to obtain a reprint from 1966). As one of my most treasured possessions, this rare repository of history, copies of certificates, pictures, and excerpts from letters, pamphlets, course curriculum guides, and so on is something you should own if you are truly interested in the history of women's education. No other scholar even comes close. However, since Woody did not have access to information on Native American institutions in 1929, of particular importance in this list are the schools associated with Native Americans. Just as the opportunity for women to preach allowed room for African American women to gain a voice, educating Native American women would allow room for them to have a voice as well. These are pieces of history that are often addressed separately and not put into the context of each other. It is significant that the histories which only share information on boarding schools for Native Americans do not usually address those institutions which were built and run by the tribes themselves. African Americans also laid claim to their own education, and thus their own potential for success, in institutions such as Spellman University (originally the Atlanta Baptist Female Seminary) later on.[24]

As an example, young women at the Cherokee National Female Seminary (CNFS) wrote the articles, essays, and poems for the school's newspaper, *A Wreath of Cherokee Rosebuds*. In fact, the first edition, published in 1854, begins with a poem by Corrinne. It is titled "Our Wreath of Rose Buds." After asking where the "roses"—a metaphor for the young, female students—originate, she writes, "No, our simple wreath is twined / from the garden of the mind / where bright thoughts like rivers flow / and ideas

---

22. Welch and Ruelas, *Role of Female Seminaries*, 47–58.
23. Woody, *History of Women's Education*, vol. 1, 329.
24. Welch and Ruelas, *Role of Female Seminaries*, 88.

like roses grow" in order to celebrate the opportunity to be educated.[25] It is also of note that the article immediately following is written entirely in the Cherokee syllabary, a sign of cultural pride.

Despite this, Devon Mihesuah points out that the "curriculum of the Cherokee seminary did not include any aspect of Cherokee culture."[26] It was also not an institution full of full-blood Cherokees, but had both mixed-blood and full-blood students, with many who appeared Caucasian "yet were acutely aware of themselves as Cherokees."[27] In fact, "a number of Cherokee females were economically, socially, and physiologically nearly identical to Victorian society's white women, and many seminary students subscribed to the same value system as whites even before they enrolled."[28] Chief John Ross himself was mostly white.[29] Noting the diversity of the students, Mihesuah asks, "Could there be more than one Cherokee culture?"[30] The school newspapers communicated a national pride that Mihesuah describes as not bicultural, but part of a "highly acculturated subculture."[31]

Education was a tool of assimilation, but not all went as lambs to the slaughter, as the young women at the Cherokee National Female Seminary clearly demonstrate. Assimilation had begun long before the school was built and would continue for long after. So this moves the conversation away from the subjugation of women in general and into a complex topic of how education was used as a means of control. Knowing that the entire field of English literature was once rooted in the ideology of British imperialism and that educational systems were used by colonizers to force assimilation, the "taste," or higher cultural sensibility, displayed in the school newspapers reflect assimilation, but they also show that "colonized cultures have often been so resilient and transformative that they have changed the nature of imperial culture itself. This "transcultural" effect has not been seamless or unvaried, but it forces us to reassess the stereotyped view of colonized peoples' victimage and lack of agency."[32] While some postcolonial scholars try to find some version of culture prior to colonization, Bill Ashcroft argues that this is a mistake, since culture and identity are linked so that one's culture can never be destroyed because it is the way people "make sense of" and "inhabit"

---

25. Gunter and Hicks, "Our Wreath," 1.
26. Mihesuah, *Cultivating the Rosebuds*, 2.
27. Mihesuah, *Cultivating the Rosebuds*, 2.
28. Mihesuah, *Cultivating the Rosebuds*, 3.
29. Faulk and Welge, *Oklahoma*, 53.
30. Mihesuah, *Cultivating the Rosebuds*, 5.
31. Mihesuah, *Cultivating the Rosebuds*, 107.
32. Ashcroft, *Post-Colonial*, 11, 3.

the world, no matter the fate of the way that culture is expressed in various forms.³³ Thus, the CNFS newspapers capture ways that the young Cherokee women saw life, made sense of life, and understood life and each other, and do not serve as evidence of the mere imitation of Euro-American culture.

The essays and poems in these papers also represent a "standpoint," which is an important theory used by many feminist scholars today. Standpoints "emerge when those who are marginalized and relatively invisible from the vantage point of the epistemically privileged become conscious of their social situation with respect to socio-political power and oppression and begin to find a voice."³⁴ While not overtly political, the young women writing for the school newspapers asserted themselves in a variety of important ways, including attempts to define themselves through the rhetoric of "taste" as defined by the rhetoricians of the time (Blair, Campbell, and Newman—Newman's textbook was used to educate teachers at Mount Holyoke and was thereby infused into the curriculum of the CNFS, since their teachers came from that school).³⁵

Education and religion were intimately intertwined at the CNFS, as they were at most female seminaries and academies of the eighteenth and nineteenth centuries. The distinctly Christian beginnings of American education are well documented. For example, Mary Lyon, who founded Mount Holyoke, felt women should be both teachers and missionaries. "As 'missionary-educators,' women were sent to the West and the South as 'cultural and civilizing influences.'"³⁶ In fact, Mary Lyon was converted to Christianity by Joseph Emerson and ended up converting about 25 percent of her students over the course of her career. She was, in effect, a woman minister. Thomas Woody, author of two volumes on *A History of Women's Education in the United States*, wrote:

> Though religion played a prominent role in the life of most schools of the early part of the last century, and Christian character and usefulness were almost without exception reckoned as true objectives . . . there is no exaggeration in saying that at Mount Holyoke there was probably more personal religious fervor than in any other single institution. Miss Lyon was prone to regard the success of her efforts to create the school as sealing a covenant with God for the advancement of His Kingdom.³⁷

33. Ashcroft, *Post-Colonial*, 3.
34. Bowell, "Feminist Standpoint Theory."
35. Mihesuah, *Cultivating the Rosebuds*, 28.
36. Welch and Ruelas, *Role of Female Seminaries*, 133.
37. Woody, *History of Women's Education*, 1:362.

Catharine Beecher—sister to the famous Harriet Beecher Stowe and founder of Hartford Female Seminary—was certainly no exception. Her famous essay "American Women, Will You Save Your Country?" argued that women should work to convert people in the West. On the University of Michigan's "Religion in Schools" webpage, they write:

> Evangelism was a significant cultural force during the first half of the nineteenth century and schools provided centers for revivals. Ministers preached and prayed over women students hoping the students would be converted; and some students came to school expecting and hoping for religious experiences. Because of the close association between seminaries and revivals, almost every denomination built their own seminaries and colleges where revivals were led by ministers from their own denomination. These schools were open to students from any religious persuasion, but attendance at weekly religious services and daily prayers were mandatory.[38]

So how did women in the eighteenth and nineteenth centuries win the right to an education beyond the lower grades when they could not justify it by preparing for a job outside of the home? How did women—who themselves supported and reinforced the patriarchal structures that defined them as "less than" men intellectually, morally, spiritually, legally, and socially—find a way to gain an education and to justify it while remaining in their "place"? Possible answers to these questions include: To justify it through a desire to improve oneself as a Christian, to work as a missionary to convert others, and to educate one's children, converting them as well. Another answer is more political.

Just as with women preachers, these women deferred to and used those social structures by—whether intentionally or not—subverting them to make a place for themselves. One tactic used to argue that a woman should be educated was to define her education as useful for attending to her family better.[39] Another was to be a better "gentleman's companion." Eventually, however, it would be justified by the ideals of Republican motherhood, often referred to as the "Fourth Branch of Government," which dictated that a mother was essential for creating good citizens and thus needed to be educated.

Let's look at one example. Emma Willard, founder and leader of Troy Female Seminary (established in 1821) spoke before the New York Legislature in 1819. Part of her argument for funding her seminary was this:

---

38. "Religion, Race, and Culture; Religion in Schools," quoted in Welch and Ruelas, *Role of Female Seminaries*, 38–40.

39. Welch and Ruelas, *Role of Female Seminaries*, 43.

It is the duty of a government, to do all in its power to promote the present and future prosperity of the nation, over which it is placed. This prosperity will depend on the character of its citizens. The characters of these will be formed by their mothers; and it is through the mothers, that the government can control the characters of its future citizens, to form them such as will ensure their country's prosperity. If this is the case, then it is the duty of our present legislators to begin now, to form the characters of the next generation, by controlling that of the females, who are to be their mothers, while it is yet with them a season of improvement.[40]

To sum up:

[In the US, three seminaries] are often used to characterize the whole era: Emma Willard and Troy Female Seminary (1821), Catharine Beecher and Hartford Female Seminary (1823), and Mary Lyon and Mount Holyoke Female Seminary (established in 1837 and included in the list of "Seven Sisters" below), although there were hundreds of female seminaries and academies across the North and the South. Horowitz would add Zilpah Grant's in Ipswich, Massachusetts (1828) to the list because of its profound influence. Later, the "Seven Sisters" would come to represent the best of female education, with only one of the original three still a part of the group. These are: Barnard College (1889), Bryn Mawr College (founded by Quakers) (1885), Mount Holyoke College (1837), Radcliffe College (1879), Smith College (1871), Vassar College (1861), and Wellesley College (1875).[41]

In 1926, the Seven Sisters College Conference began. This conference gave these institutions their nickname. This is important because in the history of women's education in the United States, Christianity played a starring role in the achievement of equal rights for women. Education was a key component in achieving the rights we enjoy today. In fact, many Christian women were devoted to education. Abraham Ruelas recovered and documented the history of Pentecostal women in his book *Women and the Landscape of American Higher Education: Wesleyan Holiness and Pentecostal Founders*. His work is important because the idea that obtaining an education for women was antithetical to Christianity is not true in practice, and in fact, creating institutions of higher education was seen as Christian work designed to help convert the lost and to train future mothers

---

40. Welch and Ruelas, *Role of Female Seminaries*, 124.
41. Welch and Ruelas, *Role of Female Seminaries*, 124.

and leaders as Christians, knowledgeable in scriptures and doctrines that defined their faith.

Although Emma Willard is not considered a first-wave feminist, in response to the idea that she thought a woman's highest goal was to please a man, Willard once wrote that for a Christian "the will of God . . . is the only standard for perfection."[42] Like the women mystics and women preachers, she too recognized that deifying men was a barrier to living a full life.

Education and work are interrelated, and it was through these female academies and seminaries that women got the opportunity to do work that was not manual labor outside of the home. As teachers, women embraced the first real working opportunity made available to them, although the pay was low and women were expected to quit once they were married. Education helped women form and lead reform societies that gave them a chance to display their intelligence and leadership skills. Education gave women a chance to open female seminaries and academies, to create and publish textbooks, and to teach in those classrooms as well.

Within the schools, young women were given the opportunity to be much like the Bluestockings (a derogatory term used for intelligent women), putting their knowledge on full display in written and spoken contexts. For example, in *Learning to Stand and Speak*, Mary Kelley describes the role literary societies played in giving women an opportunity to exercise their critical thinking skills. These societies, usually housed in female seminaries, offered women a place to speak authoritatively on a variety of subjects.[43]

We also briefly touched on the fact in chapter one that many women preachers published their autobiographies, sermons, and other types of texts. However, this is only a thin slice of a much bigger pie. Increased access to education led to the desire to write for many women. As Mary Kelley explains in *Learning to Stand and Speak*, in the last decade of the eighteenth century, "an expansive literary marketplace brought thousands of women into the world of print between the American Revolution and the Civil War.[44] They wrote "travel literature, biographies, novels, and histories," but it was the explosion of the periodicals that really helped women gain a voice. Women had their work published in publications that were often edited by other women. In fact, when *Godey's Lady's Book* appeared in 1830, there were already "scores" of other women's magazines in circulation.[45] Kelly estimates there were about one thousand four hundred of them in circulation by 1840.

---

42. Welch and Ruelas, *Role of Female Seminaries*, 39.
43. Kelley, *Learning to Stand*, 16.
44. Kelley, *Learning to Stand*, 56–57.
45. Kelley, *Learning to Stand*, 58.

Also, the nature of publishing itself changed from local printers hired to print and distribute texts to printers who "collaborated and shared in the profits and its attendant risks," making the printed word into a business very different than it was before.[46] The power of print became one of the most useful tools there was for breaking the silence of women, but it would have been less useful if these women weren't using the education they gained at the female seminaries and academies that proliferated in the eighteenth and nineteenth centuries.

Also significant is that at a time when men and women persisted in the belief that women should not speak publicly, oral examinations were given to female students before graduation, as Mary Kelley discusses. These were performed before "an audience of assembled dignitaries, including trustees, parents, teachers, and classmates," on a stage and then interrogated. One student recalled it lasted five hours. In this student's particular case, she was questioned, sent to the board to display her command of math, commissioned to speak in Latin, Greek, or French, and read a composition as a "grand finale."[47]

In the nineteenth century, a visitor to a women's school in Ohio wrote:

> One word only in regard to your institution. Everything indicates that you have been well and faithfully trained not only to perform regularly certain exercises, but to think and acquaint yourselves with history. You cannot but know, then, that in all ages and in all countries, up to a very recent period, your half (and the common parlance is equally complimentary and true) the better half of the species was viewed, *as a race holding to man the relation of butterflies to eagles.* Cast by the beneficence of Providence in a more delicate mould, you were considered in the light of statues, in which grace and beauty were the chief requisites, gaudy playthings in which mind was by no means necessary.
>
> All that has passed away, and we hope, forever. A new era has dawned upon you, not the mental deliverance and independence of Miss Frances Wright, separating you from God and eternity, as it would emancipate you from this base thralldom of the past. But it has been proved, no longer to be contested, that you have minds capable of illimitable progress, differing, indeed in some respects, from the male mind, but differing, perhaps in your favor. It has been shown, in innumerable instances, that you are quite as susceptible of intellectual, and more docile to

---

46. Kelley, *Learning to Stand*, 61.
47. Kelley, *Learning to Stand*, 96.

moral training than man; that thus you can become, what you were formed to be, an helpmate for him, his intellectual companion, his guide, philosopher, and friend, cheering existence with a mental radiance all your own, a mental radiance differing from that of many, only by that beautiful diversity, which marks all the works of God."[48]

Again, education led to working opportunities, but these would be experienced on a small scale in the eighteenth century and on a broader scale after World War II. As America became industrialized in the latter nineteenth century and as more working opportunities emerged, some women chose to work in the mills and factories. These jobs required long hours and hard manual labor. These experiences were part of the battle against employers who worked their people into early graves and endangered them in other ways. Rebecca Harding Davis wrote *Life in the Iron Mills* in 1861 and Fanny Fern (Sarah Payson Willis Parson) wrote "The Working Girls of New York" in 1868 to document these hardships.

However, although opportunities were limited for both men and women in the nineteenth century, after women took over men's jobs in World War II they found opportunities to work in a variety of roles, albeit under the sexist social paradigms that characterized the 1940s and '50s.

In fact, injustice in the workplace was part of what begged second-wave feminists to flourish in the 1960s and '70s. The pressure placed on women to stay home was another instigating factor. Betty Friedan's *The Feminine Mystique*, published in 1963, would not have held such sway over women if they had not been experiencing social pressure to stay home and raise kids and to completely reject the option of a career. This book expressed the boredom and lack of fulfillment echoed by many women who wished for greater opportunities in work and in education. Friedan will be discussed in my next chapter on politics.

Indeed, education was a deciding factor in the liberation of women. Or at least it was for white women. What about women of other races, though? One of the defining factors of third-wave feminism was the legitimate complaint that only white, middle- or upper-class women were being heard. To a lesser extent, the voices of Black women were heard in women preachers in the nineteenth century, but also in the seminaries and academies that emerged after the Civil War for the purpose of educating young, Black women.

It was a long battle. Black women had to fight not only prejudice against their gender but against their race, something that characterizes

---

48. Welch and Ruelas, *Role of Female Seminaries*, 37–38.

"intersectionality," or multiple forms of oppression that are intertwined into the challenges some women face. These challenges might include class, economic status, age, or religion.

Mary Kelley recalls that Frederick Douglass's daughter Rosetta was denied admission to Lucilia Tracey's Seward Seminary in 1847.[49] She also found articles written in *Colored American* arguing that Black women should be educated, including one article called "Female Education," which was published in 1839 by an anonymous author. She quotes the writer as saying, "We expect our females to be educated and refined; to possess all the attributes which constitute the lady."[50] Of course, these were the words of free Black women in the North. We can't forget that before the Civil War, any sort of opportunities for Black women were limited.

Abraham Ruelas's chapter in *The Role of Female Seminaries on the Road to Social Justice for Women* focuses on the "Talented Tenth." It was a term coined by Henry Morehouse in 1896 referring to those the community felt were most likely to succeed and in whom they invested their financial resources. Because of limited resources and limited opportunity, the Black community wanted the very best to "have the best opportunity to make the most of himself for humanity and for God."[51]

Also, Black missionary groups emphasized the education of women for these reasons: 1) They wanted women to educate the poor and illiterate among them; 2) they wanted these women to model refined behaviors and values by emulating the white middle class; and 3) they wished to create a "buffer" class that would be between them and the whites.[52]

One of the most famous Historically Black Colleges and Universities (HBCU) is Spelman College, located in Atlanta, Georgia. Originally, it was the Atlanta Baptist Female Seminary, which was established in 1881 in the basement of a Baptist church.[53] Interestingly, John D. Rockefeller provided funds to the founders, Sophia Packard and Harriet Giles, to purchase the nine acres where Spelman Seminary was built. Spelman was Rockefeller's wife's maiden name. Like most other schools, they produced a school newspaper, the *Spelman Messenger*, to give the students a voice. In 1924, the seminary became Spelman College.[54]

---

49. Kelley, *Learning to Stand*, 32.
50. Kelley, *Learning to Stand*, 31.
51. Welch and Ruelas, *Role of Female Seminaries*, 85.
52. Welch and Ruelas, *Role of Female Seminaries*, 86.
53. Welch and Ruelas, *Role of Female Seminaries*, 88.
54. "About Spelman College."

The takeaway from this history is that the first institutions to educate women were created by and governed by Christian women and they created distinctly Christian epistemologies that viewed the role of women as one that served others, in particular, the family. As teachers, they served the community, and as missionaries, they furthered the goal to convert others. Education was to help them serve others better, not to realize their full potential as human beings. Yet that is exactly what happened as the curriculum for women moved from ornamental subjects like painting, music, and French to subjects that mirrored the curriculum offered to men, which included history, science, rhetoric, literature, and so on. While bowing to societal norms, women such as Catharine Beecher found ways to argue for an equal education for women, thus eventually freeing women from those norms.

It was education that helped pave the road toward second-wave feminism in the 1960s as well as the civil rights movement because the increase of education led to an increased ability to strategize ways to obtain the types of power women wanted for diverse goals in order to lead a fulfilled life. Also, higher education for women transitioned from female seminaries and academies to "normal schools" designed to educate teachers. Normal schools flourished mostly in the late nineteenth and early twentieth centuries, with most becoming teacher's colleges in the 1930s and then moving into departments of education at universities in the 1950s.[55] Also, community colleges played a huge role in the education of women from all socioeconomic classes after World War II. According to the Education Encyclopedia:

> The community college evolved from at least seven sources of educational innovation. Two began in the 1880s and 1890s: (1) community boosterism and (2) the rise of the research university. Three came from the educational reforms of the Progressive Era (1900–1916): (3) the advent of universal secondary education, (4) the professionalization of teacher education, and (5) the vocational education movement. The final two, (6) open access to higher education, and (7) the rise of adult and continuing education and community services, were primarily post–World War II phenomena. The seeds of all seven of these innovations can be found even in the earliest junior colleges.[56]

Also, "the American Association of Junior Colleges (AAJC), begun in 1921, provided a forum for the motley assemblage of emerging institutions, including high schools providing two-year collegiate programs, women's colleges, military institutes, private junior colleges, and technical

55. "Normal School."
56. "Community Colleges."

institutes."[57] Therefore, opportunities for women to get an education have been varied and they have been significantly important for opening the door to opportunities and for giving a place from which second-wave feminist ideas could emerge, be discussed, and be furthered.

So where are we at today? Today has seen the rise of power within the university. As a major factor in the shaping of culture, professors reach America's best and brightest at an opportune moment. The American Association of University Women states that as of 2016 about 27 percent of tenured faculty at four-year institutions are women.[58] So as women have moved into the corporate world and every other facet of society, they have also claimed a place within colleges and universities, giving them a chance to shape the scholarship and to articulate their place within the disciplines they teach, thereby feeding into the next generation who will open an even wider door for women.

It is mostly from their places in the universities, not only as professors but as graduate students, that third-wave feminists of the 1990s have flourished. Third-wave feminism gave a voice to women from different races, but it also gave women a chance to subvert, ridicule, and confront socially constructed sexism in all its forms.[59] In their hands, feminism becomes playful and powerful in groups such as the punk rock riot grrrls and the Guerilla Girls.

Fourth-wave feminists, said to have been started around 2010 or so, focus on confronting injustices associated with sexual harassment and rape. Body shaming—or insulting women who dress provocatively—is tied into this wave as well. While it is my position that women who dress with style and modesty are much more powerful and respected than those who do not, most recently the Me Too movement has put feminists in the spotlight as rapists at every level have been called out. This has had both positive and negative outcomes by bringing some men to justice but also by promoting false accusations against others, such as Brett Kavanaugh. In short, education in the twenty-first century is also political and our colleges and universities provide opportunities for confronting sexism. In this context, education is an effective weapon.

Finally, women's studies programs began in the 1970s and have profoundly changed the nature of higher education for many.[60] Known as the "academic arm" of the "women's movement," women's studies programs

---

57. "Community Colleges."
58. Kelly, "Though More Women."
59. "Third Wave of Feminism."
60. Jaschik, "Evolution."

promote the "idea of learning for social change and action." Mostly interdisciplinary, there are currently about eight hundred programs nationwide. Students can earn a doctorate in women's studies—or "gender studies," as many programs are now called—if they wish. The National Women's Studies Association gave these scholars a place to share knowledge and resources. Their website lists numerous academic journals. A few in the list are:

*Asian Women*

*Feminism & Psychology*

*Feminist Economics*

*Feminist Formations*

*Feminist Legal Studies*

*Frontiers: A Journal of Women's Studies*

*Gender & Society*

*Hypatia: A Journal of Feminist Philosophy*

*Journal of Women, Politics, & Policy*

*Women's Studies Quarterly*[61]

So what should you take away from this discussion?

- Women who had the benefit of an education argued that it should be a privilege for all women to enjoy as far back as the early fifteenth century in Christine de Pizan's work.
- Women who displayed their education or touted their scholarly accomplishments in the eighteenth and nineteenth centuries were often ridiculed. The Bluestockings are one example and the term was used to try to silence women for decades afterward.
- Education was originally offered to women with a proliferation of ornamental courses designed to make them better wives and mothers. Later, courses equivalent to those offered in male universities allowed women to enter the teaching profession, lead reform societies, and create and teach in seminaries specifically for women.
- Scriptures had to be confronted in the arguments justifying an education for women. Later, it became convenient to draw on the ideals of Republican motherhood, which also had a strong Christian basis.

---

61. "Journals."

- Women who wanted an education recognized they were missing out on a way to reach their full potential. For whatever purposes they wished to be educated, their arguments repeated the belief that they were not capable of full personhood without an education.
- The printing press gave women a way to display and share their knowledge as well as a way to break their silence. For students, this appeared in school papers. For women in general, it manifested itself in magazines and periodicals of all sorts, as well as books.
- Literary societies provided women with a way to embrace a life of discussion and to sharpen their intellectual skills while in conversation with each other about important texts.
- Second-wave feminists were responsible for starting the recovery of women's history through archival work and the establishment of groups of professors and graduate students where papers on women's history and issues could be shared; journals that published scholarship on women's history and issues could be disseminated; and books on women's history and issues could be discussed, analyzed, and used as part of the scholarship being circulated in the conferences and journals they had established.
- Schools for women that were established in the eighteenth and nineteenth centuries were openly Christian, offered courses that drew on one aspect of Christianity or another, and required church attendance. Scripture was used to establish and defend institutions opened to educate women. The history of first-wave feminism should acknowledge the ironic role that Christianity played in obtaining an equal education for women through such institutions.
- The university, roughly from the mid-twentieth century to today, provides a way for feminist ideas to circulate. Education has become political, empowering women to argue for change at every level of society.
- As a result of first-wave feminism, the denial of an education and working opportunities for women was no longer possible in the nineteenth century; female seminaries and academies became a gateway to a college education. This education allowed women to apply for jobs that were outside the realm of manual labor.

# 3

## "What Shall I Say with Regard to Daughters?"
*Politics and Feminism*

The Battlefield: The push for political power and influence, primarily by nineteenth-century women, and for the vote.

The Opponents: Men and women who believed in coverture laws that denied women equal legal status and equal status as persons because of cultural norms; those who believed that Christianity supported men's "headship" in the home; and those who knew the implications of allowing women to have full political participation as politicians and in legislation. On the other side were those men and women who formed social reform groups to push for positive societal change. These groups focused on issues such as temperance, abolition, the reform of mental health institutions, the rescue and reform of prostitutes, and orphanage work, among others. These reform groups were based on both cultural and Christian principles. Some advocated for a woman's right to enjoy full citizenship in America through picketing, arguments, protests, publications, and speeches.

*Guiding questions for chapter 3*

1. Where did the fight for women's rights begin in America? What challenges to a woman's ethos, or credibility, can be found in arguments for continuing to deny women their rights? What challenges to ethos do the women address in their texts?
2. How were arguments for an education incorporated into arguments for equal political rights? Why was it still necessary to argue for a woman's right to preach in the late eighteenth century?
3. What can you learn about temperance, abolition, and suffrage? How did women establish groups to address concerns with these broad areas?
4. What was the Seneca Falls Convention and what was the guiding document used to argue for women's rights?
5. Once women gained legal and political rights, what rights did second- and third-wave feminists fight for? What role does race play in the identity politics that characterize feminist thought and action?

Let's begin the story of how women gained political power in regard to women's rights with Abigail Adams, our second First Lady in the United States. Descended from Puritans, she did not receive any formal schooling.[1] John Adams was considered to be from a lower social class, but she gained permission to marry him and they were wed in 1764. John Adams would later go on to sign the Declaration of Independence and become the president of the United States. Their oldest son, John Quincy Adams, became the sixth president of the United States.

Because he was gone so much, Abigail wrote him many letters. She often signed them as Portia, after Shakespeare's character in *The Merchant of Venice*. This character was beautiful, sought-after, and resourceful. She also disguised herself as a man in the play, but let's set that to the side for now.

On August 14, 1776, Abigail wrote to her husband:

> You remark upon the deficiency of Education in your Countrymen . . . If you complain of neglect of Education in sons, What shall I say with regard to daughters, who every day experience the want of it. With regard to the Education of my own children, I find myself soon out of my debth, and destitute and deficient in every part of Education . . . If we mean to have Heroes, Statesmen and Philosophers, we should have learned women. . . . If much depends as is allowed upon the early Education of youth and the first principals which are instilld take

---

1. Warhol-Down, *Women's Worlds*, 281.

the deepest root, great benifit must arise from litirary accomplishments in women.²

She had written her often-quoted "Remember the Ladies" letter just a few months before on March 31, 1776. She makes a distinctly political appeal:

> In the new Code of Laws which I suppose it will be necessary for you to make I desire you would Remember the Ladies, and be more generous and favorable to them than you ancestors. Do not put such unlimited power in the hands of the Husbands. Remember that all Men would be tyrants if they could. If perticuliar care and attention is not paid to the Ladies we are determined to foment a Rebelion, and will not hold ourselves bound by any Laws in which we have no voice, or Representation.³

Unfortunately, Abigail Adams's remarks had no effect on her husband. Later, in 1792, Mary Wollstonecraft spoke of both education and equality in her quite long and rambling piece *A Vindication of the Rights of Woman*, written in England. In it she suggests that access to education would allow women to be "physicians as well as nurses," "to study politics," to read history, and to pursue "business of various kinds they might likewise pursue." If allowed to work, "women would not marry for support," she points out. She draws on biblical language when she says women should be a "help-mate" and argues that "would men but generously snap our chains, and be content with rational fellowship instead of slavish obedience, they would find us . . . better citizens."⁴ She continues: "But we shall not see women affectionate until more equality be established in society . . . nor will the important task of education ever be properly begun till the person of a woman is no longer preferred to her mind."⁵ In other words, Wollstonecraft objected to the way some men preferred a mindless body over a woman who was educated and who knew her own mind.

Though their arguments ran along similar lines, whereas Abigail Adams was a highly respected, Christian woman, Mary Wollstonecraft was not. However, it is interesting to note that Wollstonecraft and a friend of hers began a school in their town and that she wrote *Thoughts on the Education of Daughters* in 1787, several years before her more famous piece, reaching

---

2. Warhol-Down, *Women's Worlds*, 284. Misspellings in this and the following passage are in the original text, as Abigail Adams did not have a formal education.

3. Warhol-Down, *Women's Worlds*, 284.

4. Mary Wollstonecraft, *A Vindication of the Rights of Woman*, quoted in Freedman, *Essential Feminist Reader*, 32.

5. Mary Wollstonecraft, *A Vindication of the Rights of Woman*, quoted in Freedman, *Essential Feminist Reader*, 34.

far beyond what Abigail Adams did or perhaps could do with her limited education.[6] Educational reform was what was needed for social reform, in her opinion. Also, she wrote the scandalous *Maria, or the Wrongs of Woman* in 1798, which is said to have explained that women have sexual desires. Additionally, she became pregnant and did not choose to marry Captain Gilbert Imlay, an American who was a merchant. He left her a few years later. She then became pregnant outside of wedlock a second time but married soon after. Her daughter, Mary, was only ten days old when she died, leaving her father and later a stepmother to raise her.

Her daughter would lead a similar life to her mother's troubled one and author the famous, deeply engaging, and utterly profound book, *Frankenstein*, which was published in 1818. Like her mother, Mary (Wollstonecraft) Shelley was deeply reflective and her novel brought out questions we still wrestle with today: What is the nature of a creator? How much should the creator determine our lives? What are the ethics of creating a rational being and placing him in a troubled world? The true monster is the creator, Frankenstein, not the monster he created (who people have mistakenly named Frankenstein). Both Mary Wollstonecraft and Mary Shelley pushed past the restrictions of society to ask important questions. They don't bring us comfort or coddle our imaginations, but they both did important, lasting, timeless political work by challenging our complacency with social and religious structures that were in place then and, in some ways, now.

Another important figure is Maria Miller Stewart, a Black woman, who gave her famous speech "Lecture Delivered at Franklin Hall" in 1832 to an audience of both men and women, white and Black.[7] In her speech, she argues:

> As far as our merit deserves, we feel a common desire to rise above the condition of servants and drudges. I have learnt, by bitter experience, that continual hard labor deadens the energies of the soul, and benumbs the faculties of the mind; ideas become confined, the mind barren, and, like the scorching sands of Arabia, produces nothing; or like the uncultivated brings forth thorns and thistles.[8]

She begs her audience to consider their Christian beliefs and "make some mighty efforts to raise your sons and daughters from the horrible state of servitude and degradation in which they are placed."[9] In other words, as a

---

6. "Mary Wollstonecraft."

7. Ritchie and Ronald, *Available Means*, 109–10.

8. Maria W. Stewart, "Lecture Delivered at the Franklin Hall," quoted in Ritchie and Ronald, *Available Means*, 111.

9. Maria W. Stewart, "Lecture Delivered at the Franklin Hall," quoted in Ritchie and

Black woman her situation is far more dire than that of the white feminists that we have been reading. Her hope for equality is challenged by sex, race, and economic class, making it seem almost impossible to achieve in her time.

Also enormously influential were the Grimké sisters. They were an interesting pair of abolitionists. According to *The Essential Feminist Reader*, the "woman question" went from the topic of education to politics in the early nineteenth century and "inspired by Protestant revivals, social reformers in America and England campaigned to rid society of sins ranging from intemperance to slavery." The Grimké sisters were raised in a family that had slaves but converted to Quakerism and headed North. These sisters were "condemned" for speaking to groups of men and women as well as for encouraging women to call for the abolition of slavery, thereby transcending "their domestic and religious realms." Their letters defend women's rights, both Black and white.[10]

Sarah Grimké's "Letters on the Equality of the Sexes" were published in the US in 1837 and argued for women's education and against low wages for women's labor and the "sexual vulnerability of female slaves."[11] In it, Grimké blames a lack of education as well as the practice of shunning women who display intellectual superiority to men for the desire of young women to get married and for the way that one goal represented their highest achievement in life.[12]

Make no mistake, Grimké uses these letters to do battle. Just a mere thirteen years before the Fugitive Slave Act passed in 1850, she wrote:

> The virtue of our female slaves is wholly at the mercy of irresponsible tyrants, and women are bought and sold in our slave markets, to gratify the lust of those who bear the name of Christians . . . she is either bribed or whipped into compliance, or if she dares resist her seducer, her life . . . has been sacrificed to the fury of disappointed passion . . . the sufferings of some females on this account, both physical and mental, are intense.[13]

So here, she labels "Christian" men as rapists, murderers, and tyrants. And, as we know from the well-documented facts in our history books, some of them were.

---

Ronald, *Available Means*, 112.

10. Freedman, *Essential Feminist Reader*, 47.

11. Freedman, *Essential Feminist Reader*, 47.

12. Sarah Grimké, "Letters on the Equality of the Sexes," cited in Freedman, *Essential Feminist Reader*, 48–49.

13. Sarah Grimké, "Letters on the Equality of the Sexes," quoted in Freedman, *Essential Feminist Reader*, 50.

But she doesn't leave it there. Oh no. She points her finger at the white women who pretended to be blind to these abuses. She goes on to say:

> Nor does the colored woman suffer alone; the moral purity of the white woman is deeply contaminated. In the daily habit of seeing the virtue of her enslaved sister sacrificed without hesitancy or remorse she looks upon the crimes of seduction and illicit intercourse *without horror*, and although not personally involved in the guilt, she loses that value for innocence in her own.[14]

At the end of her letter, she says "the Equality of the Sexes" would mean that men would find that "woman, as their equal, was unspeakably more valuable than woman as their inferior, both as a moral and an intellectual being."[15]

So her argument is three-pronged: Education is needed. Protection from rape is needed for African American women. Equality between men and women is needed.

Margaret Fuller is another famous feminist. She only lived to be forty years old and was "educated at home in the classics and fluent in several languages."[16] In 1843, she published an essay called "The Great Lawsuit: Man versus Men, Woman versus Women" in the periodical she co-founded with Ralph Waldo Emerson, *The Dial*. This was expanded into her more famous piece, *Woman in the Nineteenth Century*, published in 1845.

I admit that reading this piece in full requires more patience than I possess. It is badly written and scattered; it is a miracle that it ever achieved any sort of popularity, in my opinion.

However, here are some excerpts:

> The irritated [slave] trader asks if it's not enough that the abolitionists, such as herself, try to destroy the profitability of the country, but they also wish to "break up family unions," to take women "away from the cradle and the kitchen hearth to vote at polls, and preach from a pulpit." He argues, "She is happy enough as she is. She has more leisure than I have, every means of improvement, every indulgence."[17]

---

14. Sarah Grimké, "Letters on the Equality of the Sexes," quoted in Freedman, *Essential Feminist Reader*, 50. Italics mine.

15. Sarah Grimké, "Letters on the Equality of the Sexes," quoted in Freedman, *Essential Feminist Reader*, 51.

16. Ritchie and Ronald, *Available Means*, 125.

17. Margaret Fuller, *Woman in the Nineteenth Century*, quoted in Ritchie and Ronald, *Available Means*, 126.

Fuller goes on to write: "Have you asked her whether she was satisfied with these *indulgences*?" She remarks on some key themes: Women have taken up the pen, so to speak, gaining a voice in public. They have been represented as having no capacity for reason—i.e., "You cannot reason with a woman"—and woman has been thought of as a lesser creature, one made for man and not made as a creature of value in her own right.[18]

She argues for the education of girls and of women, for the option to have "a much greater range of occupations than they have," for the option to be independent instead of pushed into marriage, and for the right to be a woman and not "an overgrown child."[19]

As influential as Margaret Fuller was in her time, it was in 1848 that the official beginning of feminism was truly born at the Seneca Falls Convention. In the "Declaration of Sentiments and Resolutions" by Elizabeth Cady Stanton, the beginning of political power for women in America was birthed in a formal way and women never let it go. It was a time when words were finally followed by concrete actions performed by a group.

The "Declaration" was born of out anger, but it was righteous anger. In 1840, Stanton and Lucretia Mott were denied the right to be delegates at the World Anti-Slavery Convention held in London in 1840 because they were women. In 1848, these two "issued a public invitation to a convention to discuss 'the civil and political rights of women.'"[20] It was held for two days and ran by James Mott, Lucretia's husband. More than three hundred were in attendance, both men and women.

At the Seneca Falls Convention, held in Seneca Falls, New York, Stanton presented her declaration, clearly built by imitating the Declaration of Independence, and no less than sixty-eight people signed it. In Stanton's full recognition of the great need for political power, this was where the battle for suffragism really began.

The "Declaration" begins:

> When, in the course of human events, it becomes necessary for one portion of the family of man to assume among the people of the earth a position different from that which they have hitherto occupied, but one to which the laws of nature and of nature's God entitle them, a decent respect to the opinions of mankind

---

18. Margaret Fuller, *Woman in the Nineteenth Century*, quoted in Ritchie and Ronald, *Available Means*, 128–29.

19. Margaret Fuller, *Woman in the Nineteenth Century*, quoted in Ritchie and Ronald, *Available Means*, 132, 135–36.

20. Elizabeth Cady Stanton, "Declaration of Sentiments and Resolutions," quoted in Freedman, *Essential Feminist Reader*, 57.

"WHAT SHALL I SAY WITH REGARD TO DAUGHTERS?" 61

requires that they should declare the causes that impel them to such a course.[21]

Echoes of the Declaration of Independence continue in the next lines: "We hold these truths to be self-evident: that all men and women are created equal."[22] The addition of the word "women" here is essential to her argument. Stanton goes on to quote the Declaration of Independence word for word for quite a few lines.

The parallels are clear: Just as the colonists cast off the unfair governance of the British crown, so should women cast off the unfair constraints of a government that sanctioned their inferior status and allowed them no political representation.

What does Stanton want?

- The vote.
- Representation in the government and a voice.
- The overturn of coverture laws—to count in the "eye of the law."
- The right to own property.
- To reject unfair domination in marriage.
- To have a chance at "profitable employments" and equal pay.
- To obtain a "thorough education."
- To have equal status in both church and state. To not be excluded from the ministry.
- To overturn the idea that is "moral" to "exclude women from society."
- To reject the "sphere of action" that men used to limit women.
- To reject the way men undermined "her [a woman's] confidence in her own powers, to lessen her self-respect, and to make her willing to lead a dependent and abject life."[23]

Stanton's list of resolutions that follows echoes this list, but the last one points to the power of the pulpit, which we covered in chapter one of this book: "Resolved, That the speedy success of our cause depends upon the zealous and untiring efforts of both men and women, for the overthrow of

---

21. Elizabeth Cady Stanton, "Declaration of Sentiments and Resolutions," quoted in Freedman, *Essential Feminist Reader*, 58.

22. Elizabeth Cady Stanton, "Declaration of Sentiments and Resolutions," quoted in Freedman, *Essential Feminist Reader*, 58.

23. Elizabeth Cady Stanton, "Declaration of Sentiments and Resolutions," quoted in Freedman, *Essential Feminist Reader*, 59–60.

the monopoly of the pulpit, and for the securing to woman an equal participation with men in the various trades, professions, and commerce."[24]

Another feminist of note is Susan B. Anthony, who decided to vote on November 5, 1872. She was arrested for doing so three weeks later. After her arrest, she gave the lecture "Is it a Crime for a Citizen of the US to Vote?" in every nearby village. It must have been good because they moved her trial to a different county. So she gave the same speech in every district there. Perhaps knowing he could not win, the judge simply declared her guilty and fined her one hundred dollars. She never paid the fine.[25]

In *Available Means: An Anthology of Women's Rhetoric(s)*, the exchange between the judge, the inspector, and Anthony is excerpted.

Here are a few lines:

> *The Court:* The prisoner will stand up. Has the prisoner anything to say why sentence should not be pronounced?
> *Miss Anthony:* Yes, your honor, I have many things to say; for in your ordered verdict of guilty, you have trampled underfoot every vital principle of our government. My natural rights, my civil rights, my political rights, are all alike ignored. Robbed of the fundamental privilege of citizenship, I am degraded from the status of a citizen to that of a subject; and not only myself individually, but all of my sex, are, by your honor's verdict, doomed to political subjugation under this so-called Republican government.
> *Judge Hunt:* The Court cannot listen to a rehearsal of arguments the prisoner's counsel has already consumed three hours in presenting.
> *Miss Anthony:* May it please your honor, I am not arguing the question, but simply stating the reasons why sentence can not, in justice, be pronounced against me. Your denial of my citizen's right to vote is the denial of my right of consent as one of the governed, the denial of my right of representation as one of the taxed, the denial of my right to a trial by a jury of my peers as an offender against the law, therefore, the denial of my sacred rights to life, liberty, property, and—
> *Judge Hunt:* The court cannot allow the prisoner to go on.[26]

---

24. Elizabeth Cady Stanton, "Declaration of Sentiments and Resolutions," quoted in Freedman, *Essential Feminist Reader*, 62.

25. Ritchie and Ronald, *Available Means*, 151.

26. Susan B. Anthony, *The United States of America v. Susan B. Anthony*, quoted in Ronald and Ritchie, *Available Means*, 154.

Susan B. Anthony and Elizabeth Cady Stanton formed the National American Women's Suffrage Association in 1869, and Anthony argued tirelessly for the vote all of her life until her death in 1906, fourteen years before the Nineteenth Amendment gave women the right to vote on a federal level.

So when did women win the right to vote? Most quote the year 1920, when the Nineteenth Amendment passed making it federal law, but the history is a little more complex. According to the National Constitution Center, "While seeking to amend the US Constitution, the women's suffrage movement also waged a state-by-state campaign."[27] The territory of Wyoming was the first to give women the vote in 1869. Other western states and territories followed.

States that gave full voting rights before the Nineteenth Amendment and before statehood are as follows:

Territory of Wyoming, 1869

Territory of Utah, 1870

Territory of Washington, 1883

Territory of Montana, 1887

Territory of Alaska, 1913

States granting women the right to vote prior to the Nineteenth Amendment include:

Wyoming, 1890

Colorado, 1893

Utah, 1896

Idaho, 1896

Washington, 1910

California, 1911

Arizona, 1912

Kansas, 1912

Oregon, 1912

Montana, 1914

Nevada, 1914

New York, 1917

---

27. "Centuries of Citizenship."

Michigan, 1918

Oklahoma, 1918

South Dakota, 1918

States where a woman could vote for president prior to the Nineteenth Amendment include:

Illinois, 1913

Nebraska, 1917

Ohio, 1917

Indiana, 1917

North Dakota, 1917

Rhode Island, 1917

Iowa, 1919

Maine, 1919

Minnesota, 1919

Missouri, 1919

Tennessee, 1919

Wisconsin, 1919[28]

The right to vote was a key issue, but racism was intertwined with it and with the general subject of women's rights in the nineteenth century. It is worth discussing Sojourner Truth, as she has become a vital part of our American history. She was once a slave in New York and gave a legendary speech called "Ar'n't I A Woman?" in 1851 at the women's rights gathering in Akron, Ohio.[29] In this short speech, she points out that Christ himself came from God and a woman. "Man had nothin' to do wid Him!" She wraps up by saying that now women want their rights and "de men better let 'em."[30] Another of her speeches, called "When Woman Gets Her Rights Man Will Be Right" and given in 1867, is an overtly feminist statement. Sojourner Truth says that there has been a lot of attention paid to Black men getting their rights, but not to Black women getting theirs. "I want women to have their rights," she says. "In the courts women have no right, no voice; nobody

---

28. "Centuries of Citizenship."
29. Guy-Sheftall, *Words of Fire*, 35.
30. Sojourner Truth, "Ar'n't I A Woman?" quoted in Guy-Sheftall, *Words of Fire*, 36.

speaks for them."³¹ She points out she has done the same work as men but only received half the pay. She argues, "Men have got their rights, and women have not got their rights. That is the trouble. When woman gets her rights man will be right. How beautiful that will be."³²

In 1892, the first book-length feminist text by a Black woman was published by Anna Julia Cooper. She graduated from Oberlin College in 1884, taught modern languages at Wilberforce University, and a few years later began a long career at M Street High School in Washington, DC. In 1900, she gave her paper "The Negro Problem in America" at a Pan-African Conference in London. She earned her doctorate at the Sorbonne. Her dissertation, written in French, was titled "Slavery and the French Revolutionists, 1788–1805."³³

In her speech "The Status of Woman in America," she mentions the upcoming fair in Chicago where women will be speaking and says, "This of itself marks the dawn of a new day."³⁴ She succinctly identifies continuing areas of struggle in the workforce and in politics, but then sings a high note:

> But to be a woman of the Negro race in America, and to be able to grasp the deep significance of the possibilities of the crisis, is to have a heritage, it seems to me, unique in the ages. In the first place, the race is young and full of the elasticity and hopefulness of youth. All its achievements are before it. It does not look on the masterly triumphs of nineteenth-century civilization with that *blasé* world-weary look which characterizes the old washed-out and worn-out races which have already, so to speak, seen their best days.³⁵

In 1893, Frances Ellen Watkins Harper, who was in Boston when the National Association of Colored Women formed in 1896 and who eventually became their vice president, gave a speech at the World's Congress of Representative Women at the Columbian Exposition in Chicago. She was a free Black, a member of the Underground Railroad, a board member of the Women's Christian Temperance Union, and a founding member of the American Woman Suffrage Association.³⁶ She was an obviously eloquent

---

31. Sojourner Truth, "When Woman Gets Her Rights Man Will Be Right," quoted in Guy-Sheftall, *Words of Fire*, 37.

32. Sojourner Truth, "When Woman Gets Her Rights Man Will Be Right," quoted in Guy-Sheftall, *Words of Fire*, 38.

33. Guy-Sheftall, *Words of Fire*, 43.

34. Anna Julia Cooper, "The Status of Woman in America," quoted in Guy-Sheftall, *Words of Fire*, 44.

35. Anna Julia Cooper, "The Status of Woman in America," quoted in Guy-Sheftall, *Words of Fire*, 49.

36. Guy-Sheftall, *Words of Fire*, 39.

speaker, as evident in "Woman's Political Future," a speech that begins with a reference to the Garden of Eden, using the biblical language of "it was not good for man to be alone" but then moving on to the argument for women's suffrage and the education of the "children of those who were born under the shadow of institutions which made it a crime to read."[37] Later she says, "Today, women hold in their hands influence and opportunity." She notes that woman has entered the workforce and is also the "priestess" of her home, "in society the queen," a "power" in literature, and a political force that has changed laws to benefit women. She argues that "the press has felt the impress of her hand. In the pews of the church she constitutes the majority; the pulpit has welcomed her, and in the school she has the blessed privilege of teaching children and youth." She ends with a reference to Eden as she calls on women to lift their hearts.[38]

In 1893 Lucy Stone gave a speech at the same World's Fair in the Woman's Building at the World's Columbian Exposition in Chicago. Titled "The Progress of Fifty Years," it is one of the best iterations of all that women had accomplished toward women's rights in the nineteenth century.[39]

Stone begins with the fact that in 1833 Oberlin College became the US's first coeducational institution. Education is cast into a metaphor as the "new Messiah." She then lists Mount Holyoke and Amherst College as examples. Lucy herself was educated at Oberlin and Mount Holyoke.

She says:

> But, whatever the reason, the idea was born that women could and should be educated. It lifted a mountain load from woman. It shattered the idea, everywhere pervasive as the atmosphere, that women were incapable of education, and would be less womanly, less desirable in every way, if they had it. However much it may have been resented, women accepted the idea of their intellectual inequality.[40]

Next, she describes women's role in the abolitionist movement and how men tried to silence them—men in the church and men in society.

> Some of the abolitionists forgot the slave in their efforts to silence the women. The Anti-Slavery Society rent itself in twain over the subject. The Church was moved to its very foundation in

---

37. Francis E. W. Harper, "Woman's Political Future," quoted in Guy-Sheftall, *Words of Fire*, 40–41.

38. Anna Julia Cooper, "The Status of Woman in America," quoted in Guy-Sheftall, *Words of Fire*, 42.

39. Stone, "Progress of Fifty Years."

40. Stone, "Progress of Fifty Years."

opposition. The Association of Congregational Churches issued a "Pastoral Letter" against the public speaking of women. The press, many-tongued, surpassed itself in reproaches upon these women who had so far departed from their sphere as to speak in public. But, with anointed lips and a consecration which put even life itself at stake, these peerless women pursued the even tenor of their way, saying to their opponents only: "Woe is me if I preach not this gospel of freedom for the slave."[41]

She emphasizes that "the right to education and to free speech having been gained for woman, in the long run every other good thing was sure to be obtained." Next, she describes the opposition of men who wished for women to stay in their "sphere" and did not want their words in print, but she then describes how women overcame these obstacles. She describes women who won a place in fields and occupations outside of the home: as physicians, artists, businesswomen, ministers, and lawyers. She describes the terrible effects of coverture laws, particularly on widows, and how women have overturned those laws, gaining freedom. She then celebrates the places where women had won the right to vote at that point.

Here is her conclusion:

> The last half century has gained for women the right to the highest education and entrance to all professions and occupations, or nearly all. As a result we have women's clubs, the Woman's Congress, women's educational and industrial unions, the moral education societies, the Woman's Relief Corps, police matrons, the Woman's Christian Temperance Union, colleges for women, and co-educational colleges and the Harvard Annex, medical schools and medical societies open to women, women's hospitals, women in the pulpit, women as a power in the press, authors, women artists, women's beneficent societies and Helping Hand societies, women school supervisors, and factory inspectors and prison inspectors, women on state boards of charity, the International Council of Women, the Woman's National Council, and last, but not least, the Board of Lady Managers. And not one of these things was allowed women fifty years ago, except the opening at Oberlin. By what toil and fatigue and patience and strife and the beautiful law of growth has all this been wrought? These things have not come of themselves. They could not have occurred except as the great movement for women has brought them out and about. They are part of the eternal order, and they have come to stay. Now all we need is to continue to speak the

---

41. Stone, "Progress of Fifty Years."

truth fearlessly, and we shall add to our number those who will turn the scale to the side of equal and full justice in all things.[42]

This conclusion brings me to my next topic: nineteenth-century women's reform societies. Intensely both religious and political, these societies gave women the opportunity to serve as leaders of large organizations, and they did so successfully. In the nineteenth century, women engaged in prison reform, orphanage work, asylum reform, and abolitionism. The Female Moral Reform Society focused on prostitutes. There was the National Woman Suffrage Association and the American Woman Suffrage Association.[43]

Perhaps one of the groups that is most interesting and representative of the political power afforded to women in the nineteenth century is the Woman's Christian Temperance Union (WCTU), led by Frances Willard from 1879 until her death in 1898.[44] Prior to this role, she taught for Northwestern Female College until it merged with Northwestern University, and her former fiancé—who did not take the breakup well—made her life so difficult that she was forced to resign in 1874.[45] After that, she became involved in the Chicago chapter of the WCTU and became secretary of the national WCTU after being sent as a delegate to the convention.[46] Under Willard's leadership, the WCTU went on to become "one of the largest and most influential women's groups of the 19th century by expanding its platform to campaign for labor laws, prison reform and suffrage."[47] After her "death in 1898, the WCTU began to distance itself from feminist groups, instead focusing primarily on prohibition. Though its membership steadily declined following the passage of the Eighteenth Amendment in 1919, the WCTU continued to operate through the 20th century."[48]

However, Willard did not limit her political activity to fighting the evils of intemperance, which was blamed for spousal abuse, among other things. As a Methodist, she believed in a woman's right to preach and wrote *Woman in the Pulpit* in 1888. She fought for what she called "Do Everything Reform."[49] "She attached temperance work to a range of social issues, including stronger laws against rape, laws raising the legal age of consent (which was age ten in twenty states), improved conditions for female factory

---

42. Stone, "Progress of Fifty Years."
43. "Women's Rights Movement."
44. Bizzell and Herzberg, *Rhetorical Tradition*, 1117.
45. Bizzell and Herzberg, *Rhetorical Tradition*, 1114–15.
46. Bizzell and Herzberg, *Rhetorical Tradition*, 1115.
47. "Women's Christian Temperance Union."
48. "Women's Christian Temperance Union."
49. Bizzell and Herzberg, *Rhetorical Tradition*, 1117.

workers and female prison inmates, improved enforcement of anti-child-labor laws, free kindergartens and what we would call day care programs for working mothers, and more."[50] In addition, she supported women's suffrage. She also believed in "Christian Socialism."[51]

In *Woman in the Pulpit*, as you may well imagine, she confronts the same Pauline scriptures calling for women's silence that so many before her had confronted. She created a table of scriptures comparing Paul's, which limited women, to others which did not. She argues for a woman's right to speak publicly and heralds the many occupations she can fill in her time. She argues that "the entrance of woman upon the ministerial vocation will give to humanity just twice the probability of strengthening and comforting speech, for women have at least as much sympathy, reverence, and spirituality as men, and they have at least equal felicity of manner and of utterance. Why, then, should the pulpit be shorn of half its power?"[52]

While Frances Willard was a notable feminist in the nineteenth century, also of note is Alice Dunbar-Nelson, who was secretary of the National Association of Colored Women in 1915 and field organizer for the Middle Atlantic States in the fight for women's right to vote. In 1920 she was chair of the League of Colored Republican Women. In 1922 she was head of the Anti-Lynching Crusaders in Delaware. They fought for the Dyer federal Anti-Lynching Bill. In her essay "The Negro Woman and the Ballot," published in *The Messenger* in 1927, she asks what Black women had done since women won the right to vote.[53]

Dunbar-Nelson specifically mentions the Dyer Bill in that piece.[54] This bill would have punished those who lynched Blacks, but while Dunbar-Nelson commends women for coming together in support of this bill, history tells us it did not pass. Dunbar-Nelson writes, "When the Negro woman finds that the future of her children lies in her own hands—if she can be made to see this—she will strike off the political shackles she has allowed to be hung upon her, and win the economic freedom of her race." She concludes, "Perhaps some Joan of Arc will lead the way."[55]

Although I have left out many significant voices, the next person I would like to discuss is Virginia Woolf, who wrote "Professions for Women"

50. Bizzell and Herzberg, *Rhetorical Tradition*, 1117.
51. Bizzell and Herzberg, *Rhetorical Tradition*, 1118.
52. Bizzell and Herzberg, *Rhetorical Tradition*, 1133.
53. Guy-Sheftall, *Words of Fire*, 85.
54. Alice Dunbar-Nelson, "The Negro Woman and the Ballot," cited in Guy-Sheftall, *Words of Fire*, 87.
55. Alice Dunbar-Nelson, "The Negro Woman and the Ballot," quoted in Guy-Sheftall, *Words of Fire*, 88.

in 1942. This piece was a speech delivered to the Women's Service League. This group was founded by "seven Sunday School girls" in 1931 and was originally a sorority called Tau Sigma, or "truth seekers." The group is still in existence and focuses on "aid to civic and charitable causes."[56]

Woolf begins her speech by saying, "When your secretary invited me to come here, she told me that your Society is concerned with the employment of women and she suggested that I might tell you something about my own professional experience." Woolf explains, however, that she does not really have a "profession," per say, but that she is a writer. As a writer, she also writes critiques of others' writing. To do so, she has had to struggle with "The Angel in the House."[57]

Who is the angel in the house? It is a woman who exists in her imagination; a woman who sacrifices all her comfort and integrity for the purpose of pleasing others. This woman says to her: "Never let anybody guess that you have a mind of your own." The pressure to please others instead of to emerge with her true opinions inspired Woolf to kill the angel in the house. "Had I not killed her," she says, "she would have killed me."[58] Why? Because taking away someone's true voice is a kind of death. That's why Woolf was so important. Many of the battles fought for equality were inward battles experienced by women who had been shaped by their culture.

The problem, Woolf writes, is that "even when the path is nominally open—when there is nothing to prevent a woman from being a doctor, a lawyer, a civil servant—there are many phantoms and obstacles, I believe, looming in her way." In other words, Woolf was trying to explain to the women of the Women's Service League that many of the biggest obstacles to their success in the working world began within their own minds. Because the prejudice against women was largely internalized, they faced challenges, such as earning less pay, because of the effects of this. She goes on to say, "You have won rooms of your own in the house hitherto exclusively owned by men." She ends with encouragement, saying they are well able to "pay the rent" but they need to do more than occupy a space—they need to decorate and share the room. She asks, "How are you going to furnish it, how are you going to decorate it? With whom are you going to share it, and upon what terms? These, I think are questions of the utmost importance and interest.

---

56. "Leadership and Members."

57. Virginia Woolf, "Professions for Women," quoted in Ritchie and Ronald, *Available Means*, 242–43.

58. Virginia Woolf, "Professions for Women," quoted in Ritchie and Ronald, *Available Means*, 244.

For the first time in history you are able to ask them; for the first time you are able to decide for yourselves what the answers should be."[59]

As feminist concerns began to include more introspective issues, second-wave feminism captured some of the political activities that were tied to ideas that won equality for women. In *Feminist Thought*, Rosemarie Tong and Tina Fernandes Botts write that "between the passage of the Nineteenth Amendment and the advent of the second wave of US feminism during the 1960s, only two official feminist groups—the National Woman's Party and the National Federation of Business and Professional Women's Clubs—promulgated women's rights."[60] But this was not because women had won the battle for equality. Instead, Tong and Botts argue, the mindset of people had not changed and sexism continued. The civil rights movement would disrupt the sexist and racist structures that were in place. It was in 1961 that President John F. Kennedy "established the Commission on the Status of Women," which Eleanor Roosevelt chaired.[61] This produced the Citizens' Advisory Council, states that also put in place commissions on the status of women, and the Equal Pay Act. In 1964, the Civil Rights Act included Title VII, a provision to prevent discrimination on the basis of sex, but the courts were reluctant to enforce it.

What happened as a result was the National Organization for Women (NOW), which formed in 1966. The first president was Betty Friedan. Echoing Seneca Falls, they wrote a Bill of Rights in 1967 which included demands to:

1. Pass the Equal Rights Amendment.
2. Give women equal employment opportunities.
3. Protect women's jobs after having a baby.
4. Let working parents deduct childcare expenses from their taxes.
5. Establish public childcare facilities.
6. Give women the right to obtain an equal education.
7. Reform welfare programs to help women who needed job training, housing, and family allowances.
8. Stop limiting women's contraceptive choices.[62]

---

59. Virginia Woolf, "Professions for Women," quoted in Ritchie and Ronald, *Available Means*, 246.
60. Tong and Botts, *Feminist Thought*, 22.
61. Tong and Botts, *Feminist Thought*, 23.
62. Tong and Botts, *Feminist Thought*, 24.

Friedan responded to the lesbians who wished to join the movement as a "lavender menace" since they were taking attention away from (these are her words) "employment and education and new social institutions."[63] Even so, by 1984, NOW held its first Lesbian Rights Conference, its first Global Feminist Conference in 1992, its first Women of Color and Allies Summit in 1998, and its first Women with Disabilities and Allies Summit in 2003.[64] Friedan's desire for a narrow focus for NOW did not last long.

Yet Betty Friedan published one of the most famous milestones in feminist history, *The Feminine Mystique*, in 1963.[65] Keeping in mind that her book is over five hundred pages, it was enormously influential nevertheless. Her book found some resonance with part of the population, although I think it is important to note that not all were dissatisfied with their situation. She starts the first chapter, titled "The Problem That Has No Name," by writing:

> The problem lay buried, unspoken, for many years in the minds of American women. It was a strange stirring, a sense of dissatisfaction, a yearning that women suffered in the middle of the twentieth century in the United States. Each suburban wife struggled with it alone. As she made the beds, shopped for groceries, matched slipcover material, ate peanut butter sandwiches with her children, chauffeured Cub Scouts and Brownies, lay beside her husband at night—she was afraid to ask even of herself the silent question, "Is this all?"[66]

Friedan goes on to explain the different types of dissatisfaction women were experiencing sexually, mentally, and socially, along with the reasons being offered for their dissatisfaction, such as too much education. In fact, she writes that in 1920, 47 percent of women were in college and in 1958, only 35 percent.[67] Women went to college to find husbands and only worked to support husbands going through college.[68] Women stayed home sewing clothes, baking bread, and serving others. But many were unhappy. Why? Friedan writes, "Sometimes a woman would say, 'I feel empty somehow... incomplete.' Or she would say, 'I feel as if I don't exist.'"[69]

In the 1960s, articles in newspapers and magazines began reporting on the unhappiness of women. Friedan quotes *Newsweek*'s March 7, 1960 issue:

63. Tong and Botts, *Feminist Thought*, 25.
64. Tong and Botts, *Feminist Thought*, 30–31.
65. Friedan, *Feminine Mystique*.
66. Friedan, *Feminine Mystique*, 15.
67. Friedan, *Feminine Mystique*, 16.
68. Friedan, *Feminine Mystique*, 16–17.
69. Friedan, *Feminine Mystique*, 20.

"She is dissatisfied with a lot that women of other lands can only dream of. Her discontent is deep, pervasive, and impervious to the superficial remedies which are offered at every hand." She complains she's "just a housewife." The article continues, "A good education, it seems, has given this paragon among women an understanding of the value of everything except her own worth."[70]

Indeed, a lack of material goods does not lead to a woman's dissatisfaction. Friedan argues that "it is no longer possible to blame the problem on loss of femininity: to say that education and independence and equality with men have made American women unfeminine."[71] She echoes Woolf when she writes, "It is easy to see the concrete details that trap the suburban housewife, the continual demands on her time. But the chains that bind her in her trap are chains in her own mind and spirit. They are chains made up of mistaken ideas and misinterpreted facts, of incomplete truths and unreal choices. They are not easily seen and not easily shaken off."[72] In the end, Friedan says, women simply want something more.

Tong and Botts put Friedan in their chapter on liberal feminism in *Feminist Thought*. It is in second-wave feminism that the number of feminist theories multiplies heavily. They split radical feminism into two camps: radical-libertarian and radical-cultural.[73] The radical-libertarians focus on "consciousness-raising," or helping people see the problems of women. Among these are Joreen Freeman, who celebrates androgynous women; Gayle Rubin, who sees gender as a fluid category; Kate Millett, who suggests that men and women should temporarily separate from each other in order to completely break male control of institutions and also to embrace androgyny; and Shulamith Firestone, who wanted to be able to reproduce outside of the body and who embraced incest and all forms of sexual pleasure.[74] These theories bring to mind 2 Pet 2:19: "While they [false teachers] promise them liberty, they themselves are slaves of corruption" (NIV). These women seem to get lost in their ideas, circling ever deeper into theories that bring them attention through the "shock factor." They do not recognize that the liberties they celebrate also bring destruction.

Tong and Botts outline key differences between the radical-libertarian and the radical-cultural camps: On the radical-libertarian side, sex is seen as complete freedom in practice, whereas the radical-cultural side says sex is free unless it supports male violence. Other points of division include

---

70. Quoted in Friedan, *Feminine Mystique*, 24.
71. Friedan, *Feminine Mystique*, 26–27.
72. Friedan, *Feminine Mystique*, 31.
73. Tong and Botts, *Feminist Thought*, 40.
74. Tong and Botts, *Feminist Thought*, 40–43.

pornography as a good way to enjoy sexual pleasure versus pornography as the "sexual objectification" of women; prostitution as a legitimate profession versus prostitution as the abuse of women; and artificial means of reproduction versus the natural means of reproduction as something to value.[75] In addition, radical-libertarian feminists came up with lesbian separatist feminism.[76] Instead of defining one's sexual preferences as something innate, women were encouraged to embrace lesbianism because a "truly sexually liberated woman would not want to have sex with men."[77]

*If anyone teaches otherwise and does not agree to the sound instruction of our Lord Jesus Christ and to godly teaching, they are conceited and understand nothing. They have an unhealthy interest in controversies and quarrels about words that result in envy, strife, malicious talk, evil suspicions and constant friction between people of corrupt mind, who have been robbed of the truth and who think that godliness is a means to financial gain.—1 Tim 6:3–5, NIV*

As a representative of radical-cultural feminism, the Catholic Mary Daly is an interesting voice. Daly's *Beyond God the Father: A Philosophy of Women's Liberation* was published in 1973. She objects to being called a theologian but writes that her "task is to study the potential of the women's revolution to transform human consciousness and its externalizations, that is, to generate human becoming."[78] She explains her political stance here:

> Women have been extra-environmentals in human society. We have been foreigners not only to the fortresses of political power but also to those citadels in which thought processes have been spun out, creating a net of meaning to capture reality. In a sexist world, symbol systems and conceptual apparatuses have been male creations. These do not reflect the experience of women, but rather function to falsify our own self-image and experiences. Women have often resolved the problems this situation raises by simply not seeing the situation. That is, we have screened out experience and responded only to the questions considered meaningful and licit within the boundaries of prevailing thought structures, which reflect sexist social structures.[79]

75. Tong and Botts, *Feminist Thought*, 47–53.
76. Tong and Botts, *Feminist Thought*, 64.
77. Tong and Botts, *Feminist Thought*, 65.
78. Daly, "Document 12," 6.
79. Daly, "Document 12," 6–7.

What does this have to do with being "beyond God"? Here is one piece of a long, complicated answer:

> It should be apparent, then, that for women entrance into our own space and time is another way of expressing integrity and transformation. To stay in patriarchal space is to remain in time past. The appearance of change is basically only separation and return—cyclic movement. Breaking out of the circle requires anger, the "wrath of God" speaking God-self in an organic surge toward life. Since women are dealing with demonic power relationships, that is, with structured evil, rage is required as a positive creative force, making possible a breakthrough, encountering the blockages of inauthentic structures. It rises as a reaction to the shock of recognizing what has been lost—before it had even been discovered—one's own identity. Out of this shock can come intimations of what human being (as opposed to half being) can be. Anger, then, can trigger and sustain movement from the experience of nothingness to recognition of participation in being. When this happens, the past is changed, that is, its significance for us is changed. Then the past is no longer static: it too is on the boundary. When women take positive steps to move out of patriarchal space and time, there is a surge of new life. I would analyze this as participation in God the Verb who cannot be broken down simply into past, present, and future time, since God is form-destroying, form-creating, transforming power that makes all things new.[80]

The Combahee River Collective Statement published in 1977, Audre Lorde's "The Master's Tools Will Never Dismantle the Master's House," the 1979 Convention on the Elimination of all Forms of Discrimination Against Women, and the 1995 Fourth World Conference on Women hosted by the United Nations are also key milestones as well. These will be addressed in the next chapter.

To sum up, first-wave feminists fought for more concrete goals: the vote, societal reform, an equal education, and opportunities in the workplace. Second-wave feminists took on the mindset of Americans which supported limitations in education, society, the workplace, and other contexts. They saw a return to the ideology of the domestic sphere in the 1950s and they saw the dissatisfaction that resulted for some who wanted the opportunities that come with choices. While some of the solutions to this were quite liberal, they are still interesting, particularly as feminists such as Daly redefined God, taking on the voice of authority that moved beyond "preacher"

---

80. Daly, "Document 12." 43.

to "theologian." So what inspired third-wave feminists of the 1980s and '90s? In short, these women drew attention to race and economic status.

Currently, feminism is all about politics. Everything is political: art, poetry, fiction, speeches, essays, memoirs, film. Some feminists trade heavily on vulgarity and their ability to shock audiences to gain more attention for themselves and for their message. The Broadway production of *The Vagina Monologues* in the 1990s is one of the most well-known examples. However, a list of events for women in 2020 include a great deal of variety. For example, there is the Women of the World Festival (guest speakers and performances), SheFest (art, music, theater, film, guest speakers, panels), *The Enchanted Interior* (art), *The Guilty Feminist* (comedy show), *Unfinished Business* (showcases political activists through history), and New Suns (literary festival), among others.[81] It is also about marches and other traditional activities associated with political action.

Recent publications show a range of topics addressed by feminists, such as:

Naomi Kline, *No Logo*, 2000

Ofelia Schutte, "Cultural Alterity," 2000

Cherrie Moraga, "From a Long Line of Vendidas: Chicanas and Feminism," 2001

Virginie Despentes, *King Kong Theory*, 2004

Chao-Ju Chen, "The Difference that Differences Make: Asian Feminism and the Politics of Difference," 2007

Leslie Bow, "Racial Interstitiality and the Anomalies of the 'Pardy Colored': Representations of Asians under Jim Crow," 2007

Luana Ross, "From the 'F' Word to Indigenous/Feminisms," 2009

Kate Bornstein and S. Bear Bergman, *Gender Outlaws: The Next Generation*, 2010

Mitsuye Yamada, "Asian Pacific American Women and Feminism," 2013

Maile Arvin, Eve Tuck, Angie Morrill, "Decolonizing Feminism: Challenging Connections between Settler Colonialism and Heteropatriarchy," 2013

Tristan Taormino (collection of essays by those in the porn industry), *The Feminist Porn Book: The Politics of Producing Pleasure*, 2013

---

81. "Your 2020."

Melissa V. Harris-Perry, *Sister Citizen: Shame, Stereotypes, and Black Women in America*, 2013

Cheryl Sandberg, *Lean In: Women, Work, and the Will to Lead*, 2013

Jill Lepore, *The Secret History of Wonder Woman*, 2014

Rebecca Solnit, *Men Explain Things to Me*, 2014

Leslie Jameson, *The Empathy Exams*, 2014

Roxanne Gay, "Confessions of a Bad Feminist" (TED Talk), 2015

Emma Watson, "HeforShe" speech at the United Nations, Switzerland, 2015

Kate Harding, *Asking for It: The Alarming Rise of Rape Culture—And What We Can Do About It*, 2015

Sady Doyle, *Trainwreck: The Women We Love to Hate, Mock, and Fear . . . and Why*, 2016

Janet Mock, film, *The Trans List*, 2016

So what should you take away from this discussion?

- Education and political power were often essential parts of the argument for women's equal rights.
- Political arguments were espoused by both Christian women and some notable non-Christian proponents with the same goal: to give women real power by giving them the vote.
- African-American women played an important role in first-wave feminism but had to address much more than just a desire for political power.
- Woolf showed that the battle for equality was often inward, not just a battle for changed laws and additional rights. For women to be free, they needed to kill the "woman in the house."
- In second- and third-wave feminism, the number of theories and their proponents multiplied, often contradicting each other or espousing radical views.
- Currently, feminists use every available outlet to spread messages about equality, protection for women, education, sexuality, gender, violence, and so on by using art, film, poetry, events, political marches, and more to bring women together for action, entertainment, and education.

# 4

# The Ultimate Feminist DIY Project

## Constructing Realities in the Age of the Cyborg

The Battlefield: The mind and higher education in the time of second-and third-wave feminism

The Opponents: Those who believe that humans are the basis of identity and freewill, dichotomous categories are too reductive and promote hierarchy, reality is constructed, truths are relative to time and to situation, capitalism promotes patriarchy and even racism, technology has been subsumed into our identities, teaching should be political, and language and meanings attached to words are arbitrary relationships and allow for multiple meanings to be attached to words, versus those who believe that Christ is the basis of our identity and the source of freedom, some aspects of reality are discovered, there are absolute truths, Christ is the living location of truth, capitalism promotes social mobility, teaching should be balanced and not overtly political, and language allows some room for multiple meanings to be attached to words but not an unlimited range of meanings.

*Guiding questions for chapter 4:*

1. As the fight for women's rights shifted onto an intellectual and academic plane mostly experienced inside of the university, why did African American women feel the need to issue the Combahee River Collective in 1977?
2. How did lesbians influence feminism in the second and third waves? How does the theory of intersectionality reveal the intersecting layers of oppression twentieth-century women had to address?
3. Why is capitalism identified as a problem by some feminists? How are the concerns of feminists grouped into themes?
4. What is transnational feminism?
5. What is standpoint theory and how does it reveal the limits of colonialism? How is education sometimes a tool of assimilation?
6. How would you define postmodernism, poststructuralism, and a "technoscience" society? What is networked feminism?
7. How are language and identity embedded in social power structures? How are they embedded in technology?
8. How have college classrooms become a site for political influence imposed upon students?

With the goals of first-wave feminists addressed in the story of how women achieved equality through the right to speak publicly, the right to receive an equal education and to put it to good use in jobs not based on manual labor, and the right to have legal rights and political representation, you might be asking, Well, what's left? In many ways, the battle for women's equality moved from these concrete goals to addressing the mindsets of men and women who clung to outdated and erroneous beliefs on the abilities of women and their status in society, and to forming and supporting academic research into the histories and contributions of women through work done by second-wave feminist scholars in the university. However, there is a mix of both concrete goals and those that have to do with inspiring inner changes in second-wave feminism, and as you can see from the lists in Appendix A of this book, these have changed because the historical, social, and political contexts have changed between the nineteenth and the twentieth centuries.

You will perhaps quickly notice that Christianity does not provide either much of a help or much of a challenge to feminist thought in this chapter. It is mostly ignored. What was once so central to arguments for women's rights in first-wave feminism and some of second-wave feminism appears to be noticeably absent as we merge into third- and fourth-wave feminist thought. Why is this so?

In the university, many regard Christianity as opposition to be defeated. In the *Atlanta Journal Constitution*, Maureen Downey republishes an article by Robert Moranto on the prejudice against Christians in the university. In his article, Moranto offers a description of a student rejected for a graduate school program but changes details on religious disposition to race. At the end, he points out the sense of outrage at the student, who was clearly more than qualified, being rejected on the basis of race. Then he tells us to substitute *Christian* for race. "The bigotry," he writes, "has at least four costs to academia, and to society."[1]

The first of these four costs includes limiting the talent hired into the university. Many identified as "conservative" do not make it into graduate school programs, as he shows. I would add that it is well documented in *The Chronicle of Higher Education* that many conservatives are denied tenure—if they are fortunate enough to be hired in the first place.

The other three costs of excluding Christians and conservatives are easy to see. As Moranto argues:

> Second, exiling dissenters retards research. On subjects from family life to foreign policy, academia has scores of professors asking questions of interest to the secular left for every one doing so from the religious right. This limits our understanding of a complex world.
>
> Relatedly, when intellectual elites celebrate the traditionalism of most Muslims and Hindus while castigating it among some Christians, their support for multiculturalism seems highly selective, even hypocritical.
>
> Finally, an unrepresentative intelligentsia leads many of our fellow Americans to distrust us and our research. When traditional Christians find the media and academic and cultural institutions closed to people like them, they see little reason to believe those authorities.[2]

Yet I would not let these facts discourage my Christian readers, and I hope I have not inspired you to skip this chapter. There is much to be learned from secular thought, especially as we bring it into relationship with the insights given to us as Christians through prayer, meditation, and revelation. Also, how will the weaknesses of secular thought be exposed if

---

1. Robert Moranto, quoted in Downey, "Is Higher Education Biased?"
2. Robert Moranto, quoted in Downey, "Is Higher Education Biased?"

never subjected to critique by those who use a different lens for seeing the world? Honestly, efforts to exclude conservatives and Christians from the university are futile so long as we continue to study religion in the university, although—let's be honest—some theologians or professors who teach religious histories are not Christians either. Yet there are many institutions of higher education that are Christian—including Hillsdale College, which offers free courses online and serves to use education to help correct the errors and omissions so common in other places where histories are severely reduced and fragmented; where philosophical thought that runs contrary to liberalism is openly ridiculed and harshly criticized; and where scholarship that truly questions the theories and those theorists is often undermined.

We have colleges and universities that are largely defined by Christian denominations that produce graduates who go into the workforce, some within the university. These institutions remain a threat to the dominance of liberalism and provide a needed balance to liberal thought.

> Oh, how I love Your law! It is my meditation all the day. You, through Your commandments, make me wiser than my enemies. For they are ever with me. I have more understanding than all my teachers. For your testimonies are my meditation. I understand more than the ancients because I keep your precepts. I have restrained my feet from every evil way that I may keep Your word." (Ps 119: 97–101 NKJV)

In fact, these institutions are such a threat that the decidedly liberal news organization *NPR* published an article on fears expressed as Christian universities are accused of Title IX violations on the basis of sexual orientation.³ What this means, of course, is that those liberals who disagree with freedom of religion wish to shut down Christian universities by taking away financial aid funds students need to attend based on a Title IX violation. Christianity is, indeed, still the enemy. As my pastor pointed out last week, Muslim bakeries are not being sued for discrimination. In general, Christians are the ones who find themselves targeted.

To begin this chapter, it is helpful to review the goals of second-wave feminists, who:

- Sought to add women to history within the university by forming their own journals, conferences, and eventually, academic programs. This work continues in the concerns of third-wave and, if you choose to use the term, fourth-wave feminists. The pursuit of recovering the histories

---

3. Gjelten, "Christian Colleges."

and contributions of women continues. Also, for about the last decade or so, you can earn a master's or a doctorate in women's studies.

- Criticized a sexist, patriarchal mindset and sought to challenge it within whatever context it existed.
- Opened the doors to divergent views on sexuality, reproduction, and women's roles. Some included incest and embracing lesbianism to avoid men. Others embraced pornography and prostitution; others did not. Some valued a woman's ability to bear children; others wished for an alternative. Some considered gender to be fluid.
- Fought for equality in the workplace.
- Wanted their jobs protected while on maternity leave.
- Wanted access to birth control. Also, abortion was legalized in 1973.
- Wanted to pass the Equal Rights Amendment but ended up with the Civil Rights Act and Title VII instead.
- Wanted to redefine the gender category "woman" and to abolish the category in favor of freedom to define themselves as they chose.
- Wanted to redefine God to fit their new emphasis on equality. This means many things. For some it meant creating a whole new god, complete with a female counterpart. For others, it meant getting rid of anything that disrupted their politics. For others, it meant a new interpretation of Scripture. For yet others, it meant contextualizing Scripture so that the requirement voiced by Paul for women to learn in silence became time bound. Also, they wanted to restructure Christian thought and practice. This was continued from first-wave feminists who, intentionally or not, did something similar—although not in the language of the university, as the highly educated second-wave feminists did.
- Sought political representation, such as through Kennedy's Commission on Women. They formed political groups—in particular, the National Organization of Women (NOW).

In sharp contrast to first-wave feminism, the battlefield for third-wave feminists was an intensely political one with entirely different concerns for concrete action, but it was also an intensely intellectual one. Ideas about truth, the social construction of reality, the nature of language (semiotics), capitalism, and so on are part of third-wave feminism because the battles are taking place at the university and then being disseminated into political action beyond those doors. The benefits of an education in the history of women's rights can be seen in third-wave and in fourth-wave feminist writings as women draw upon complex theories and posit their own complex theories. If education was once a tool that society tried to use to force immigrants and the colonized to assimilate, and if education was once used to enforce the subjugation of women, in the hands of women inside the university today it is now a weapon—and it is a formidable weapon, to be sure.

To further simplify this discussion, the themes for the table of contents in *Contemporary Feminist Theory* by Mary F. Rogers, published in 1998, helps us see the main areas third-wave feminist scholars explored (and fourth-wave or contemporary feminists continue to explore).[4] These include:

- Hierarchy, Domination, and Oppression
- The Politics of Knowledge
- Women and Popular culture
- Schooling, Pedagogy, and Learning
- The State, Politics, and Public Policy
- The Economy, Work, and Money
- Partnering, Parenting, and Family Making
- Caring and Community
- Identity and Selfhood
- Embodied Consciousness
- Social Change and Cultural Transformation
- Feminist Theorizing[5]

Many of the feminist theories we have covered in this book can fit under one or more of these themes.

Third-wave feminists can claim many different starting points, but one of the most useful is the Combahee River Collective, published in 1977 in a collection titled *Capitalist Patriarchy: The Case for Social Feminism*.[6] They introduce themselves by saying:

> We are a collective of Black feminists who have been meeting together since 1974. During that time we have been involved in the process of defining and clarifying our politics, while at the same time doing political work within our own group and in coalition with other progressive organizations and movements.

---

4. Rogers, *Contemporary Feminist Theory*.
5. Rogers, *Contemporary Feminist Theory*, iv-vi.
6. Ritchie and Ronald, *Available Means*, 291.

> The most general statement of our politics at the present time would be that we are actively committed to struggling against racial, sexual, heterosexual, and class oppression, and see as our particular task the development of integrated analysis and practice based on the fact that the major systems of oppression are interlocking. The synthesis of these oppressions creates the conditions of our lives. As Black women we see Black feminism as the logical political movement to combat the minefield and simultaneous oppressions that all women of color face.[7]

Three important things come up here: (1) A critique of capitalism because it is "patriarchal"; (2) A critique of feminists (like Betty Friedan) who have ignored the goals of women who are not white, middle-class, and educated; and (3) a realization that oppression comes at women from many different angles (which goes with the theory of intersectionality, defined best in 1989 by Crenshaw).

What constitutes the problem with capitalism? To briefly explain, Marxist feminists blame classism, not sexism, as the cause of women's oppression. Socialist feminists take a broader view by investigating "women's subordination in a coherent and systematic way that integrates class and sex, as well as other aspects of identity such as race/ethnicity or sexual orientation."[8] In 1981, Gloria Joseph, a "black revolutionary spirited feminist of West Indian parents," wrote "Black Feminist Pedagogy and Schooling in Capitalist White America."[9]

Here she criticizes schools because they convey capitalist knowledge that keeps in place "inequalities and hierarchies that characterize capitalist America." She explains that the curriculum in her time could be accurately characterized as a "white studies" and a "male studies" program that leaves out the "histories, experiences, cultures, and perspectives of people of color, and women of all colors."[10] Ultimately, capitalism is to blame for the oppression of her people and for others who are disenfranchised by a system that heavily favors the "slave captor, power makers," and "corporate monsters."[11]

As for the second point where women of color have been excluded from feminist organizations and theories, Joseph tackles that from the

---

7. Combahee River Collective, "The Combahee River Collective Statement," quoted in Ritchie and Ronald, *Available Means*, 292.

8. Tong and Botts, *Feminist Thought*, 73.

9. Guy-Sheftall, *Words of Fire*, 461–62.

10. Gloria Joseph, "Black Feminist Pedagogy and Schooling in Capitalist White America," quoted in Guy-Sheftall, *Words of Fire*, 466.

11. Gloria Joseph, "Black Feminist Pedagogy and Schooling in Capitalist White America," quoted in Guy-Sheftall, *Words of Fire*, 467.

definition of what she thinks education should be. She argues that "black feminist pedagogy is designed to raise the political consciousness of students by introducing a worldview with an Afrocentric orientation to reality, and the inclusion of gender and patriarchy as central to an understanding of all historical phenomena." She goes on to explain that it is not only the existence of flawed truths that is a problem, but the system of creating knowledge labeled as truth that is a problem. She suggests using an "alternative epistemology." Teaching should be political and it should "generate a new political consciousness."[12] Other third-wave feminists address their exclusion from feminist movements in different ways, but Joseph's captures the way that education could play a key role in liberation.

As for the third point regarding overlapping forms of oppression, Joseph also writes, "Afro-American women's lives have been greatly affected by the intersection of systems of racial, sexual, and class oppressions. However, they have developed a unique black female culture whose purpose is to foster authentic black female self-definition and self-valuation that counters and transcends the multiple structures of oppressions that they face."[13]

This comes up in several pieces by different third-wave feminists, but it was a lawyer named Kimberlé Crenshaw who defined "intersectionality," or how overlapping forms of oppression affect women.[14] These forms of oppression can include race, education, ability, class, gender, age, ethnicity, language, and culture, according to the International Women's Development Agency.[15] Of course, I would add religion to that list. In any case, understanding overlapping contexts is key to understanding the challenges a particular woman may be faced with, particularly if she is not white.

Third-wave feminists adopted a postmodernist view that reflected just how fragmented and individualistic feminist theories and practices were in second-wave feminism. For example, Black lesbian poet and literature professor Audre Lorde offered "The Master's Tools Will Never Dismantle the Master's House" in 1973.[16] In this piece, she argues that "advocating the mere tolerance of difference between women is the grossest reformism. It is a total denial of the creative function of difference in our lives."[17] She also

12. Gloria Joseph, "Black Feminist Pedagogy and Schooling in Capitalist White America," quoted in Guy-Sheftall, *Words of Fire*, 465.

13. Gloria Joseph, "Black Feminist Pedagogy and Schooling in Capitalist White America," quoted in Guy-Sheftall, *Words of Fire*, 464.

14. Tong and Botts, *Feminist Thought*, 115.

15. "What Does Intersectional Feminism?"

16. Audre Lorde, "The Master's Tools Will Never Dismantle the Master's House," quoted in Freedman, *Essential Feminist Reader*, 331.

17. Audre Lorde, "The Master's Tools Will Never Dismantle the Master's House,"

writes, "As women, we have been taught to either ignore our differences or to view them as causes for separation and suspicion rather than as forces for change. Without community, there is no liberation." When she offers her famous line as captured in her title, she argues that community and difference are the way to bring about real change.[18]

Third-wave feminism makes room for people of different races and ethnicities. Another influential feminist that brought in the third wave is Bell Hooks. An English professor at CUNY, she published *Feminist Theory: From Margin to Center* in 1984.[19] Of course, this is just one text out of many she has written. She's a prolific and influential writer and speaker.

She describes the impulse for third-wave feminism by stating, "Feminism in the United States has never emerged from the women who are most victimized by sexist oppression; women who are daily beaten down, mentally, physically, and spiritually—women who are powerless to change their condition in life. They are a silent majority."[20] She then goes on to criticize Betty Friedan and to describe how she was treated while a student at the university when she wondered where pieces by Native American, Black, Hispanic, and Asian women were because they weren't on the reading list for her course in feminist theory. The response? Anger from her classmates.[21]

As a result of third-wave feminism, those same four racial and ethnic groups also form the groups included in an anthology still used in classrooms today: *This Bridge Called My Back: Writings by Radical Women of Color*, originally published in 1981. It is edited by Cherríe Moraga and Gloria Anzaldúa. Moraga is Artist in Residence at Stanford University and Anzaldúa was a writer and poet, according to the biography on the back of this anthology. Pieces by women identifying with one of these four groups are mixed into these chapters: "Children Passing in the Streets: The Roots of Our Radicalism," "Entering the Lives of Others: Theory in the Flesh," "And When You Leave, Take Your Pictures With You: Racism in the Women's Movement," "Between the Lines: On Culture, Class, and Homophobia," "Speaking in Tongues: The Third World Woman Writer," and "El Mundo Zurdo: The Vision."[22]

---

quoted in Freedman, *Essential Feminist Reader*, 333.

18. Audre Lorde, "The Master's Tools Will Never Dismantle the Master's House," quoted in Freedman, *Essential Feminist Reader*, 334.

19. Guy-Sheftall, *Words of Fire*, 269.

20. Bell Hooks, "Black Women: Shaping Feminist Theory," quoted in Guy-Sheftall, *Words of Fire* 270.

21. Guy-Sheftall, *Words of Fire* 279.

22. Moraga and Anzaldúa, *This Bridge*.

The pieces included are poems, political statements, speeches, essays, and short memoirs. Operating from an artistic perspective instead of something like you might find in a researched essay in an academic journal, the arguments that are made throughout build the idea that the women in this anthology had something to say that was uniquely theirs. Their perspective could not be generalized within a particular group—and certainly not within feminist theories at the time. What ties them together is a celebration of individual experience and perspective along the same theme of oppression, just in different forms and to different levels and in different contexts. In other words, they bring the fragmentation and individualism associated with postmodernism to life. These individual points of view also disrupt the reality that mainstream America had constructed. The main effect of feminist thought is to interrupt a narrative that leaves them out, reduces them, or imprisons them in a physical, mental, or intellectual sense.

An emphasis on difference is what feeds into transnational feminism. Rosemarie Tong and Tina Fernandes Botts write, "Transnational feminism is sensitive to the myriad differences among women."[23] For example, intersectionality, "concrete specificity," and "self-reflexivity" are needed. It is also characterized by the tendency to come together in other movements and then to disperse when the work is done.[24] Taking the conversation onto a global stage, transnational feminists such as Chandra Talpade Mohanty object to the need to homogenize the "Third World Woman" into simple definitions and to point out that Western feminists are part of who oppresses these women. Mohanty is quoted as saying, "It is in this process of homogenization and systemization of the oppression of women in the third world that power is exercised in much of recent Western feminist discourse, and this power needs to be defined and named."[25] Unlike global feminists, transnational feminists do not seek to create one group but to work with other women in other countries on different issues, such as stopping sex trafficking.[26]

To explore transnational feminism, I would ask the question: What role does the reader play in interpreting a text by someone who experiences life in another geographical, political, social, religious, or cultural context(s)? As a reader, I would explore:

---

23. Tong and Botts, *Feminist Thought*, 145.

24. Tong and Botts, *Feminist Thought*, 146.

25. Chandra Talpade Mohanty, "Under Western Eyes," quoted in Tong and Botts, *Feminist Thought*, 146–47.

26. Tong and Botts, *Feminist Thought*, 146–47.

- Atavistic (refers to something "ancient" or "ancestral")[27] perceptions of non-Western communities and cultures
- Subaltern (refers to someone of lower status) knowledge production
- Embedded, intersectional contexts for women who are neither completely oppressed nor completely resistant to oppression (Remember the definition of intersectionality?)
- The role of grassroots struggles
- Political solidarity movements
- Media images of women, particularly those suffering or in acts of resistance
- Women's cultural, economic, and religious practices
- The relationship between the national and the specific (state/local) contexts of a text
- How a text can subvert existing political, cultural, or linguistic (language) borders
- The role of the sacred
- The relationship between place and identity

To look at transnational feminism as a reader is more about methodology and less about theory. So you might look at a text by a woman fighting for a cause on the basis of her interests related to equality and then contextualize it. In Derpal Grewal and Caren Kaplan's textbook *An Introduction to Women's Studies: Gender in a Transnational World*, topics include gender, the rise of Western science, reproductive rights, health education and advocacy, citizenship, identity politics, the border, artistic practice and reception, colonial contexts, the body and consumer culture, cyberculture, diasporas, economic globalization, and food production and consumption.

Readings that could be analyzed in a course on transnational feminism might include the following: Alexandra Kollontai, "The Social Basis of the Woman Question" (Russia, 1909); Huda Shaarawi, "Speech at the Arab Feminist Conference" (Egypt, 1944); Funmilayo Ransome-Kuti, "We Had Equality till Britain Came" (Nigeria, 1947); Hélène Cixous, "The Laugh of the Medusa" (France, 1975); Domitila Barrios de la Chungara, "The Woman's Problem" (Bolivia, 1980); Association of African Women for Research and Development, "A Statement on Genital Mutilation" (Senegal, 1980); and Monique Wittig, "One Is Not Born a Woman" (France, 1981).

---

27. "Atavistic."

Speeces given at the 1995 United Nations' Fourth World Conference on Women in Beijing are also worth reading, such as Gertrude Mongella's opening address and plenary session (Tanzania); Winona LaDuke's "The Indigenous Women's Network, Our Future, Our Responsibility" (United States); Palesa Beverley Ditsie's statement of the International Gay and Lesbian Human Rights Commission (South Africa); and Gro Haarlem Brundtland's closing address (Norway). Other sources include Jonah Gokova's "Challenging Men to Reject Gender Stereotypes" (Zimbabwe, 1998) and the Revolutionary Association of the Women of Afghanistan's "Statement on the Occasion of International Women's Day" (Afghanistan, 2004). These are just a few of the selections possible to read from *The Essential Feminist Reader*, edited by Freedman.[28]

One might also explore Nigerian Chimamanda Ngozi Adichie's TED Talk "We Should All be Feminists" (2017); Burmese Aung San Suu Kyi's article "In Quest of Democracy" (1992); Zimbabwean Marevasei Kachere's "War Memoir" (1998); and Yemeni Tawakkol Karman's Nobel Lecture (2011). The last three texts come from Michael Austin's *Reading the World: Ideas That Matter*.[29] I would add world literature selections to my reading list if I were to explore transnational feminism more, and I would add visual artifacts because, as a rhetorician, I study how these are powerful tools of definition and persuasion. It is also a key part of Patricia Hill Collins's argument that "controlling images" must be analyzed and addressed.[30] I have devoted part of the chapter on anti-feminists and visual culture in this book to this topic as well.

To sum up, instead of writing long, complex theories, transnational feminists are more interested in application and actions that are motivated by a devotion to equality on a global level.

Other ideas circulating in second- and third-wave feminism include existentialism, postmodernism, and poststructuralism. Existentialists such as Simone de Beauvoir, who published *The Second Sex* in 1958, proposed the idea that woman is "the other."[31] By this she means that man is essential and woman is nonessential. She focuses on the role of the body in forming an identity as "the other," and claims "women's liberation . . . requires nothing less than the elimination of men's desire to control women."[32]

---

28. Grewal and Kaplan, *Introduction to Women's Studies*.
29. Austin, *Reading the World*.
30. Seltzen and Tran, "Power of Controlling Images."
31. Tong and Botts, *Feminist Thought*, 234.
32. Tong and Botts, *Feminist Thought*, 237.

What or who are existentialists? The *Stanford Encyclopedia of Philosophy* lists a group of writers, including de Beauvoir, and emphasizes that this type of thought was based just as much in literature as in philosophy. Freedom was to be "the core of all human values" and the enemy was religion. Existentialists hold that humans cannot be understood only through the lens of science, nor can they be understood through a moral lens, and so new categories are needed: "All the themes popularly associated with existentialism—dread, boredom, alienation, the absurd, freedom, commitment, nothingness, and so on—find their philosophical significance in the context of the search for a new categorial framework, together with its governing norm."[33] Also useful is the dictionary definition, which is as follows: "A philosophical theory or approach which emphasizes the existence of the individual person as a free and responsible agent determining their own development through acts of the will."[34]

So what de Beauvoir contributes (or at least one thing she contributes) is a new category with an emphasis on using it to develop the individual.

De Beauvoir is mentioned as the inspiration for the work produced by many different feminists, but postmodernism is another powerful influence on third-wave feminists. Writers such as Hélène Cixous celebrated the fragmentation of categories and objected to the dichotomies that privileged one thing over the other, such as "activity/passivity," "culture/nature," "speaking/writing," and so on.[35] These categories presented a hierarchy in some cases.

What is postmodernism? Postmodernism "can be described as a set of critical, strategic and rhetorical practices employing concepts such as difference, repetition, the trace, the simulacrum, and hyperreality to destabilize other concepts such as presence, identity, historical progress, epistemic certainty, and the univocity of meaning."[36] It emphasizes difference, fragmentation, low culture, and individualism, much as third-wave feminists did in their theories. In this chapter, the phrase "epistemic certainty" stands out because it is one of the ways that scholars were exploring how reality and knowledge are constructed entities, although some would argue that there are some aspects of both that are discovered, not created.

Peter Barry defines postmodernism as a continuation of modernism with a celebration of fragmentation (not the lamenting of it); and whereas modernism was a time when "faith was full and authority intact," postmodernism is an "exhilarating, liberating phenomenon, symptomatic of our

---

33. "Existentialism" (*Stanford*).
34. "Existentialism" (*Oxford*).
35. Tong and Botts, *Feminist Thought*, 252.
36. "Postmodernism" (*Stanford*).

escape from the claustrophobic embrace of fixed systems of belief."[37] While a discussion of modernism and postmodernism can't really be reduced to a couple of paragraphs, the general characteristics of postmodernism are provided here as starting places for further study. Of course, even from this reductive take on these ideas, it is clear to see that the undermining of authority could be construed as a threat to Christians.

Poststructuralism made room for Judith Butler, who claimed that gender is "constructed through our actions" and consists of choices we make, not biology.[38] While the idea of choice in gender was not new, the idea that your sex could be chosen was new in her time. Poststructuralism's predecessor, structuralism, offered an argument that "language doesn't just reflect or record the world: rather, it shapes it, so that *how* we see is *what* we see."[39] Poststructuralism "derives ultimately from philosophy" and "emphasizes the difficulty of achieving secure knowledge about things."[40] Barry quotes Nietzsche's observation that "there are no facts, only interpretation."[41] Here we see the roots of relativism and the idea that there are no fixed or absolute truths to be discovered; there are only truths to be constructed. This makes total sense, as Nietzsche's essay "On Truth and Lies in a Nonmoral Sense," published in 1873, is a defining text for those who believe all truths are relative (which is an attempt to offer an absolute truth, but we shall move on).

To further define poststructuralism—briefly—is to say there was a movement from the study of language as a whole (see Saussure and explore semiotics for the arbitrary relationships between words and their meanings) to the idea that language and its speakers are the "product or effect of a variety of power relations manifested through a plurality of discourses."[42] So what does *this* mean?

It means that we have to look a little deeper and see how relationships between elements of power in our social context affect the way we speak or don't speak and how we express ourselves and our ideas. Foucault pointed out that power is connected to the social world and that "relations of power are interwoven with other kinds of relations: production, kinship, family, sexuality."[43] Power isn't just about "prohibition and punishment," but it has a lot of different forms. These forms and connections create "general

---

37. Barry, *Beginning Theory*, 83–84.
38. Tong and Botts, *Feminist Thought*, 247.
39. Barry, *Beginning Theory*, 61.
40. Barry, *Beginning Theory*, 63.
41. Friedrich Nietzsche, quoted in Barry, *Beginning Theory*, 63.
42. Tong and Botts, *Feminist Thought*, 244.
43. Tong and Botts, *Feminist Thought*, 244.

conditions of domination" and result in "possible resistances."[44] Foucault is known for describing how we internalize social control in our lives with his famous metaphor about the guard in the prison tower. We can't see the guard, so we self-regulate our behavior just in case.

Feminists, particularly those in the second and third save who occupy places in the university, were exploring power: Who has it? Who does not? Why? Can something be done to change this? The conversations are complex because the ideas and the thinkers were complex. As a scholar in rhetoric, I am interested in these conversations because rhetoric is ultimately about power. I look at how power is created, disseminated, challenged, and shifted. Feminist theories in all their forms are interesting to me because they are all about power—challenging it, resisting it, creating it, shifting it—but power is also interesting because of its effects on the auditors: How is rhetoric like a drug, as Gorgias once described it in a speech given in ancient Greece? How does truth get created, defined, and deployed? Many rhetoricians look at "epistemic rhetorics," or the way knowledge gets created and truths produced within different communities.

Finally, the idea of standpoint theory is helpful for understanding third-wave feminists because it is also about what is going on in our minds and how that affects what we do. Standpoint theory describes how some people know and understand some things that, because of their race, social position, class, or other characteristics, others cannot know. According to the *Encyclopaedia Britannica*, "the theory emerged from the Marxist argument that people from an oppressed class have special access to knowledge that is not available to those from a privileged class. In the 1970s feminist writers inspired by that Marxist insight began to examine how inequalities between men and women influence knowledge production."[45]

In short, standpoint theory means that your social position can "shape what you know." Sandra Harding coined the term and Dorothy Smith's book *The Everyday World as Problematic: A Feminist Sociology*, which was published in 1989, explored women's roles in the home and in society and investigated how those became the norm. A person's standpoint determines the type of knowledge produced, who it includes, who it leaves out, who has power, and who does not. Patricia Hill Collins published *Black Feminist Thought: Knowledge, Consciousness, and the Politics of Empowerment* in 1990 and explained how this theory helps us to understand why and how black women have been marginalized, particularly within the university.

---

44. Tong and Botts, *Feminist Thought*, 245.
45. "Standpoint Theory."

To understand the role standpoint plays, Khristie Dotson, who wrote the article "Inheriting Patricia Collins' *Black Feminist* Epistemology" in 2015, explains that there are "three patterns of suppression" explored in Collins' book: "omission, trivialization, and depoliticization."[46] She goes on to explain that when we create knowledge, we leave out Black women or we trivialize them. We undermine knowledge created by Black women by removing the political implications of it. Knowledge is created in a "hegemonic" society. What this means is that there is an overarching, dominant culture. She quotes Collins: "Its [culture's] significance 'lies in its ability to shape consciousness via the manipulation of ideas, images, symbols, and ideologies.'"[47]

Standpoint theory is a way of understanding that we do not all produce the same types of knowledge because there are factors that make us incapable of producing the knowledge that people of other social, racial, ethnic, economic, etc. backgrounds can produce. I would argue it's a postmodern epistemology because it admits that knowledge is partial—a hallmark of postmodern thought that recognized that fragmented, limited thinking is all that is available from one person's perspective.

Kathryn Gines adds something else in her article on Patricia Collins by pointing out the impact "controlling images" have on women, specifically Black women. She writes:

> What I find so appealing in Collins's scholarship is her emphases on the vital need and incredible power of Black women's voices as well as our agency. She juxtaposes negative controlling images of Black women imposed from the outside with our own agency for self-definition to make the case for a distinct Black feminist epistemology. I have always been especially struck by this analysis of controlling images and the power of self-definition. I recognized the pervasiveness of controlling images like the mammy (the Black mother figure in white homes), the matriarch (the Black mother figure in Black homes), the welfare mother (poor, working-class Black women) and the Black Lady (a middle-class image informed by Black respectability), and finally the jezebel (the hypersexualized Black woman). I walk out into the world, I have various interactions on campus, I go to parent-teacher conferences, I listen to music, I watch television dramas and films, and I see representations of the Obama family. In all of these contexts I think about controlling images and the power of self-definition. I often ask myself—almost

---

46. Dotson, "Inheriting Patricia," 2323.
47. Patricia Collins, quoted in Dotson, "Inheriting Patricia," 2326.

automatically—to what controlling image is society expecting this Black woman to conform and in what way is this Black woman resisting and/or defining herself because of (or despite) those controlling images?[48]

Strikingly similar to the points made in standpoint theory are the points made in the area of technoscience. This theoretical perspective critiques the relationship between science and sexist structures. In "Situated Knowledges: The Science Question in Feminism and the Privilege of Partial Perspective," Donna Haraway argues that there is no objective knowledge, that knowledge is socially created, and that it is embodied.[49] She writes, "I am arguing for the view from a body, always a complex, contradictory, structuring, and structured body, versus the view from above, from nowhere, from simplicity."[50] Published in 1988, she is an influential voice within third-wave feminism.

Another offshoot of third-wave feminism is cyberfeminism. According to the *Encyclopedia of New Media*, "Cyberfeminism is a term coined in 1994 by Sadie Plant, director of the Cybernetic Culture Research Unit at the University of Warwick in Britain, to describe the work of feminists interested in theorizing, critiquing, and exploiting the Internet, cyberspace, and new-media technologies in general." Cyberfeminism "has tended to include mostly younger, technologically savvy women, and those from Western, white, middle-class backgrounds." Some explore how technology and its uses are "embedded in structures of power."[51] Donna Haraway is also often quoted as a representative for this area too. Her essay "A Cyborg Manifesto: Science, Technology, and Socialist-Feminism in the Late Twentieth Century," which was published in 1985, explores how people and machines in various contexts interact. She is also an example of someone who completely disregards religion.

Even so, it is worth our time to take a closer look at her manifesto, as most people who study women's history or feminism have read it. We read it in my doctoral program for rhetoric. Haraway writes, "A cyborg is a cybernetic organism, a hybrid of machine and organism, a creature of social reality as well as a creature of fiction."[52] She then argues that all reality is constructed: "Social reality is lived social relations, our most important political construction, a world-changing fiction." She goes on to say that our experiences help to create this fiction and that they have political

---

48. Gines, "Ruminating," 2343.
49. Haraway, "Situated Knowledges," 575–76.
50. Haraway, "Situated Knowledges," 589.
51. "Cyberfeminism."
52. Haraway, "Cyborg Manifesto," 5.

consequences. She writes, "The international women's movements have constructed 'women's experience,' as well as uncovered or discovered this crucial collective object. This experience is a fiction and fact of the most crucial, political kind. Liberation rests on the construction of the consciousness, the imaginative apprehension, of oppression, and so of possibility. The cyborg is a matter of fiction and lived experience that changes what counts as women's experience in the late twentieth century."[53]

She goes on to write:

> The cyborg is our ontology [this deals with the nature of being, but it is also defined as a "set of concepts and categories in a subject area or domain that shows their properties and the relations between them"][54]; it gives us our politics. The cyborg is a condensed image of both imagination and material reality, the two joined centers structuring any possibility of historical transformation.[55]

She later explains the cyborg as something outside of our human histories—our constructs—as she explains its role in how we have combined ourselves with this disembodied idea of machine. She goes on:

> In the traditions of "Western" science and politics—the tradition of racist, male-dominant capitalism; the tradition of progress; the tradition of the appropriation of nature as resource for the productions of culture; the tradition of reproduction of the self from the reflections of the other—the relation between organism and machine has been a border war. The stakes in the border war have been the territories of production, reproduction, and imagination. This essay is an argument for pleasure in the confusion of boundaries and for responsibility in their construction. It is also an effort to contribute to socialist-feminist culture and theory in a postmodernist, non-naturalist mode and in the utopian tradition of imagining a world without gender, which is perhaps a world without genesis, but maybe also a world without end."[56]

These excerpts give you a taste of her prose, something that is unlike what normally appears in a journal—that is, research that is full of citations and that uses the formal, academic voice. For a theorist who thinks teaching

---

53. Haraway, "Cyborg Manifesto," 5–6.
54. "Ontology."
55. Haraway, "Cyborg Manifesto," 7.
56. Haraway, "Cyborg Manifesto," 7.

creationism is child abuse,[57] she still offers a new way of thinking about the relationship between our identities as humans and those we find in the cyborg.

I would say the next main area of feminist thought, networked feminism, carries us into fourth-wave feminism or beyond that into postfeminism. It's using social media to connect and to confront sexism where it is found. However, make no mistake; this is firmly rooted in third-wave feminism. Tong and Botts explain that these feminists "use the Internet to engage in micropolitics. They are generally against constituting organizations, networks, and institutions that have a life of their own as well as a relatively set agenda."[58] With the exception of the International Network for Feminist Approaches to Bioethics, there's no central organization. These particular feminists also reject "feminist" and "womanist" as terms that define them and replace those with "grrls."[59]

*The Essential Feminist Reader* includes two pieces by the Guerilla Girls—"When Sexism and Racism Are No Longer Fashionable" and "Do Woman Have to Be Naked to Get into the Met Museum?"—and Kathleen Hann of Bikini Kill's "Riot Grrrl Manifesto."

The two pieces included in the *Feminist Reader* by the Guerilla Girls were published in 1989 and are just posters. These are easy to find online and are worth checking out to get a sense of the playfulness mixed with serious messages that are characteristic of this group.

The 1992 "Riot Grrrl Manifesto" takes a deliberately informal voice in an attempt to be provocative. One statement comes from the other types of feminism we have just been discussing: "BECAUSE we must take over the means of production in order to create our own meanings." Sounding a lot like a teenager, she also writes: "BECAUSE we are unwilling to falter under claims that we are reactionary 'reverse sexists' AND NOT THE TRUE-PUNKROCKSOULCRUSADERS THAT WE KNOW we really are."[60] The manifesto is nothing like the scholarship of many of the other feminists we have explored, but it also has its place.

So what might fourth-wave feminism be? Well, like all of the waves, it is a continuation and it is a fragmentation of ideas. In an article in *Vox*, Constance Grady writes:

> Online is where activists meet and plan their activism, and it's where feminist discourse and debate takes place. Sometimes

---

57. Haraway, "Cyborg Manifesto," 10.
58. Tong and Botts, *Feminist Thought*, 266.
59. Tong and Botts, *Feminist Thought*, 266–67.
60. Kathleen Hanna/Bikini Kill, "Riot Grrrl Manifesto," quoted in Freedman, *Essential Feminist Reader*, 396.

fourth-wave activism can even take place on the internet (the "#MeToo" tweets), and sometimes it takes place on the streets (the Women's March), but it's conceived and propagated online. As such, the fourth wave's beginnings are often loosely pegged to around 2008, when Facebook, Twitter, and YouTube were firmly entrenched in the cultural fabric and feminist blogs like *Jezebel* and *Feministing* were spreading across the web. By 2013, the idea that we had entered a fourth wave was widespread enough that it was getting written up in *The Guardian*. 'What's happening now feels like something new again,' wrote Kira Cochrane.[61]

Finally, as for postfeminism, we can say that most agree it's the idea that feminism might no longer be needed. To be clear, the term is what is perceived as no longer being necessary, not that the need to fight for women's rights is no longer necessary.

As a conclusion for this chapter, it is important to note that there are several key areas here that directly challenge a Christian epistemology. For example, many postmodernists think all truths are relative. There are a couple of problems with that. For one, the statement that "all truths are relative" is an attempt to state an absolute truth, so they have a problem with paradox there. For another, if we agree all truth is relative and that there are no absolute truths that relate to moral or ethical behavior, then Christianity falls apart. As a Christian, I believe God is literally a living embodiment of truth, and I look to God for truth, not to people—at least not at first, anyway.

But whether or not a person believes in God, if we have no guiding principles that are based on timeless truths because all truth is tied to the idea that "it just depends on the situation," then this allows for us to say in *this culture*, adultery is not wrong; or, in *this culture* marrying children to adults is not wrong. Yet when we see the effects of adultery and the destruction it wreaks, we are sickened by it. So something tells us: *This is wrong.* When we watch middle-aged men in India take eight-year-old girls as brides, we are sickened by it. We know it is wrong. These truths might be presented as a "good" because they are created and supported by a particular culture, but we know better as human beings because there are some things that are absolutely wrong.

Another problem with postmodernism in the classroom is that it is sometimes (not always) translated into setting its political goal to present only one perspective and to ignore other perspectives. According to Stephen Hicks, professor of philosophy at Rockford University and author of *Explaining Postmodernism: Skepticism and Socialism from Rousseau to Foucault*:

---

61. Grady, "Waves of Feminism."

> Postmodernism is a sprawling movement centered on the conviction that the modern world's most distinctive achievements—among them the rise of science, technology, individualism, universal rights, democratic-republicanism, and liberal capitalism—should be treated with suspicion or outright contempt.
>
> Most of us encountered old-fashioned indoctrinators in our education. Indoctrinators think this way: There is the One Truth. I am in possession of it. So important is it that students must believe it. Alternative ideas are a waste of time—and a temptation to unformed minds—and should be shunned. So as a teacher I will use my authority and my power to instill only the correct ideas.[62]

As you can see, Hicks confronts many of the ideas of feminists we have covered in this chapter. He also brings to light the openly political work being done in the universities: Present one side only. Ridicule or squelch the other side. Push students into action. This misuse of authoritarianism in regard to feminism is why I wrote this book. Many students describe becoming a feminist in terms of a conversion experience or as an awakening. However, while actions taken to obtain equality are important and while theories for how power is established and undermined are needed, they don't rate high enough to become a form of religion. It's time to put these theories into context. They are tools; they are not a holy text.

But is Hicks overstating things? Well, in my field, where we are to teach English composition, literature, and rhetoric, he is not overstating things at all. In fact, Stephen Combs describes several cases where politics is an important part of andragogy in the English composition classroom. Drawing upon articles published in academic journals, he shares the example of composition teacher Patrick Sullivan, who states that teaching "'is also about class, gender, and race, and inequality and poverty. It is about freedom, social justice, and the ideals of a democracy.' Sullivan urges teachers to add 'activist' to their identity as teacher-scholars, 'accepting and embracing the revolutionary and inescapably political nature of our work.'" Combs also shares the example of Dale Bauer, who "admitted that her courses are dominated by 'feminist doctrines and ideas' and that she does not permit students to challenge her assumptions. 'How do we move ourselves out of this political impasse and resistance in order to get our students to identify with the political agenda of feminism?' she asked."[63]

---

62. Hicks, "Why Postmodernists Train."
63. Combs, "Freshman Comp."

To be clear, it is not possible to teach without a political point of view as we are human beings, but it is possible to allow students to choose their own position in relation to what is being taught. When that is limited or denied to them, it can be destructive. It is possible to allow students to explore texts that represent different points of view, and even if the teacher's bias is evident, at least they are given a fuller view of a topic than if all texts represent only one point of view—or worse, they represent one point of view and only include critiques of other points of view.

In response to these trends, Professor Stanley Fish wrote *Save the World on Your Own Time*, Combs notes. What the composition class should be about is composition, in Stanley's view. Combs is hardly the first to notice or to resist the politicization of the composition classroom. In fact, it is still a major focus of conferences, papers, and courses across the US because this politicization is presented as a way for professors to "do good" in light of injustice. Many professors do not question their right to present one-sided views in the name of "what's right." That's okay in many respects, but how do they handle it when their views are challenged by students who hold a different point of view? That is really the heart of the matter.

Even though I understand the arguments at hand, I believe provocative readings can be included in a classroom, provided students are presented with good arguments for each side. If the instructor makes her biases clear in a way that lets students know she is not really open to a full discussion of a particular topic, the students often mirror her opinions to get the grade they want. Some will be persuaded to actually adopt those opinions; others will not. However, the true work of teaching composition should never be lost in discussions of texts used to inspire those compositions or lost behind a professor's decision to use the classroom as a political pulpit. There is much to learn in a composition classroom about writing, research, and documentation, and that should take center stage. Yet we should not shy away from the academic freedom to discuss challenging texts that the university provides.

By keeping critical thinking at the forefront of the classroom, a professor can still allow students to have genuine agency. Critical thinking has been defined in many ways, but it is basically asking students to consider a problem, do the research needed to fully understand the problem, draw some conclusions based on that research, and then propose a solution to a problem.[64] Students are invited to question texts and authority, reflect, assess, resist, adopt, and gather evidence as they wish in the pursuit of answers. Again, critical thinking is reflective and involves gathering and

64. "Critical Thinking."

applying evidence. It requires posing and testing solutions to those problems. It's messy at times. It's a recursive sort of process. It is best done when the student is allowed freedom in that process.

That is the heart of the challenge to those who use postmodernism to justify pushing a distinct political or ideological agenda in the classroom. It can undermine the critical thinking process and put students who disagree in an untenable position against the accepted authority embodied by the professor in the classroom.

So, as my imagined readers are Christian college students, I need to ask: What should you do with this information? First, you should never shy away from taking your education into your own hands. If a professor only provides texts that support his or her opinions, there is no reason why you cannot find some on your own that challenge your professor's views. After all, as a college student, you are now an independent learner. You do not need someone to hand you everything on a silver platter. You have enough research skills to get information on your own. If you can't, ask a librarian. They have a master's degree in Library Science and can help you if you will just ask.

Second, you should find a mentor who is sympathetic with your desire to know more, such as another professor. This could be done at the university or through attending academic conferences. A mentor who has more education and experience than you can help you find texts you can study and consider that fall outside of the biases of your professor. You can also study texts written and published by Christians who are known for challenging the status quo. Perhaps they will provide ideas for you. They should have a bibliography at the end of the book that you can use as a way to see what you might read. Treat it as a reading list for your treasure hunt.

A final issue with the theories in this chapter is with the idea that *all* reality is constructed, as it gives the illusion that we, as humans, actually create and control reality. Nothing could be further from the truth. Perhaps by carefully qualifying what is and can be constructed, this fallacy could be circumvented. For example, if you run over a nail and get a flat tire, you did not "construct" the reality that you now have a flat tire. However, you can construct the narrative that describes the experience. By focusing on the illusion that we construct and therefore control reality, the argument can be made that God is nothing more than a fiction that has been invented by a group of people. However, to experience God is to know that the idea that he is nothing more than a fiction is invented by those who find the reality of God to be an inconvenience for the reality they wish were real. There will always be those who wish to live outside the boundaries of what is good.

So what should you take away from this chapter?

Takeaways:

- Second-wave feminists are to thank for the burgeoning field of study that allows professors a way to recover women's histories and texts. These women created conferences to honor and share research on women, produced journals to publish research on women and women's texts, and inspired programs in women's studies which are found in most universities today.
- Second- and third-wave feminists brought in wildly divergent theories on motherhood, sexuality, and patriarchy. They often position themselves on opposite sides of a particular point, such as on pornography.
- Second- and third-wave Feminists fought for workplace protections for women, expectant mothers, and new mothers. They also wanted women to have the right to abortion and contraceptives.
- Third-wave feminists broke the dominance of white, middle class women over feminist thought.
- Key ideas such as intersectionality and standpoint theory help us see the way overlapping contexts oppress women.
- Transnational feminism allows us to look at the work of feminists on a global scale.
- Identity politics dominate feminist thought.
- Poststructuralism reveals the arbitrary relationship between a word and its meaning and the instability of language and communication.
- Technology is analyzed as a means of creating power.
- Some believe reality is constructed and that the classroom is an appropriate place for converting students to political and social views similar to a professor's.

# 5

# "She Gets Up While It Is Still Night"

## *Theology and Feminism*

The Battlefield: The Bible and how scriptures regarding women are interpreted in the time of second-wave, third-wave, and contemporary feminism.

The Opponents: Those men and women who believe that women should be silent in religious settings, that women should always and without question submit their will to that of a husband or father, and that true Christian women stay home and raise children versus those men and women who interpret scriptures to allow women to speak, preach, educate others, and engage in a partnership with a spouse (although there is disagreement over whether it is a partnership with predetermined "male" and "female" qualities associated with each, or if it is a partnership of people who have different strengths and weaknesses that do not come from biology), and who believe that Christian women have options for work and for the home that are open and not limited.

*Guiding questions for chapter 5:*

1. How would you characterize the ethos of a theologian who is also a woman? In what ways is this different than how women were able to establish their credibility as female preachers in the nineteenth

century? In what ways is this different from the ethos of the non-Christian women in the university who are also professors?

2. Do we understand Scripture literally or is there always a process of interpretation involved?

3. How was the Bible constructed? When were common people able to read it without interference? Why did church leadership wish to deny common people the right to read the Bible?

4. How does the way we interpret Scripture affect the way we live, particularly in regard to women's rights? How does an amateur interpretation of Scripture reflect the interpreter's values, such as when I offer a reading of the Proverbs 31 woman?

5. How do the views expressed by feminist theologians challenge or affirm your views? What is most surprising to you about how they interpret Scripture? What do you agree or disagree with and on what basis?

We are returning, in some ways, to the concerns first-wave feminists had with Christianity. These women had to present themselves as Christians—and were, for the most part, sincere believers as far as we can tell. The seventeenth-, eighteenth-, and nineteenth-century American women could not achieve their goals for equality without acknowledging the fact that religion dominated the thoughts, actions, culture, and social norms of Americans. It could not be ignored. However, in the late twentieth century and now in the early twenty-first century, many Americans have moved away from Christianity and do not use it to determine their standards for living in non-religious contexts. We have increasingly made room for other religions and for the rejection of religion in its entirety.

The Pew Research Center conducted a study which clearly demonstrates the decline of Christianity in the United States. In "telephone surveys conducted in 2018 and 2019, 65% of American adults describe themselves as Christians when asked about their religion, down twelve percentage points over the past decade. Meanwhile, the religiously unaffiliated share of the population, consisting of people who describe their religious identity as atheist, agnostic or 'nothing in particular,' now stands at 26%, up from 17% in 2009." As recent as 2009, 51 percent of adults identified as Protestants. Now it is 43 percent. Twenty-three percent identified as Catholics. Now it is 20 percent, or one in every five people. Regular church attendance has dropped significantly as well, according to their research.[1]

---

1. "In US, Decline of Christianity."

Yet we still see religion as a powerful persuasive factor in our society and in American politics. That's why feminist theologians are worth our time to consider carefully. We have placed ethos, or credibility, in the hands of science and in the hands of the university. As research in social areas of study mimics that of science, it gains a place of influence, as we can see from the statistics listed above, which are an example of quantitative, not qualitative, research. The university holds influence over all young adults who wish to enter the workforce in fields that require education and specialized training. While young adults do not necessarily bow to the liberal politics preached by their professors, they are undoubtably influenced by them, and the move away from religious practices might be construed as an effect of the shift toward using the university as a place of political transformation instead of a place where ideas are considered more objectively. This shift was covered at the end of the last chapter.

So what we have with theologians are highly educated professors who are experts in the Protestant and Catholic religions that so many still hold allegiance to (and world religions—areas of specialty differ). They have the ethos of the university with all of its authoritative connotations and they can wield the ethos of science with their research. They educate the pastors that stand at the front of our churches every week. They are the root of change, our pastors the stem, and our people, the flower. To ignore their contributions to the story of feminism in the United States, however controversial they may be, is to ignore a major force of influence today.

Theologians are those with master's degrees or with doctoral degrees (in the twentieth and twenty-first centuries anyway—prior to that they were mostly men who devoted a lifetime to study and who got training, usually through the Catholic church), and they are the ones teaching your pastors. While your pastors are not mindless robots just regurgitating what their professors say, they do recognize the value of higher education (which is why most pastors these days need at least a bachelor's degree to be ordained), and they do carry into their sermons many ideas gained while in classes at a university. Your pastors share sermons with the congregation. These sermons challenge, affirm, and perhaps shape your beliefs and practices. See the connection? Theologians are pretty important people.

This is also a chance to say that so are women preachers and teachers of the twentieth and twenty-first centuries. Their public positions speaking for God have had a positive effect on women pursing doctoral degrees in theology, providing for a position of authority that includes two places of influence: the college classroom and the pulpit. Conversely, even if they are not ordained, many of the theologians of today occupy a place in the pulpit at times, and most certainly make their voices heard at academic conferences. I have done this myself with my most notable speech given on the nature of equality at the centennial celebration of the International Pentecostal Holiness Church just a few years ago. I spoke about unity but emphasized the important role women play as those who speak for God.

Despite the best efforts of some evangelical fundamentalists, women preachers and teachers persist and flourish. They are much more in the public eye than theologians who spend most of their time in the university and at academic conferences attended by other theologians. Women such as Lisa Bevere, Beth Moore, Joyce Meyer, Marilyn Hickey, Paula White, Patricia Shirer, and so many others have enjoyed enormous economic success and great visibility and influence as a result of their ministries. Books, sermons, social media, conferences—all are avenues used by these women to reach others. Some are on TV. Some author devotionals that form the basis of Bible studies around the country. A couple of years ago, I attended an annual, multi-day event in Tucson that featured Lisa Bevere as the speaker and that focused on women's issues. For non-Christians or for those who are not involved with a church, the influence and popularity of these Christian celebrities might go unnoticed. In addition to these famous examples, there are also the women leading churches who never gain much attention outside their hometowns. Yet they are teaching, preaching, and leading. They are connecting God-ordained leadership with their calling. But these women did not get there without standing on the shoulders of women preachers who had come before them.

It is worth briefly noting that leading up to the proliferation of women preachers and teachers today were many well-known women preachers, but none so colorful as Aimee Semple McPherson. Her father was a Methodist and her mother a member of the Salvation Army. Originally a Methodist, McPherson became Pentecostal when she married and then created the Foursquare Gospel denomination. As she built her denomination, she established a Bible college, offered ordination to women, and had a regular church of her own.[2] By 1922, she was preaching to crowds of more than thirty thousand and in one case, the Marines had to be called in to help with crowd control. Her flamboyant, dramatic productions meant she could build a church to seat five thousand three hundred people and hold services seven days a week. By 1926, she was a household name in the US, yet the crowds she commanded then are nothing compared to the crowds women like Bevere, White, and Shirer can command today. The influence of women preachers has been multiplied and amplified by technology.[3]

2. Hyatt, "Spirit-Filled Women," 249.
3. King, "Incredible Disappearing Evangelist."

Because women preachers so openly challenge patriarchal structures some evangelicals want to keep in place, they can face heavy criticism and have since the time of Anne Hutchinson, who was banished by the Puritans for her skill in teaching. This is a sign of their power to enact social change, to influence, and to lead. Women preachers play an important role in demonstrating the marriage of Christianity with key tenets of women's equality and, intentionally or not, are an important piece of the picture that has allowed female theologians to find a way to marry their Christianity to feminist ideals too.

All this being said, before we begin our discussion of feminist theologians, it might be worth some time to put a few things on the table for a college student to consider. For one, many fundamentalists do not believe they interpret Scripture, preferring to think they read and understand the truths of the Bible literally. Yet, we have scriptures such as this:

> The Spirit searches all things, even the deep things of God. For who knows a person's thoughts except their own spirit within them? In the same way no one knows the thoughts of God except the Spirit of God. What we have received is not the spirit of the world, but the Spirit who is from God, so that we may understand what God has freely given us. This is what we speak, not in words taught us by human wisdom but in words taught by the Spirit, explaining spiritual realities with Spirit-taught words. The person without the Spirit does not accept the things that come from the Spirit of God but considers them foolishness, and cannot understand them because they are discerned only through the Spirit. The person with the Spirit makes judgments about all things, but such a person is not subject to merely human judgments, for, "Who has known the mind of the Lord so as to instruct him?" But we have the mind of Christ. (1 Cor 2:10–16 NIV)

I think of this as having a lamp. You know all the parts to the lamp. You are an expert in how that lamp works and you see it every day. But if you don't plug the lamp in, it never lights up. You work hard, flipping the switch each day. But nothing. You advise others on the lamp, demonstrating your extensive knowledge, but they can't turn it on either. At least not until someone plugs it in. Again, it takes an external power source for the lamp to work. In the same way, for you to truly understand the Bible, you need the Spirit.

Okay, you may say. Fine. So I interpret Scripture with the help of the Spirit. But that's not all. You interpret a translation of Scripture. The words in Scripture have many possible translations, and it is a mistake to believe that somehow the King James Version of the Bible is the one, true, correct translation.

Additionally, today ordained pastors must get a college degree and part of that curriculum involves learning about the historical, political, cultural, and social contexts that situate the stories in the Bible. Furthermore, if these contexts affected the way the Bible was written and aid in understanding how it is situated in a specific culture, they certainly affect the way the Bible is interpreted and applied. It is not difficult to find examples of shifts in culture that prove this. For one, there was once the idea that dressing plainly was "holy" based on the verses like 1 Pet 3. Centuries later, for Pentecostals "holiness" was an inward change but also an outward expression in this very legalistic way they held to for decades. Then they dropped this idea. What changed? We did. Culture changed. Times changed. The interpretation changed.

So you interpret Scripture and it requires the Spirit and it requires a recognition that Scripture can be contextualized and that your response to it is affected by contexts. All of that is great, you might be saying to yourself. However, we also see that the nature of translation allows some room for understanding the Scriptures in different ways. Additionally, we must also realize that God did not dictate Scripture to a few people who then just wrote it down and handed it to us. Instead, the Bible went through centuries of being written and capturing oral histories and stories, and then was passed through the hands of Jewish priests who worked together to edit and assemble it, and then went through the hands of Catholic priests. The introduction to the Old Testament in the *Oxford Study Bible* states that "the Old Testament consists of a collection of works composed at various times from the 12th to the 2nd century B.C.E."[4] Most of these books were written in Hebrew and a few in Aramaic, and few of them survived the destruction of Jerusalem in 70 CE. After that, Jewish religious leaders created the Massoretic text. The editors go on to share a long explanation of how the Bible went through various translations and how there are places the translators had to guess at the meaning of a word.[5] So the idea of having a simple translation of the "true" text is questionable as well. Was it guided by the Holy Spirit? Yes, I believe so. But it was not simply written down and then handed to us.

In fact, according to History.com, the Bible did not settle into its accepted form until the fifth century CE.[6] Furthermore, in the sixteenth century during the Protestant Reformation, books that were originally written in Greek instead of Hebrew were kicked out of the Bible. These books are known as the Apocrypha. However, the Catholics decided to keep them. The

---

4. Suggs, *Oxford Study Bible*, 3.
5. Suggs, *Oxford Study Bible*, 4.
6. "Bible."

Gnostic Gospels, which are not used by either Protestants or Catholics as part of the Bible, come from around 120 CE and there are about fifty of them.

So now you can see why I am not beginning this chapter praising Elizabeth Cady Stanton's *Woman's Bible*. Published partially in 1895 and partially in 1898, most describe it as laughable. Ignorant of the biblical languages, untrained in exegesis, and unaware of historical contexts, she nevertheless interpreted the Bible to fit her views on equality. While we may look at her more as an example of failure than success in the battle for equality, keep in mind that a vast majority of people sitting in congregations each Sunday are (and were) just as uneducated in this area as she was. Memorizing a text does not serve as a good substitute for the type of study that goes along with putting it into historical context. Putting together aspects of historical context piecemeal is no substitute for the types of study in a university that give students the bigger picture with the intellectual depth needed to contextualize, theorize, and create knowledge using Scripture.

While all of this is valuable to address, you should know that for all our failures to agree on how to interpret the Bible, just having the opportunity to try is an enormous privilege. For all of us, Christian or not, educated or just on the way to getting a degree, it is important to understand that the freedoms you enjoy today are largely due to the Protestants winning the battle to translate and distribute the Bible in English. This battle played out over many years. According to the *Encyclopaedia Britannica*, Johannes Gutenberg published the Bible in 1455 using his new moveable type printing press.[7] The problem, of course, was that it was in Latin. Why is this a problem? Because if the only ones who can read the Bible are educated priests, then how can anyone who does not have the benefit of education challenge their interpretation? And so few people had an education. And even fewer numbers of those with an education were women.

So it was a matter of control. As Clyde Votaw wrote, "Four hundred years ago the Bible was the possession of the priests, written in an ancient language which only the learned could read; and the church considered it inadvisable for the people to know the Bible except as it was taught to them by the priests."[8] When men such as William Tyndale (1492–1536) translated the Bible into English and made it possible for anyone to read, they paid for it with their lives. Just to get it printed required great secrecy which required him to move between different places. Tyndale had to smuggle copies into England hidden in other shipments so that, despite the best efforts of the church, thousands of people gained access to the New Testament. Sadly,

---

7. "Gutenberg Bible."
8. Votaw, "Martyrs," 296.

Tyndale's life did not have a happy ending. The Roman church in England both "denounced" Tyndale and burned him at the stake before he could finish translating the Old Testament.[9] Why?

Without religious control, Rome would lose much of its political and economic power in England. So they denounced all translations of the Bible into English at the Council of Trent in 1546. Yet people persisted in putting in into the hands of the common people. Others such as Tavener, Marbuck, and Matthew were imprisoned or burned at the stake for either reading or printing the Bible in the sixteenth century.[10]

Technically, this was a battle that really began in 1380 when Wycliffe copied translations by hand. In 1391, a bill was introduced into English Parliament to prohibit people from reading Scripture in their own language, and it was defeated. However, in 1408 the church issued an edict to stop it.[11] Henry the VIII allowed the Bible to be published with a statement indicating his approval in 1537, but the Protestants Cromwell (beheaded 1540), Latimer (burned at the stake 1555), and Cranmer (burned at the stake 1556) paid with their lives for their part in distributing and printing the Bible.[12] When Queen Elizabeth took the throne in 1558, the battle was finally over and anyone who wished to read the Bible in English could do so, since Protestantism had finally won out over Catholicism and the control of England by Rome. That is, if you were literate.

Why is all of this so important? Because while you and I might not be trained theologians, we can still read, interpret, and engage with Scripture as we wish. We are allowed the opportunity of a first-hand reading and understanding of Scripture that was denied to others. For those women who were literate, with a Bible in their hands they could now circumvent the authoritarianism of priests who wished to present only a partial view of Scripture. Imagine the difficulty of trying to gain full personhood within a culture heavily controlled by a text you could not read or have access to? It is one thing to fight a culture based on secular ideas and practices. Those are more susceptible to change. It is much more difficult to fight a culture built on religious beliefs vigorously enforced by proponents who wield power over the common people as well as those in the highest places of leadership and government. With tools such as execution and imprisonment, who could win such a battle? Indeed, as we discussed in chapter one in the case

---

9. Votaw, "Martyrs," 297.
10. Votaw, "Martyrs," 297–98.
11. Votaw, "Martyrs," 298.
12. Votaw, "Martyrs," 299.

of the Puritans, this is why we must have the separation of church and state. Power amplified by religion is often misused.

Finally, it is important to realize that the Bible presents contradictory views on women. These may just be a reflection of the culture, as the Christians for Biblical Equality state.[13] There are two key places in the Bible that many like to study that illustrate this: the unnamed daughter in the book of Judges and the ideal wife in the book of Proverbs. Let's talk about these briefly and draw on the interpretations offered by a feminist theologian to see how it shapes our understanding of these scriptures. These are key pieces of Scripture for women, and much of my discussion in this chapter casually draws on religious language that those of us who were raised in church are quite familiar with. If you are reading this book and do not have much of a background in the Christian religion, you might wish to look into Letty M. Rusell and J. Shannon Clarkson's *Dictionary of Feminist Theologies*, which explains the significance of key terms as well as offering information on theologies and theologians.

One of the two passages I want to explore can be found in the book of Judges. Here we find the troubling story of Jephthah and his unnamed daughter. She ends up becoming a human sacrifice. Now before you say God does not take human sacrifice, don't forget the most glaring example: Christ. However, God never asks for this young virgin's sacrifice; instead, it is in fulfillment of a vow. It is Jephthah who sacrifices his daughter to fulfill a hastily made vow rather than lose credibility as a leader. Ah, pride.

You see, Jephthah was the son of a prostitute. We never hear of his daughter's mother, so we have to assume she is gone. Exiled in Gilead, he lives apart from his people and their customs. When they seek him out to lead them into battle, he does not know it is customary for the women to come out dancing after a victory. So when he vows to sacrifice to God the first thing he sees upon returning victorious from battle, he never imagines it will be his most precious daughter.

Unwilling to give up his newly won acceptance by his people and his status as a victorious judge, we don't see him seeking a way out of his vow by supplication to God. Instead, we see his act of mercy as he lets her go away for two months to mourn her fate and pray with her friends. Then we read that he "did with her according to his vow which he had vowed" (Judg 11: 39 KJV).

Some scholars argue that she was sent away as a prophetess, an eternal virgin, to serve God. However, the fact that her friends commemorate her each year does not make sense if she is still alive, so their actions do not corroborate this alternative story.

---

13. "CBE's Mission and Values."

The theme ends up being that she was sacrificed for the greater good to retain the goodwill of a God who expects absolute obedience. Jephthah does well ruling as a judge and is even commended in the New Testament as a hero and an example of faith. It is sexism and patriarchy at its finest.

In literature, authors reflect life. The archetype of the unnamed virgin—the woman sacrificed for the greater good—is repeated throughout human history in a variety of cultures. I found it in *Iphegenia at Aulis* and the play after, *Iphigenia in Tauris*, both by Euripedes. I found it in a text written centuries later: Barbara Kingsolver's *The Poisonwood Bible*. You can find it throughout the stories we have told as a human race, in all cultures and in all times. This is why we can call it an "archetype," or a story with universal themes that is told with culturally situated details. Carl Jung invented this concept so we could name what was going on in terms of why a particular theme or character shows up in different cultures and why a culture believes the theme or character is its own, original creation.

The point is that sacrificing the young, innocent woman for the greater good is a tragedy. When the young virgin dies in our plays and stories, we recognize that it is wrong. Yet one gift of feminism is the realization that we put young women, the virgins who seek bright futures, on the altar when we deny them the possibility of a full life—when we deny them the right to live out their calling.

Perhaps this is part of why Abigail Greves wrote "Daughter of Courage: Reading Judges 11 With a Feminist Pentecostal Hermeneutic." In this essay, she draws on two well-known Pentecostal theologians, Estrelda Alexander and Cheryl Bridges Johns, to help explain how the daughter in Jephthah may be a heroic figure instead of a tragic one, as feminists like Phyllis Trible portray. In an effort to create a heroic figure out of the unnamed daughter, Greves offers the possibility that the daughter knew of the vow before she emerged from the house alone.[14] She points out that the daughter's language reflects her father's language and exposes his manipulation and ambition.[15] Greves credits the daughter's integrity when she says the daughter was clearly not going to allow Jephthah a way out of the vow; she could have claimed it was against Jewish law to sacrifice a human, but "her willingness to hold Jephthah to his word acts as an attempt to curtail Israel's way of speaking flippantly before the Lord."[16] Greves points to an interpretation of the daughter's sacrifice as a way of saying that fathers must "learn not to sacrifice

---

14. Greves, "Daughter of Courage," 163.
15. Greves, "Daughter of Courage," 164.
16. Greves, "Daughter of Courage," 164–65.

their daughters"; she implies the story is a warning.[17] Greves describes the daughter as one who valued family and community, interpreting her decision to mourn two months as evidence of valuing a family and her decision to emerge on her own in celebration of her father's victory as evidence of her valuing community.[18] So instead of assuming that the biblical authors supported the father's actions, she argues that the story was told as an example of what not to do. She points out that God is silent in this story, something often noted by feminists who write about these scriptures, but this may be an indication that Jephthah did not have the support of a deity he had tried so hard to manipulate with his vow instead of trusting as he should have done. In the end, it is still worth noting that God did not step in to save the daughter, whether she was heroic in her actions or a victim of a man's pride.

What connections can be made with contemporary life? What does this have to do with the project of winning equal rights for women that we refer to as feminism? For one, when women argued against coverture laws, they were arguing against a living death, a half-life. When women argued for a full education, they were arguing against the intellectual death that a life without access to knowledge brings—especially when, like Sor Juana Inés de la Cruz, you are born with a passion for learning. When women argued for the right to vote, they were arguing for the right to decide what and whom would be sacrificed for the greater good in society because political power does just that—political power says whose interests will be served and whose will not. There are always winners and losers. When women gained the right to vote, they took themselves off the altar. The men who put these women on the altar often did so because, like Jephthah, they wished to rely on manipulation to achieve their goals and they wished to nurture their pride. Thus, the connections between the ways our hermeneutics become translated into a way of life should be clearer. It is the work of theologians like Greves to explore the details and depth of the scriptural passage and its contexts.

So now I would like to take you to another significant place in the Old Testament. Proverbs 31 defines the ideal woman. These verses consist entirely of words repeated by a mother to a son. It says:

> A wife of noble character who can find? She is worth far more than rubies. Her husband has full confidence in her and lacks nothing of value. She brings him good, not harm, all the days of her life. She selects wool and flax and works with eager hands. She is like the merchant ships, bringing her food from afar. She gets up while it is still night; she provides food for her family and

---

17. Greves, "Daughter of Courage," 166.
18. Greves, "Daughter of Courage," 162, 166.

portions for her female servants. She considers a field and buys it; out of her earnings she plants a vineyard. She sets about her work vigorously; her arms are strong for her tasks. She sees that her trading is profitable, and her lamp does not go out at night. In her hand she holds the distaff and grasps the spindle with her fingers. She opens her arms to the poor and extends her hands to the needy. When it snows, she has no fear for her household; for all of them are clothed in scarlet. She makes coverings for her bed; she is clothed in fine linen and purple. Her husband is respected at the city gate, where he takes his seat among the elders of the land. She makes linen garments and sells them, and supplies the merchants with sashes. She is clothed with strength and dignity; she can laugh at the days to come. She speaks with wisdom, and faithful instruction is on her tongue. She watches over the affairs of her household and does not eat the bread of idleness. Her children arise and call her blessed; her husband also, and he praises her: "Many women do noble things, but you surpass them all." Charm is deceptive, and beauty is fleeting; but a woman who fears the Lord is to be praised. Honor her for all that her hands have done, and let her works bring her praise at the city gate. (Prov 31:10–31 NIV)

Even though I don't have the benefit of a degree in theology, in my layperson's opinion, what's inconvenient for fundamentalists about the Proverbs 31 woman is that she is the voice of authority. Clearly in control of the household, the servants, and the provisions for all—who do you think they go to when they need something? As the voice of "wisdom" and "kindness," her servants and her children look to her. As someone who is trustworthy, wouldn't her husband speak to her about his thoughts? His plans? And as the voice of wisdom, would she not answer? If you've ever served in a leadership position, you know that if you are the person everyone seeks out when there's anything important to be done, you are the leader. Titles don't matter. And if you are valued and recognized—such as when the Proverbs 31 woman's children "bless her" and when "her own works praise her in the gates"—you are a successful leader. Wisdom is personified as a woman in Proverbs. Doesn't this mean something in a book of wisdom that begins with wisdom personified as a woman and ends with wisdom coming from the mouth of a woman?

What's also inconvenient for those who like to use Scripture to limit women is that she's a working mother. Not just at home—although mothers working at home deserve great recognition for all they do. The Proverbs 31 woman is into real estate. She "considers a field and buys it." The passage does not say she considers a field, asks her husband for permission and advice, and then buys it. She is trusted, intelligent, and shrewd, so she acts on her own as an equal partner in her marriage. Then what does she do with the field? "She plants a vineyard." So in other words, she starts a business. You plant a vineyard to produce wine; you produce wine to sell it or provide your family with it. Either way, you are profiting from it and overseeing a business venture. For those who claim that it is God's will that all women stay home, it is also a huge inconvenience that she has a clothing business, selling sashes "in the gates." Not from home. Not through a servant. Not through her husband. But herself. In public. Way outside the "sphere" of domesticity. And she does really well at this too. She is the epitome of excellence when it comes to her work as well as her family.

The Proverbs 31 woman is clearly an equal in her marriage: supportive, trustworthy, and treated as a competent, equal human being. She is clearly in charge of all aspects of her home, including her servants and children. She is not a victim who lives off the system or spends her life explaining why she can't do what she wants to do, but instead "she girds herself with strength" (Prov 31:17 NKJV). She is not lazy but always ahead of the game, "[rising] while it is yet night" (Prov 31:15 NKJV). She is generous to the poor and she takes care of others well. She is not stupid, gossiping, critical, or hateful. She is kind and wise. She exhibits this by what she does not say as much as by what she does. And she has power. It cannot be overstated how much power is tied to having some financial independence, which is why it was so essential that coverture laws and associated discriminatory practices be overturned in the nineteenth and twentieth centuries. If you are financially dependent and have no agency, you are little more than a child in a relationship that is supposed to be made up of two adults. If you have not experienced this, you may not understand the feelings of powerlessness that result when a husband misuses or abuses a wife. However, you can trust the stories of those who have. It is healthy to have power—to be equal.

When I look to see what feminist theologians think, however, I get a much different perspective. In *Feminist Interpretation of the Bible*, Renita Weems ridicules the idea that a woman could have written Prov 31 because it celebrates hard work, sacrifice, and a wife caring about her husband's reputation. "What woman would write this?" she asks. "Celebrating exhaustion? Celebrating being crazy out of your mind? Who would write this but a man?" Then, imagining herself in conversation with her students, she writes, "And then at the end I say to them: Maybe there is an insight here and there." She goes on to praise the text for celebrating a woman for something other than "charm"—for fearing God, not men, and for keeping the "rewards of her labor."[19]

Writing on the same text but from a completely different perspective, feminist theologian L. Juliana Claassens, who is a professor of Old Testament at Stellenbosch University in South Africa, summarizes Martha Nussbaum's "capabilities list which is at the heart of her views on human flourishing" to analyze the Proverbs 31 woman.[20] The list, quoted directly from Claassens's summary of Nussbaum's insights, is as follows:

1. Life. The ability to live a normal life, not dying before one's time.
2. Bodily health and integrity. The ability to have access to adequate food and shelter and health care.
3. Bodily integrity. The ability to be free from violent assault, including rape and domestic violence. To have opportunities to enjoy one's sexuality.
4. Senses, imagination, thought. The ability "to imagine, to think, and to reason." This includes access to education, freedom of expression and religious experience in addition to the ability "to have pleasurable experiences."
5. Emotions. The ability to freely love and grieve significant others. The freedom to express human emotions such as longing, gratitude, and anger without fear of recrimination.
6. Practical reason. The ability to form one's own conception of what is good and apply it to one's own life.
7. Affiliation. The ability to form meaningful relationships with others and engage freely in various forms of social interaction: "Being able to be treated as a dignified being whose worth is equal to that of others."
8. Other species. The ability to show concern and be in relation to animals, plants, and nature.
9. Play. The ability to laugh, play, and have time for recreational activities.
10. Control over one's environment. The ability to engage in politics, possessing "the rights of political participation, free speech, and the freedom of association." The ability to own property both individually and/or collectively. The right to seek employment on an equal basis with others.[21]

---

19. Bietenhard and Schroer, *Feminist Interpretation*, 18.
20. Claasaans, "Woman of Substance," 8.
21. Claassans, "Woman of Substance," 8–9.

By analyzing the Proverbs 31 woman with this list, Claassens puts the activities of this woman in a completely different light. Yet she brings out the many negative interpretations as well. For example, she points out that the text was written with a male audience in mind, and she questions how much culture plays a role in what this woman chooses to do. Even so, she highlights the freedoms and privilege this woman enjoys.[22]

To sum up, from my layperson's point of view, the interpretation by Claassens was positive. From Renita Weems' point of view, the interpretation is negative. Claassens, by using the benefits of her education, explores and analyzes the passage and presents a point of view that sees both the strengths and the weaknesses of the text. Out of the brief interpretations provided so far, hers seems to be the one with the most authority.

So what do you do when you are trying to interpret these important scriptures as they come to you through the words of a feminist theologian? First, evaluate the authority of a text by examining its author and his or her credentials. Then examine where, when, and how the text was published. Who is the target audience and how does this author speak to them? This is known as the "rhetorical situation." You'll find this advice in any freshman composition textbook, but it is well worth remembering in this book which is designed to help students navigate texts drawn from different time periods and written by women of varying levels of education and authority. If you quote something from Lisa Bevere, it has one type of authority because of her wide-spread influence. If you quote something from L. Juliana Claassens, who is a professor of Old Testament, it has quite a different type of authority. A student should accurately represent the information as well as where it came from in college work. In other words, explain and qualify an author and her credentials. To do otherwise is academic dishonesty. Don't make more of one person's text in terms of its authority just because you prefer that point of view.

After you understand the type of credibility the author has and the type of audience he or she is writing to, you can determine what you will accept, negotiate, or reject from that person's interpretation of Scripture. But there are other passages that are far more contentious that these two Old Testament scriptures.

So let's get to it. Here is a list of the most often cited scriptures at the center of the debate over a woman's place:

First Corinthians 14:34–35, NIV: "The women should keep silent in the churches. For they are not permitted to speak, but should be in submission,

---

22. Claassans, "Woman of Substance," 17–19.

as the Law also says. If there is anything they desire to learn, let them ask their husbands at home. For it is shameful for a woman to speak in church."

First Timothy 2:11–14, NIV: "Let a woman learn quietly with all submissiveness. I do not permit a woman to teach or to exercise authority over a man; rather, she is to remain quiet. For Adam was formed first, then Eve; and Adam was not deceived, but the woman was deceived and became a transgressor."

First Peter 3:5, NIV: "For this is how the holy women who hoped in God used to adorn themselves, by submitting to their own husbands."

First Peter 3:1, NIV: "Likewise, wives, be subject to your own husbands, so that even if some do not obey the word, they may be won without a word by the conduct of their wives."

Galatians 3:28, NIV: "There is neither Jew nor Greek, there is neither slave nor free, there is no male and female, for you are all one in Christ Jesus."

Acts 2:16–21, NIV: "But this is what was uttered through the prophet Joel: 'And in the last days it shall be, God declares, that I will pour out my Spirit on all flesh, and your sons and your daughters shall prophesy, and your young men shall see visions, and your old men shall dream dreams; even on my male servants and female servants in those days I will pour out my Spirit, and they shall prophesy. And I will show wonders in the heavens above and signs on the earth below, blood, and fire, and vapor of smoke; the sun shall be turned to darkness and the moon to blood, before the day of the Lord comes, the great and magnificent day.'"

First Peter 3:7, NIV: "Likewise, husbands, live with your wives in an understanding way, showing honor to the woman as the weaker vessel, since they are heirs with you of the grace of life, so that your prayers may not be hindered."

Ephesians 5:22–33, NIV: "Wives, submit to your own husbands, as to the Lord. For the husband is the head of the wife even as Christ is the head of the church, his body, and is himself its Savior. Now as the church submits to Christ, so also wives should submit in everything to their husbands. Husbands, love your wives, as Christ loved the church and gave himself up for her, that he might sanctify her, having cleansed her by the washing of water with the word."

While many try to read these passages literally, there are some problems. For one, many verses that communicate a patriarchal social and spiritual structure may have been added later and not by Paul himself. As Barbara MacHaffie shares in *Her Story: Women in Christian Tradition*, "in the eyes of many contemporary interpreters, the material that does come from Paul himself reflects a marked ambivalence toward women." She goes on to say, "Keep in mind, too, that his letters were occasional pieces to specific mission situations and not intended to present a systematic position."²³ As a theologian and professor of religion at Marietta College, MacHaffie is able to bring us important historical information that shapes how we can view these scriptures. Again, the work of a theologian is vital in the ongoing battle for equality for women in all aspects of life. We will encounter these verses in the work of feminist theologians in this chapter.

At this point, it is also helpful to define the work of a theologian. Pentecostal African American professor of theology Estrelda Alexander teaches us about the important work of a theologian when she writes:

> No theologian within the contemporary academy approaches the theological task simply for the glory of God. All theology is political, some of it more blatantly so than other theology. But all theology is crafted within the context of specific social, cultural, and political realities that not only color how it is formulated, developed, and refined, but also seek to protect, resist, or destroy specific views of that reality. There is always some vested interest at stake in doing theology, employing a specific theological method, or insisting that certain theological methods are legitimate and others are not. A theology of the nature of humankind, for example, that would allow a society to enslave or otherwise abuse any race or class of people while providing biblical sanction for such an endeavor is a political theology. The fact that such a theology is couched in esoteric terms obscuring a desire to uphold a supposedly God-ordained order does not deny its political nature.²⁴

After arguing against the idea that homosexuality is somehow bigger than other sins and that it is okay to target homosexuals in the church, she says that "we [theologians and Christians] are called to use our intellectual gifts to assist the church in modeling the already but not yet reality that the Holy Spirit makes possible in lives lived out in authentic obedience to the dictate to work for justice."²⁵

Echoing third-wave feminists, Alexander also points out that theologians either preserve or dismantle "a social reality that is presumed to be God-ordained or against the will of God."²⁶ In other words, while secular feminists focus on the social construction of reality that affects them

---

23. MacHaffie, *Her Story*, 6.
24. Alexander, "Presidential Address," 346–47.
25. Alexander, "Presidential Address," 350.
26. Alexander, "Presidential Address," 350–51.

politically, economically, and socially, theologians focus on the construction of a social reality as it becomes embedded in religious doctrines. Those holding to faith-based belief will not regard change as a possibility, as it feels like a betrayal of something deeper than just what happens to be the norm. Theologians shape deeply embedded patterns of belief and behavior to bring about change in the church.

How does theology do important political work? Theologians are to do more than talk; they are to take action. Alexander also writes:

> Any theology that provides a foundation for the sanctioning of bigotry or injustice or provides a base for disengagement from the vital work of justice seeking is unscriptural and unsound. Any theological system that props up existing structures of oppression is inauthentic in its claim to be biblical. Any theological system that does not take seriously the liberative work of the Holy Spirit and the implications of Jesus' assertion, "I have come that you might have life, more abundantly" is inauthentic. Any theology that does not enter into Jesus' project of proclaiming and pushing forward the possibility of that abundant life within the already present manifestation of the kingdom, while being cognizant that its full presentation is only possible in the undetermined not-yet, is impotent. Further, whenever an individual or group hides behind the Bible as an excuse to ignore the cause of justice, it is an inauthentic use of the sacred text.[27]

Now that you have a working definition of theology, as a Christian student this chapter might be important to you because you need to ask yourself some questions that inspire critical thinking:

1. Is complementarity an acceptable substitute for full equality?
2. If I serve a "male" God, then am I supporting a patriarchal social structure?
3. How do I scripturally support the claim that women are equal to men?
4. What is my purpose as a Christian? Does biology limit those choices? What about ability and calling?
5. The Bible does not offer a picture of the fair treatment of women consistently, nor does it offer a picture of the unfair treatment of women consistently. How do I understand and navigate these contradictions? How does this shape my belief?
6. What is Christ's role in defining how women should be treated? Is he more or less important than the apostle Paul?

27. Alexander, "Presidential Address," 352.

7. Am I comfortable with women in leadership within certain areas in the church but not in others? Why?

8. What are the different ways scriptures in the New Testament have been interpreted, and how do they affect the doctrines in the church I attend or the denomination I am affiliated with?

9. If a feminist theologian rejects Christianity, is it possible that his or her beliefs are still something to consider? Or do I reject non-Christian ideas when it comes to theology?

10. If I identified with the perspectives of other feminists already covered in this book, do I see overlap with the feminist theologians in this chapter? How does that affect my identity?

To begin a discussion of feminist theologians, let's start with their opposition. The Council on Biblical Manhood and Womanhood came into existence in 1987 in response to the threat of feminist influence on the church.[28] Led by John Piper and Wayne Grudem, this group decided that egalitarianism was a result of "unbiblical teaching" and that complementarianism, which affirms the hierarchy of man over woman, was the "created divine order." Complementarians view the man's role as "leader, provider, protector" and the woman's role as "homemaker, nurturer, and supporter." They affirm that "men and women are completely equal in dignity, value, worth, and honor; however, men and women are different in role and function."[29]

The Council on Biblical Manhood and Womanhood did not go unchallenged. In the same year (1987), *Priscilla Papers* began. It is a journal for papers on equality. The following year the organization Christians for Biblical Equality (CBE) formed out of the same group who began the journal. In contrast to the Council, this group "affirms and promotes the biblical truth that all believers—without regard to gender, ethnicity, or class—must exercise their God-given gifts with equal authority and equal responsibility in church, home, and world."[30] Whereas the Council reorganizes scriptures in Genesis to prove that hierarchy was God's plan, CBE views hierarchy as a result of the fall into sin. Genesis 3 does not prescribe hierarchy but instead predicts it. Instead of being born into leadership based on the fact that you are male, CBE recognizes that people of both genders are "gifted" for leadership, not born into it. Unlike the Council, roles defined in CBE are "flexible and negotiable."[31] Gender is a construct, not just a given—although

28. Archer and Archer, "Complementarianism," 71.
29. Archer and Archer, "Complementarianism," 72.
30. Archer and Archer, "Complementarianism," 76.
31. Archer and Archer, "Complementarianism," 78.

this in no way resembles what Judith Butler means by "gender fluidity."[32] As discussed in a previous chapter, Butler thinks you can choose male, female, or some other combination. CBE thinks you can have giftings that are stereotypically defined as "male" or "female" regardless of your sex.

CBE's Statement of Faith and Core Values, which I have copied here, is instructive:

Statement of Faith

- We *believe* in one God, creator and sustainer of the universe, eternally existing as three persons equal in power and glory.
- We *believe* in the full deity and the full humanity of Jesus Christ.
- We *believe* that eternal salvation and restored relationships are only possible through faith in Jesus Christ who died for us, rose from the dead, and is coming again. This salvation is offered to all people.
- We *believe* the Holy Spirit equips us for service and sanctifies us from sin.
- We *believe* the Bible is the inspired word of God, is reliable, and is the final authority for faith and practice.
- We *believe* that women and men are equally created in God's image and given equal authority and stewardship of God's creation.
- We *believe* that men and women are equally responsible for and distorted by sin, resulting in shattered relationships with God, self, and others.

"Core Values

- Scripture is our authoritative guide for faith, life, and practice.
- Patriarchy (male dominance) is not a biblical ideal but a result of sin.
- Patriarchy is an abuse of power, taking from females what God has given them: their dignity, and freedom, their leadership, and often their very lives.
- While the Bible reflects patriarchal culture, the Bible does not teach patriarchy in human relationships.

---

32. Archer and Archer, "Complementarianism," 79.

- Christ's redemptive work frees all people from patriarchy, calling women and men to share authority equally in service and leadership.

- God's design for relationships includes faithful marriage between a man and a woman, celibate singleness, and mutual submission in Christian community.

- The unrestricted use of women's gifts is integral to the work of the Holy Spirit and essential for the advancement of the gospel in the world.

- Followers of Christ are to oppose injustice and patriarchal teachings and practices that marginalize and abuse females and males.[33]

While CBE's values point directly at the areas of controversy and create a useful starting place for us, Anne Clifford breaks feminist theology into three main categories: revolutionary, reformist, and reconstructionist.[34] Mary Daly would be in the revolutionary category as a radical, post-Christian feminist. Clifford traces the origins of these feminists back to Matilda Joslyn Gage (1826–93), whose research on other cultures led her to advocate for goddess worship.[35] Gage had little real influence in her time but was recovered by second-wave feminists who have adopted her "theory of matriarchy" and rejection of Christianity.[36]

*But there were also false prophets among the people, just as there will be false teachers among you. They will secretly introduce destructive heresies, even denying the sovereign Lord who bought them— bringing swift destruction on themselves. Many will follow their depraved conduct and will bring the way of truth into disrepute. In their greed these teachers will exploit you with fabricated stories. Their condemnation has long been hanging over them, and their destruction has not been sleeping.—2 Pet 2: 1–3, NIV*

Although the passage quoted above can be applied to different feminist theologians in whole, in part, or for some, not at all, it was Mary Daly and her work that inspired me to include it in this chapter. Best known for her 1973 publication *Beyond God the Father: Toward a Philosophy of Women's*

33. "CBE's Mission and Values."
34. Clifford, *Introducing Feminist Theology*, 32–33.
35. Clifford, *Introducing Feminist Theology*, 32.
36. Clifford, *Introducing Feminist Theology*, 33.

*Liberation*, Mary Daly taught for thirty-three years at Boston College, a Jesuit institution, until she was forced into retirement after refusing to allow male students into her upper-level classroom.[37] I would consider her to a be a "false teacher," as Paul warns us about in 2 Pet. The chapters in the book are titled "The Problem, the Purpose, and the Method," "After the Death of God the Father," "Exorcising Evil from Eve: The Fall into Freedom," "Beyond Christolatry: A World Without Models," "Transvaluation of Values: The End of Phallic Morality," "The Bonds of Freedom: Sisterhood as Anti-Church," "Sisterhood as Cosmic Covenant," and "The Final Cause: The Cause of Causes."[38] Just the titles should give you the flavor of a work written by a woman who is celebrated by the Freedom From Religion Foundation as having left Catholicism behind in 1968 with the publication of another famous work: *The Church and the Second Sex*.[39] Here is a taste of her work from the chapter called "After the Death of God the Father":

> With the rise of feminism, women have indeed come to see the necessity of conflict, of letting rage surface and of calling forth a will to liberation. Yet—partially because there is such a contrast between feminism and patriarchal religion's destructive symbols and values, and partially because women's lives are intricately bound up with those of men—biologically, emotionally, socially, and professionally—it is quite clear that women's liberation is essentially linked with full human liberation. Women generally can see very well that the movement will self-destruct if we settle for vengeance. The more imminent danger, then, is that some women will seek premature reconciliation, not allowing themselves to see the depth and implications of feminism's essential opposition to sexist society. It can be easy to leap on the bandwagon of human liberation without paying the price in terms of polarization, tensions, risk, and pain that the ultimate objective of real human liberation demands.[40]

Rejecting "complementarity," she argues for "androgynous integrity and transformation."[41] Although much of the chapter explores the philosophy of "being," her point seems to be that the patriarchal God used to reinforce social structures must be rejected and replaced. As she argues, "Since women are dealing with demonic power relationships, that is, with

---

37. "Mary Daly, Quite Contrary."
38. Daly, *Beyond God the Father*.
39. "Mary Daly," (Freedom from Religion Foundation).
40. Daly, *Church*, 25–26.
41. Daly, *Church*, 26.

structured evil, rage is required as a positive creative force, making possible a breakthrough, encountering the blockages of inauthentic structures." These "inauthentic structures" correspond to the different symbols associated with God and then associated with men. Daly argues that "it [rage] rises as a reaction to the shock of recognizing what has been lost—before it had even been discovered—one's own identity." She also writes that "when women take positive steps to move out of patriarchal space and time, there is a surge of new life." Finally, she thinks of God more as a verb than as a noun, an agent of change.[42]

Clearly, Daly anticipates the identity politics of the third-wave feminists who would follow her in the next couple of decades. Another interesting figure is the Catholic Rosemary Radford Ruether. As a feminist who is still committed to Christianity but believes it is in major need of reconstruction, Ruether would probably fit in the reconstructionist category of feminism. Tied to liberation theology (a term coined by Gustavo Gutierrez in 1968), which embraces the connection between theology, experience, and praxis, reconstructionist theology pays attention to the experience "of patriarchy and androcentrism," brings "these experiences into dialogue with a feminist reading of the Bible and/or other Christian texts," and develops "strategies for transformative action or praxis that are liberating."[43]

As a professor of feminist theology at the Pacific School of Religion and a professor of applied theology at Garrett Evangelical Theological Seminary, Ruether wrote a total of forty-seven books during her career. In her works, she has developed "her signature method: 'What is the problem? How has injustice been created by inadequate or false ideology? How can we improve the system with better thinking and acting?' It is a deceptively simple approach, and it works."[44]

*Sexism and God-Talk: Toward a Feminist Theology*, published in 1983, has the following chapters: "The Kenosis of the Father: A Feminist Midrash on the Gospel in Three Acts," "Feminist Theology: Methodology, Sources, Norms," "Sexism and God-Language: Male and Female Images of the Divine," "Woman, Body, and Nature: Sexism and the Theology of Creation," "Anthropology: Humanity as Male and Female," "Christology: Can a Male Savior Save Women?," "Mariology as Symbolic Ecclesiology: Repression or Liberation?," "The Consciousness of Evil: The Journeys of Conversion," "Ministry and Community for a People Liberated From Sexism," "The New

---

42. Daly, *Church*, 43.
43. "Rosemary Radford Ruether."
44. Hunt, "Life."

Earth: Socioeconomic Redemption from Sexism," "Eschatology and Feminism," and "Postscript: Woman, Body, and the Divine."

In "Act 1: The Kenosis of the Father"—from the first chapter of *Sexism and God-Talk*—it is helpful to know that the word "kenosis" means "the renunciation of the divine nature, at least in part, by Christ in the Incarnation."[45] Instead of the esoteric, philosophical journey Daly embarks on, Ruether begins with a new creation story that includes an overtly misogynist God and a Queen of Heaven who rules him as his mother. The Queen of Heaven says, "I am the Mother of gods and humans, the Creatrix of all things. I am your Mother too. Even when you deny me, I am still here. Beyond your knowledge and your decrees, there is another before You, who is greater than You, and who will survive the death of Your Reign in the heavens."[46]

If you enjoy fiction, you will enjoy how she revises key parts of the Bible in the following pages. After that, she gets more to the point. Writing as a theologian instead of as a creative writer, in the chapter "Feminist Theology," she begins to make some very good points: (1) Until feminist theology, all of the experiences that informed "codified tradition" were male. (2) "Scripture and tradition" are "codified collective human experience." (3) Since all theology is rooted in experience, it is clear there is no "objective" theology versus feminist theology. It is clearly male versus female theology.[47] Later, she points out that a "radical crisis of tradition occurs when the total religious heritage appears to be corrupt."[48] "Marxism," she writes, "teaches that religion is an instrument the ruling class uses to justify its own power and to pacify the oppressed." However, she sees feminist theology as a chance to recover "the full humanity of women" who have previously been denigrated and marginalized.[49]

Anticipating some of the concerns of third-wave feminism and the values of transnationalism, Ruether writes: "Any principle of religion or society that marginalizes one group of persons as less than fully human diminishes us all." Ruether goes on to say, "In rejecting androcentrism (males as norms of humanity), women must also criticize all other forms of chauvinism: making white Westerners the norm of humanity, making Christians the norm of humanity, making privileged classes the norm of humanity."[50]

---

45. Dictionary.com.
46. Ruether, *Sexism and God Talk*, 2.
47. Ruether, *Sexism and God Talk*, 12.
48. Ruether, *Sexism and God Talk*, 17.
49. Ruether, *Sexism and God Talk*, 17–18.
50. Ruether, *Sexism and God Talk*, 20.

She even advises against making humans the norm of humanity and advocates for a "mutuality" instead. Recognizing that there are many iterations of feminism, she explicitly states that she is not defining *the* feminist theological method but *a* feminist theological method.[51]

Another voice central to the development of feminist theology is that of Delores Williams, who published *Sisters in the Wilderness: The Challenge of Womanist God-Talk* in 1993. Using the case of Hagar out of the Old Testament, Williams makes the point that the Bible does not always show God favoring the oppressed and freeing the slave and that is a problem, particularly for Black women.[52] By laying out the discrepancies in the Bible that show a support for slavery and for the annihilation of whole peoples for the benefit of the Hebrews, she demonstrates that the Bible should not be drawn upon without critical examination.

Williams writes:

> If black liberation theology wants to include black women and speak in behalf of the most oppressed black people today—the poor homeless, jobless, economically "enslaved" women, men and children sleeping on American streets, in bus stations, parks and alleys—theologians must ask themselves some questions. Have they, in the use of the Bible, identified so thoroughly with the theme of Israel's election that they have not seen the oppressed of the oppressed in scripture? Have they identified so completely with Israel's liberation that they have been blind to the awful reality of victims making victims in the Bible? Does this kind of blindness with regard to non-Hebrew victims in the scripture also make it easy for black male theologians and biblical scholars to ignore the figures in the Bible whose experience is analogous to that of black women?[53]

Williams argues that ignoring the oppressed means they become invisible. She suggests "theologians should initially engage a womanist hermeneutic of identification-ascertainment that involves three modes of inquiry: subjective, communal and objective." For subjective, it is important to examine who you identify with in the Bible and why. For communal, which communities does your community connect with and why? For objective, how can you analyze Scripture critically to see who is really the oppressed?[54]

In terms of liberation theology, she writes:

---

51. Ruether, *Sexism and God Talk*, 22.
52. Williams, *Sisters in the Wilderness*, 148.
53. Williams, *Sisters in the Wilderness*, 149.
54. Williams, *Sisters in the Wilderness*, 149–50.

The works of the black liberation theologians used in this study agree that racial oppression helped create what they refer to as the black experience. Black liberation theology presents blackness as an important qualitative, symbolic and sometimes sacred aspect of the black experience. It portrays the experience as a holistic reality with four active constituents.[55]

1. The Horizontal Encounter. This is interaction between black and white groups in a socio-historical context . . . From this encounter, suffering has become a characteristic of African-American community life.

2. The Vertical Encounter. In this category black liberation theologians speak of the meeting between God and oppressed people. This meeting not only results in the creation of sustaining and nurturing cultural forms, like black religion, but the oppressed also achieve positive psychological and physical states of freedom and liberation.

3. Transformations of Consciousness . . . They are positive when oppressed people arrive at self or group-identity through awareness of self-worth and through the appreciation of the value of black people and black culture. Transformations of consciousness are negative when black people give up positive black consciousness and identify with alien and destructive forms of consciousness.

4. An Epistemological Process. This is a special way the mind processes data on the basis of action in the three categories above.[56]

Known best for her use of womanism in theology, Delores Williams, who is a professor of theology at Union Theological Seminary in New York City, quotes Ada María Asasi-Díaz and Yolanda Tarango when she says that theology is not an "objective science" but rather "a heuristic device." Key differences between womanism and feminism include the idea of the ideal or acceptable woman, how patriarchy is defined and the extent of its reach, different methods of biblical interpretation, and different perspectives on how God treats the oppressed.[57] Williams then carefully explains each of these in turn, drawing out differences between the two broad perspectives. In her view, Christ refused to accept the oppression of others and criticized

---

55. Williams, *Sisters in the Wilderness*, 153–54.
56. Williams, *Sisters in the Wilderness*, 154–55.
57. Williams, *Sisters in the Wilderness*, 179–80.

culture. Likewise, "to be a Christian in North America is to wage war against the white cultural, social and religious values that make the genocide of black people possible. To be a Christian is to wage this war in the name of Jesus and his ministerial vision of relationship, which involved whipping the money changers (read those in charge of genocidal values) out of the Temple."[58] As a voice for Black feminist theology, Williams sets a course that draws upon secular Black feminism but recovers faith in the process. Activism is about the strong resistance of oppression.

Another feminist theologian is Elisabeth Schüssler Fiorenza, whose "teaching and research focus on questions of biblical and theological epistemology, hermeneutics, rhetoric, and the politics of interpretation, as well as on issues of theological education, radical equality, and democracy." She is a "co-founder and co-editor of the *Journal of Feminist Studies in Religion* and has been a founding co-editor of the feminist issues of *Concilium*. She was elected the first woman president of the Society of Biblical Literature," among many other accomplishments.[59]

In *But She Said: Feminist Practices in Biblical Interpretation*, Schüssler Fiorenza credits the feminist movement for bringing to light how interpretation has been dominated by men and the effects of this.[60] As a revisionist feminist, she seeks to both critique and recover the Bible, as it both challenges and helps women.[61] She writes:

> This first approach in feminist biblical interpretation, however, not only seeks to recover forgotten traditions about women, but also to remove the layers of centuries of androcentric interpretation that cover up the supposed original meaning of the biblical text. Feminist scholars have for instance shown that biblical commentaries have either neglected women's presence in the text or distorted the original meaning of female characters in biblical stories. A feminist revisionist strategy asserts that biblical texts themselves are not misogynist. To the contrary, biblical texts have been patriarchalized by interpreters who have projected their androcentric cultural bias onto biblical texts. Consequently, the Bible must be "depatriarchalized" because, correctly understood, it actually fosters the liberation of women.[62]

---

58. Williams, *Sisters in the Wilderness*, 201.
59. "Elizabeth Schlüssler Fiorenza."
60. Fiorenza, *But She Said*, 20.
61. Fiorenza, *But She Said*, 21.
62. Fiorenza, *But She Said*, 23.

The second tenet of a feminist approach is to question the translation of Scripture, investigating choices made that privilege men.[63] The third tenant has to do with reimagining biblical stories: "From its inception, feminist/womanist/mujerista interpretation has sought to actualize biblical stories in role-play, storytelling, bibliodrama, dance, and song. In order to break the marginalizing and obliterating tendencies of the androcentric text, feminists tell biblical stories in which women are silenced or not present at all differently."[64] A fourth tenet is that we should recover works by women.[65] A fifth tenet is about history: "A feminist historical interpretation conceptualizes women's history not simply as the history of women's oppression by men but as the story of women's historical agency, resistance, and struggle against patriarchal subordination and oppression. Recognizing the absence and marginalization of women in androcentric texts, feminist historians address the problem of how to write women back into history, of how to recapture women's historical experience and contributions."[66]

A sixth tenet is to recognize that history is constructed, not just a reflection.[67] A seventh focuses on how interpretation is androcentric.[68] An eighth tenet is to highlight the work of women as readers and, by default, as interpreters. To elaborate:

> By showing both how patriarchal discourse constructs the reader, and how gender, race, and class affect the way we read, such an approach underlines the importance of the reader's textual and sociocultural location. Reading and thinking in an androcentric symbol-system entices biblical readers to align themselves and to identify with what is culturally normative, that is, culturally "male." Thus reading the Bible can intensify—rather than challenge—women's embeddedness in the cultural patriarchal discourses which alienate us from ourselves.[69]

A ninth tenet is the work of investigating contexts.[70] Finally, a tenth tenet is to approach the text from different perspectives.[71] Schüssler Fiorenza

---

63. Fiorenza, *But She Said*, 24.
64. Fiorenza, *But She Said*, 26.
65. Fiorenza, *But She Said*, 28.
66. Fiorenza, *But She Said*, 30.
67. Fiorenza, *But She Said*, 31.
68. Fiorenza, *But She Said*, 34.
69. Fiorenza, *But She Said*, 35.
70. Fiorenza, *But She Said*, 37.
71. Fiorenza, *But She Said*, 39.

draws on Latin American feminist theology, Asian American feminist theology, and African American theology to do this.

While there are many other feminist theologians, these few give you a good idea of what their concerns are and how they approach feminism from a completely different angle while being inspired by and making use of secular feminist theories at the same time. Other women of note include Jacquelyn Grant, who wrote *White Women's Christ and Black Women's Jesus: Feminist Christology and Womanist Response* in 1989, and, of course, Phyllis Trible, whose *Texts of Terror* helped shape the field. Before completing this chapter, I would like to point out a few Pentecostal feminist theologians.

While Catholic feminist theologians were the first to shape this field, Pentecostals are becoming increasingly recognized for their work. As a member of the Society for Pentecostal Studies, I know that many of my acquaintances in that organization—both male and female—claim to be feminists or hold beliefs that fit with a belief in equality between men and women. Most of us have a doctorate; a few just have a master's. The Society provides a way for scholars to meet annually to share their research. *Pneuma*, a scholarly journal, is published a few times each year as well for this very small organization. Yet Pentecostals are very important in the landscape of contemporary Christianity.

In fact, Pentecostals are the fastest growing group worldwide. While the numbers of Christians are declining in the US, Wes Granberg-Michaelson claims one billion people in Latin America and Africa are now Christians. "One out of four Christians in the world presently is an Africa, and the Pew Research Center estimates that will grow to forty percent by 2030," he writes. In addition, "Asia's Christian population of 350 million is projected to grow to four hundred and sixty million by 2025." Grandberg-Michaelson notes the growth of Pentecostals in Latin America is three times what it is for Catholics, and he claims "one out of twelve people alive today has a Pentecostal form of Christian faith." He then goes on to discuss how immigration is actually bringing more Christians back into the US, but the point is that Pentecostalism, which began in revivals held on Azusa Street in California and was led by a son of former slaves who was blind in one eye, has exploded into a worldwide passion for charismatic faith. In 1906, William Seymour was the very essence of the downtrodden in American society.[72]

As an African American, Seymour faced poverty, racism, and all of the limitations that went with life in America in the early twentieth century. With the help of women, a religion was launched that carried both the message of anti-racism and baptism in the Holy Spirit with speaking in tongues

---

72. Granberg-Michaelson, "Think Christianity Is Dying?"

to every corner of the US and now, the world. These women include Anna Hall, Mable Smith, Neely Terry, Julia Hutchins, Lucy Farrow, Clara Lum, Florence Crawford, Lucy Featherman, Ophelia Wiley, Lillian Garr, Susie Valdez, Rosa de Lopez, Ardella Meade, May Evans, Daisy Batman, Jennie Moore Seymour, Emma Cotton, and Rachel Sizelove, and their stories are shared in Estrelda Alexander's 2005 book *The Women of Azusa Street*.[73] With the inclusion and support of women preachers, Pentecostals (until they became more mainstream in the US in the mid-twentieth century) even allowed for the leadership of women. After a return to a more conservative approach in the mid-twentieth century, now they have again embraced women in leadership and in the pulpit.

Pentecostal theologians include Kimberly Ervin Alexander and Cheryl Bridges Johns. Alexander argues for the affirmation of women who want to serve as ministers in "Pentecostal Women: Chosen for an Exalted Destiny," and she explores the stories of women preachers in her latest book *What Women Want: Pentecostal Women Ministers Speak for Themselves*. Cheryl Bridges Johns has contributed many articles, including "Finding Faith in the Margins" and "Pentecostals and the Praxis of Liberation: A Proposal for Subversive Theological Education." She also wrote "Grieving, Brooding, and Transforming: The Spirit, the Bible, and Gender."

In addition to these articles, which were published in academic journals, there are many others. For example, Lisa Stephenson wrote "A Feminist Pentecostal Theological Anthropology: North America and Beyond"; Andrea Hollingsworth wrote "Spirit and Voice: Toward a Feminist Pentecostal Pneumatology"; Yolanda Pierce wrote "Womanist Ways and Pentecostalism: The Work of Recovery and Critique"; Miriam E. Figuero Aponte wrote "Pneumatology: Toward a Model of Pastoral Theology for Puerto Rican Women"; Muse Dube wrote "Between the Spirit and the Word: Reading the Gendered African Pentecostal Bible"; and the list goes on and on. The titles give a good indication of some of the wildly diverse topics feminist theologians explore.

Obviously, while feminists in the third and fourth waves have discovered and are exploring transnationalism, so are Christian feminist theologians. The difference is that Christians have been evangelizing the world for centuries and Pentecostal converts in the twentieth and twenty-first centuries have been able to draw from messages of equality in addition to the central message of salvation. Because Pentecostalism allows for greater freedom in worship, provides an avenue for female leadership, and rejects racism, it is attractive to many as a way to obtain greater liberty. The roots

---

73. Alexander, *Women of Azusa Street*.

of Pentecostalism include a veneration for the common man, often poor, uneducated, or powerless. Pentecostalism provides a way for people to feel valued and empowered. In conclusion, while Catholic feminist theologians are still a vital force shaping this field today, it would be a great loss to overlook the Pentecostals engaged in this work, particularly as more and more of the world's population claims to adhere to charismatic faith.

Key takeaways:

- Even in a "post-Christian" society, Christianity still matters to many people and shapes how we live.
- The Bible is a text that went through a process to get to its present form. It was something that was not available to be read by many people until the sixteenth century. Religious leaders jealously guarded it because it was a source of authority for them to wield.
- The status of women in the Bible is hotly contested. Some scriptures can be interpreted to support women's subjugation and others can be interpreted to support women's equality and role as prophets or preachers. The Proverbs 31 woman can be interpreted in many ways and can support more than one view of what a woman might wish to aspire to as a person in her community and in her home.
- Theology is a way to construct a viewpoint and can follow the will of God or challenge it. Some Christians oppose women's equality because they feel that male dominance is the correct interpretation of leadership in the home. Others support equality but only as male and female roles are defined stereotypically. This is known as complementarianism.
- Feminist theology fits into three main categories: revolutionary, reformist, and reconstructionist. The revolutionary feminist seeks to overthrow traditional tenets of Christianity. The reconstructionist seeks to rebuild it to fit a preferred paradigm. The reformist or revisionist seeks to critique the Bible and recover it.
- Feminist theologians often offer a process for interpreting Scripture that reveals the work of androcentrism and patriarchy.

# 6

# Tallyho on all the Ballyhoo!

## *The Anti-Feminists and the Treachery of Visual Culture*

The Battlefield: In third-wave and contemporary feminism, who gets to define who is a feminist and who is not.

The Opponents: Those who do not support women's equality as well as those who do but who provide a critique of feminist ideas and theories or political practices associated with feminism versus those who argue that feminists must accept defined political positions (pro-abortion, for example) and abstain from offering a critique of feminist thought that in any way supports or acknowledges the worth of men (I know this is a bit of an overstatement).

The Battlefield: Portrayals of women in the media, in literature, in advertisements, and in art.

The Opponents: Men and women who believe that sexual representations of women empower them and who try to create a fiction through visual images that sidesteps or undermines true historical identities and experiences of women versus those who support the idea that women should be portrayed fairly, accurately, and respectfully.

*Guiding questions for chapter 6:*

1. What is an anti-feminist? Who claims to be a feminist but is not defined as one by other feminists and why?
2. Why do some women challenge feminist accomplishments such as the right to vote? Why do they politically oppose feminists seeking legal protections of equality?
3. How do images both support and challenge the cause of women's rights? What role does race play in how images are created and interpreted by the public?
4. What is the "manosphere" and how do extremist groups differ greatly from most anti-feminists?

*And as they [Mary Magdalene and Mary the mother of James and Joseph] went to tell His disciples, behold, Jesus met them saying, "Rejoice!" So they came and held Him by the feet and worshiped Him.—Matt 28:9, NKJV*

The first Christians, or Christ followers, included women. Two women, both named Mary, were the first ones to visit the tomb and find it empty. Their response to seeing Christ was one of immediate and total submission—of worship. We can imagine them weeping as they "held Him by the feet," faces pressed into the dirt, crying in joy as they worshiped. Their hearts were not full of doubt. They *knew*.

Since feminism's main theme in all of its divergent forms is overcoming male authority, when we have a picture of women prostrate at the feet of Christ, we can clearly see why most feminist scholars do not look to Christian women when they look for ways to escape the bonds of subjugation to men. Feminists have openly criticized Christians for trading subjugation to men for subjugation to a Trinity of male figures: God, Christ, and the Holy Spirit. After all, how can such women experience freedom through subjugation to these three? They miss the fact that the Trinity is a conduit for freedom in all its purest forms. It is through worship that freedom is achieved, and a fruit of true Christian devotion is that of equality. Lacking experience with this, they have ignored, underestimated, or belittled the role Christianity played in what has retroactively been labeled as first-wave feminism.

Yet it was through Christian women that the initial goals for equality were achieved. Without an appeal to Christianity and the exegetical tools that uncovered scriptures supporting women's public speaking, leadership, and spiritual equality, these goals and many other goals that first-wave feminists had—such as the right for women to vote, the right to have their testimony count in court, the right to divorce and to retain custody of their children, the right to not be raped or abused by their husbands, and the right to own and inherit property—might not have been achieved.

Are all Christians "anti-feminists" because they serve a Trinity defined as male? Are all feminists non-Christians? Do all Christians who believe in equality want to be defined as feminists? It is reductive to pretend there are only two categories: feminist and anti-feminist? To pretend there is unity even in these two categories is incredibly naïve. We see non-Christians rejecting the term "feminist" in the twenty-first century, claiming it is no longer needed or of real use, yet they clearly follow the belief that women and men are equals. We see Christians who refuse to define themselves as feminists but who also clearly follow the belief that women and men are equals as well. Does the refusal to adopt the name make them anti-feminists? If a person believes in equality but does not support the political agenda held by liberals, is that person now an anti-feminist? Some believe so. To be labeled as anti-feminist by some is often a political move intended to exclude those who criticize key political trends, who criticize weaknesses in feminist scholarship, who point out flaws in feminist leaders, and who do not rush to adopt the latest trends in identity politics that some feminists use for political or social gain. These are the anti-feminists we should respect and support. Yet there are also those who, motivated by the hatred of women, fall into this category as well. These are anti-feminists we should worry about. Let's explore a few of the people and groups who are anti-feminists so we can see the differences.

*My soul has dwelt too long with one who hates peace. I am for peace; but when I speak, they are for war.—Ps 120:6–7, NKJV*

How exactly does one get labeled an "anti-feminist"? For some, it is opposition on a key political issue, such as abortion or homosexuality. For others, you are an enemy if you believe in capitalism, that gender is not fluid but fixed, or that truths—some, if not all—can be fixed instead of relative to time and place. Feminism is one of the least unified groups of theories there are. Enemies stake out camps within by articulating theories based on race, sexuality, religion, and so on. It would not seem possible for these groups of theorists who defy unity in all its forms to boot someone out of the club. Yet some earn the lofty moniker "anti-feminist" when they get the wrong kinds of attention from those who are less interested in unity and are in control; some earn the title by exhibiting misogynistic behavior or support misogynistic words; and some earn the title when they give it to themselves.

In an article published on Aol.com on August 26, 2020, Josephine Harvey reported on the views of a speaker for the Republican National Convention, Abby Johnson.[1] By allowing "head of household voting," women would somehow be following a godly plan for men to be head of the household. Her "new" kind of feminism is really anti-feminism, according to her critics, and it is anything but new.

Harvey reported that "Johnson claimed on Tuesday that she would 'never' prevent women from voting. Yet when commenters noted that men would have the final say under her proposed system, she responded: 'Yes. So shocking! A husband and wife who are in agreement and a wife who honors her husband as the head of the home.'"[2]

My intention here is not to attack Johnson. I love that she is young and so in love with her husband that when she looks at him, she might think, "I would trust you with anything." However, we live in a time where we have a *choice*. And that choice was hard won.

Johnson is hardly the first to object to a woman's right to vote, however. The Women's National Anti-Suffragist League was formed in 1908.[3] Groups formed to oppose women's right to vote beginning in the 1860s and were populated by women who felt that "because they took care of the home and children . . . women did not have time to vote or stay updated on politics. Some argued that women lacked the expertise or mental capacity to offer a useful opinion about political issues. Others asserted that women's votes would simply double the electorate, thus voting would cost more without adding any new value."[4]

None of these reasons fit the educated women I know: Women who will make the time to vote, who do not shy away from being informed politically, and who have enough expertise to hold the highest positions in companies, universities, and the government. Indeed, we see again the role education has played in increasing women's rights because these arguments which apparently many found persuasive in the late nineteenth and early twentieth centuries seem ridiculous now.

But then, here we are in 2021 and we have Abby Johnson, who seems not to have heard the arguments on full personhood advanced by feminists in her time or those that came before, many of whom were argued by

1. Harvey, "RNC Speaker."
2. Harvey, "RNC Speaker."
3. "Anti-Suffrage Review."
4. "National Association."

Christians, and who does not seem to have the same tools for exegesis that support the equality of women that so many Christians have these days. As a result, many have gleefully booted Johnson out of the feminist club, but others see her as a champion for women and the integrity of the family.

Speaking of suffragism, ridicule is an effective tool in feminist and anti-feminist visual rhetoric, as can be seen in political cartoons from the nineteenth century. In "The Weird Familiarity of 100-Year-Old Feminism Memes," Adrienne LaFrance shares several anti-suffragist political cartoons, and in "Fighting for the Vote" Anna Diamond shows cartoons supporting suffragism, showing how this cultural war was being fought through visually persuasive images. In a triptych cartoon, the heading at the top says "What Breaks Up the Home?" The panel on the left shows a man with his head on the kitchen table. Underneath it says, "Unemployment for Men." The middle panel shows two women and a child who is frowning and doing hard manual labor. Underneath it says, "Bad Employment for Women and Children." The panel on the right shows a couple reaching out to a young woman. The sign behind her says, "No Hands Wanted Today." Beneath the panel it says, "The Easiest Way." The large heading at the bottom reads, "What Will Save the Home?" Small print beneath it reads, "The participation of the homemaker in all governmental control of these problems. For this reason we demand"; and in large print, "Votes for Women." At the bottom, the flyer is accredited to the National American Woman Suffrage Association in New York City.[5]

Much of the visual rhetoric was published on postcards. This may seem odd to us now, but LaFrance points out the following:

> As Palczewski points out in an essay accompanying her web collection of suffrage postcards, it was common for people to display albums filled with postcards in their homes in the early 20th century. So it made sense that postcards both supporting and opposing the women's vote were ubiquitous, especially between 1890 and 1915 in the United States. About 4,500 different suffrage-themed postcards were designed during that time, she wrote.[6]

LaFrance also offers examples of postcards with cats, explaining that this was because of the 1913 "Cat and Mouse Act" in the U.K., which hoped to discourage hunger strikes by suffragettes who had been imprisoned. So in this context, the drawing of a cat next to a sign that reads "We Demand the Vote" makes sense. While there are several of interest, including one of an elderly, female Uncle Sam, one of the most interesting is of a young woman yoked with two heavy buckets on each side facing a ladder. From bottom to

5. Diamond, "Fighting for the Vote."
6. LaFrance, "Weird Familiarity."

top, the rungs read: "Slavery, House Drudgery, Shop Work, Clerks-Agents-Maids, Teachers-Caretakers, Bookkeeping-Stenography [Someone who takes notes on what someone else says using shorthand], Nurse-Governess, Private Secretary, Arts-Crafts-Science, Business Affairs, School Affairs, Church and Charities, War Workers," and so on until at the top it reads "President." The phrase "Equal Suffrage" divides the bottom rungs from the top rungs of the ladder. All the top rungs have a position in government listed.[7]

Although the article shows many images, the one at the end catches my eye. A woman's skull is drawn large and objects within it represent what is in her mind. There is a box of chocolates, a ring, two men, a baby, a puppy, a dress, and a fancy hat. The phrase "A Woman's Mind Magnified" is at the bottom. This 1906 postcard drove home the idea that women were not intellectually sophisticated enough to vote. While all this rhetoric is interesting, though, not many people object to women having the right to vote these days.

Other anti-feminists are worth discussing. Some (not all) anti-feminists are absolutely vital for the types of corrections that the sometimes outlandish feminist theories demand. For example, can one really suggest that the male population be reduced to no more than 10 percent and then honestly not think anyone will object? Can someone suggest that incest is desirable in the name of equality and think no one will push back? Even other feminists critique such ideas. Yet some feminists do not embrace and engage with criticism. Instead, some feminists operate as Medusa—ready to destroy all who criticize them with the long look of their gaze—and many who are named "anti-feminists" are like Perseus, eager to destroy what is wrong with feminist thought and theory by trying to destroy the whole body of ideas associated with feminism as well.

At the heart of those like Perseus is an objection to the shift in power. Some anti-feminists engage in a deliberate act to tie feminists to only the most radical ideas and ignore the need for equality in politics, the church, the home, and the workplace, for example. In fact, when Rush Limbaugh coined the term "feminazi," it was to tie feminists to radical political ideals and then pretend such a term represented the whole group, not just a segment.[8] Women such as Abby Johnson grasp onto conservative views of headship in the home. This means that many women do not really understand that God's original plan was for equality. After sin, hierarchy and subjugation were part of the curse. We can't blame these women for buying into

---

7. LaFrance, "Weird Familiarity."
8. "Antifeminism."

what seems simple: Let the man lead, make all the big decisions, manage the money, and work outside the home. This allows women to avoid so much stress. I can see why women eagerly buy into this.

Anti-feminists include some very famous, influential scholars. For example, Charles Darwin argued that men were superior to women. In *The Descent of Man* (1871), women were presented as "a less developed man, her anatomy more childlike or 'primitive,' her mental qualities (such as intuition and imitation) harkening back, as Darwin phrased it, to 'a past and lower state of civilization.'"[9] Other "scientists" followed, such as Herbert Spencer and Thomas Huxley.[10] As Encylopedia.com states, "the influential nineteenth-century social philosopher and social scientist Herbert Spencer (1820–1903) held an even dimmer view of women's evolution, asserting that women had not taken part of the final step in human development, the acquisition of the ability to reason."[11]

In *Sex in Education: or, a Fair Chance for the Girls* (1873), Harvard professor Edward Clarke wrote that women should not be trained the same way as men because if they were they would suffer from "neuralgia, uterine disease, hysteria, and other derangements of the nervous system."[12] Education, in his opinion, was the entire upbringing of an individual, not just the curriculum in school.[13] Because women were delicate, when educated too soon, their ovaries might not develop properly. He wrote, "They [two women] graduated from school or college excellent scholars, but with underdeveloped ovaries. Later, they married and were sterile."[14] The threat is clear: Women should be limited in their educational opportunities, you know, for their own good.

But these are old arguments, ridiculous to the modern ear. With the rise of "science" in the twenty-first century, though, which never hesitates to ridicule people of faith through the voices of the media, the voices of entertainers, and the bombast of political leaders, it is much more convenient to overlook such pieces of history—such as where a highly educated doctor from one of our most prestigious institutions wrote an entire book arguing eloquently with the full benefit of a doctor's diction that women were going to suffer physically if educated the same way as men. On the title page, Spencer claimed to be a member of the Massachusetts Medical Society,

---

9. Brilmyer, "Darwinian Feminisms," 21.
10. Brilmyer, "Darwinian Feminisms," 21.
11. "Antifeminism."
12. Clarke, *Sex in Education*, 18.
13. Clarke, *Sex in Education*, 20–21.
14. Clarke, *Sex in Education*, 39.

fellow of the American Academy of Arts and Sciences, and late professor of Materia Medica at Harvard College. How many scientists today offer their credentials in the same way and, in the time of COVID-19, request that they not be questioned but simply be believed and obeyed?

What is more common today are those who make other claims. According to an entry on antifeminism, "more common early in the twenty-first century are utilitarian social science arguments, offering anecdotal and statistical evidence that women who choose not to be wives and mothers are unhappy, that the children of working mothers are damaged, and that society suffers when women pursue any path but motherhood."[15] In addition to this are claims by anti-feminists that all or most feminists support promiscuity, abortion, lesbianism, and birth control, and that they are "unsexed." Yet there are also the decidedly patriarchal and sometimes misogynistic Old and New Testament scriptures to contend with as well as more contemporary scholarship, such as the work of the famous psychiatrist Sigmund Freud, who described female inferiority in scientific terms.[16]

Some make their name defining themselves as anti-feminists. Phyllis Schlafly is perhaps one of the best known in that category. Known as the one who led the movement to defeat the Equal Rights Amendment, Schlafly stood on the shoulders of feminists who fought to give her the right to speak publicly, to earn her degree in law, to publish her books, to work in the public sector and hold leadership positions, to run for Congress, and—oh yes—to vote.

Even so, according to Encyclopedia.com:

> Throughout the 1970s she barnstormed the country with her supporters, lobbied state legislatures, and debated feminist leaders. Schlafly founded the Eagle Forum, a national organization of volunteers to champion conservative causes, in 1976. *The Positive Woman*, in which she compared a traditional wife and homemaker, pro-family and pro-defense ideal, to feminist ideals and values, was published in 1978.[17]

Schafly is currently gaining national attention again as the subject of the show *Mrs. America*, which airs on FX on Hulu and captures her work in the '70s, which resulted in a political shift towards the "silent majority," or conservativism.[18]

---

15. "Antifeminism."
16. "Antifeminism."
17. "Phyllis Schalfly."
18. "Phyllis Schalfly."

Young Kate Roiphe, only twenty-four when she published *The Morning After: Sex, Fear, and Feminism* in 1994, brought out what tends to happen when a "victimized" group gains a bit of speed in American culture, particularly within the university: It cannot be criticized. Yet when Kate attended Harvard in the mid-nineties, she found that the feminists' focus on sexual harassment and date rape portrayed women as weak victims, such as in films she had to watch where female characters were reminiscent of women in the 1950s.[19] With an overabundance of focus on women as victims, the feminists she had hoped to encounter as bastions of strength within the university were instead playing the role of fearmongers. To criticize them meant she was anti-feminist, even though she clearly felt that nothing was further from the truth.

Christina Hoff Sommers is another famous anti-feminist, but she is one who is fully capable of playing on an even field with feminist scholars who portray America as full of "white supremacists" and a "violent patriarchy," and who present inaccurate statistics to support their positions. She is the author "of three books exploring the political and philosophical issues surrounding gender: *Who Stole Feminism? How Women Have Betrayed Women*; *The War Against Boys: How Misguided Policies Are Harming Our Young Men*; and *Freedom Feminism: Its Surprising History and Why It Matters Today*. She has also compiled an anthology of essays, *The Science on Women in Science*."[20]

Sommers's critique of feminists includes questioning the argument that we should throw history away because it is made too much out of men's accomplishments. Instead, Sommers suggests building on it. She also critiques the overemphasis on a lack of power experienced by women. In his article, Christian Alejandro Gonzalez explains Sommers's argument:

> "The vast majority of people," she [Sommers] writes, "including *most* men and almost *all* women, have had a disproportionately small share in the history-making decisions about war, politics, and culture that historians count as momentous." It would be disingenuous for historians to falsify past evidence and assign to ordinary people a greater influence over the course of events than they exerted. In the end, there is little historians can do about the historical role of "the 'common people' whom God made so numerous."[21]

---

19. Roiphe, *Morning After*.
20. Gonzalez, "Freedom Feminist."
21. Gonzalez, "Freedom Feminist."

For Sommers, the theory that a woman who does not support a feminist point of view—such as those who are pro-life, for example—is the victim of a "false consciousness" and self-deception is problematic.[22] Sommers points out that these assertions are a dangerous tool used to "open the door to the authoritarian dismissal of popular preferences."[23] In *Freedom Feminism*, Sommers offers something important for truly understanding the book I've written: there were left-wing and right-wing feminists within first-wave feminism. She puts Mary Wollstonecraft on the left for advocating for full equality and denying any differences between men and women, and she puts Hannah More on the right for valuing both equality and difference.[24]

> Sommers calls the left-feminists "egalitarian feminists" and the right-feminists "maternal feminists," and she holds that both exerted a positive force on the women's movement. The two wings, for example, worked together to promote women's suffrage. Left-feminists, such as Elizabeth Cady Stanton, demanded the vote by using the language of universal rights and appealing to thinkers such as Thomas Paine and Thomas Jefferson. Right-feminists, such as Frances Willard, were proud of women's role as caretakers of the home; they argued for suffrage on the grounds that granting women the vote would extend their benign moral influence over the rest of society.[25]

Like me, Sommers argues that conservative, Christian women were essential to the success of first-wave feminist causes.

> Conservative feminists were more successful at convincing people to join the cause, and hence far more effective at promoting women's suffrage. "In 1890," Sommers writes, "the two leading egalitarian suffragist groups merged because they were worried that the cause was dying." Their combined forces numbered no more than 13,000 members. "By comparison," Sommers continues, "Willard had built an organization with 150,000 dues-paying members, along with an additional 50,000 branches for young women.[26]

Today, Sommers has a website hosted by the American Enterprise Institute where she republishes her articles. One is from June 5, 2020 and

---

22. Gonzalez, "Freedom Feminist."
23. Christina Hoff Sommers, quoted in Gonzalez, "Freedom Feminist."
24. Gonzalez, "Freedom Feminist."
25. Gonzalez, "Freedom Feminist."
26. Gonzalez, "Freedom Feminist."

is titled "Fact Checking 'Mrs. America.'" It was originally published in the *Washington Examiner*. She accuses the show's creators of inventing a lot that did not happen, including a scene where Phyllis Schlafly, played by Cate Blanchett, emerges onto the stage before other Republicans at a fundraiser clad in a sexy bikini. In essence, the show is a character assassination, as Sommers explains, and is riddled with errors and unflattering portrayals that don't line up with reality. Furthermore, while the show's creators vigorously defend their portrayals of the debates as accurate, Sommers found errors there as well. Schlafly's main issue with the ERA (Equal Rights Amendment) was that under that law everyone, including women, would be subject to be drafted into the military if needed. Sommers writes, "Schlafly was able to organize her historic grassroots campaigns not by misrepresenting the ERA feminists but by quoting them."[27]

Although labeled as an anti-feminist because her critiques landed on their targets, Sommers is a much-needed intellectual who can reveal the fractures in feminist thought and bring forth the truth when feminists rely on flawed statistics, twisted facts, and hyperbole. She is not really an enemy of feminism so much as a deep thinker who has the courage to speak and back up her claims with research. When feminists describe Sommers as an enemy, they are attempting to silence her, knowing she is not against equality for women but that she also does not support every theory or "fact" feminist thought produces.

Anti-feminists converge into groups. These are usually political, as Dr. Nicole Hemmers describes in her 2019 article on why all anti-abortionists are anti-feminists. She also offers an interesting analogy between the identity politics of liberals and conservatives. When describing the rise of women against abortion, she writes:

> These women were vital players in a new era of conservative politics that would fundamentally transform the United States. That they were women mattered: their ability to leverage their authority as mothers, wives, and women—identities that gave them authority in the spheres of sex, reproduction, and education that they lacked in other parts of American politics. (Identity politics, usually ascribed as a quality of the left, has long been just as prevalent, if not as obvious, on the right.)[28]

Dr. Hemmers's political views are falsely presented as an all-or-nothing sort of position that makes her a feminist and pro-lifers not, but when one attempts to pose a single definition for feminism, the response is that

27. Sommers, "Fact Checking."
28. Hemmers, "Anti-Feminist Women."

it is not unified. So which is it? All feminists must subscribe to the political perspective that women have a right to an abortion and if you don't, you are anti-feminist? This either-or fallacy is part of what makes critiquing feminism so difficult.

If we are to look at the visual rhetoric surrounding the controversy over abortion, particularly in the age of Facebook, we can begin to understand that this fight is deeply personal and deeply emotional for women on both sides. Memes, videos, and ultrasounds that are now possible due to advances in technology populate social media. Conservatives criticize liberals for valuing women's rights except when they are in the womb. They point out the hypocrisy of valuing the children of undocumented immigrants and in the same breath condoning the right to murder the unborn. On the other hand, we have the BBC series *Call the Midwife*, which has characters who die after getting backstreet abortions, making it clear that outlawing abortion doesn't actually stop it and that getting an unsafe abortion could result in unnecessary death for the mother.

Rosalind Pollack Petchesky's "The Power of Visual Culture in the Politics of Reproduction," published in *Theorizing Feminism* in 2001, brings up one of the most powerful anti-abortion films, *The Silent Scream*, and critiques it as a non-scientific piece of propaganda. It is not possible, she argues, for a fetus to feel pain at only twelve weeks, so the film and the scream at the end are a work of fiction.[29] Her scathing critique of the film and the power it held over viewers in the 1980s was an attempt to silence pro-lifers. Yet pro-lifers will not yield their position. Ultimately, the battle is not one of feminist versus anti-feminist, though—not if you listen closely to both sides. It is not even Christian versus non-Christian. To pretend either side can be reduced to simple terms misses a great deal of the complexity of this ongoing battle and the visual tools used by each side.

Hemmer's point about the Right's identity politics leads to another, much more extreme, group of anti-feminists. In August of 2019, Helen Lewis reported on the manosphere in an article published in *The Atlantic*. While most Americans agree that Islamic terrorists and their need to subjugate women is disturbing, Lewis sees a parallel between the way terrorists justify their right to dominate as "divinely ordained" and the way those affiliated with the manosphere, an American group comprised of white men, see it as a biological fact that they are indeed superior to women and feel that for the world to be right, women must be put in their place. The manosphere is an online group with anonymous members which draws participants toward racism as well. Linking far-right extremists to mass shootings, Lewis

---

29. Petchesky, "Power," 419.

reveals how hatred poisons the minds of those who take superiority to the extreme and try to push others down. As the "gateway to white nationalism," "anti-feminist rhetoric" also serves to draw men into believing that whites are being replaced by minorities in "The Great Replacement." Lewis shares this view, which she encountered in manifestoes written by three mass shooters.[30]

Of course, many anti-feminists are not part of extremist groups, nor are they going to be. There is also a vast difference between hating women and wanting to limit a woman's rights. In the case of anti-abortionists, killing the unborn is not seen as a right. This is not part of what characterizes a hate group like the manosphere. Conservative religious groups such as Pentecostals were against racism from their earliest beginnings, but many believe in having a male leader in the home and are against abortion. Does this make them anti-feminists? At the same time, Pentecostals support women preachers and form different political, social, and religious ideologies that sometimes contrast with the overarching doctrines espoused by many different denominations.

Many religious groups are not extremists, and espousing a belief in male leadership does not necessarily mean these men and women have crossed into the extremist propaganda Lewis describes, but the fearmongering makes all those who are "religious" suspicious. It implies Christians are not able to think freely for themselves. Liberals who believe this are blind to the fact that they too are in a fundamentalist "church" with key beliefs that can't easily be questioned. The only difference is that their church is the university, where they regularly get rid of those who hold opposing views. This is well-documented in *The Chronicle of Higher Education*, which has been reporting on this for decades.

Yet Christians often become part of the battle over women's rights as they try to reconcile the Bible and religion with an imperfect society in an imperfect world. A Christian might grapple with the dilemma of whose life is worth more: the mother's or the baby's? If outlawing abortion produces backstreet, illegal abortions, has the problem really been solved?

Realizing I've left you with nothing clear-cut so far in this chapter, I am now going to move on to a different type of anti-feminist: those who produce stereotypical or overly sexualized images in American visual culture. In *Black Feminist Thought*, Patricia Hill Collins writes, "Portraying African-American women as stereotypical mammies, matriarchs, welfare recipients, and hot mommas helps justify US black women's oppression. Challenging these controlling images has long been a core theme in black feminist thought." The

---

30. Lewis, "To Learn."

ultimate goal of these images is to make "racism, sexism, poverty, and other forms of social injustice appear to be natural, normal, and inevitable parts of everyday life."[31] Visual culture shapes us. That is why Collins recognizes it is dangerous. There is an entire field of study referred to as "visual rhetoric." Visuals are persuasive. They tell us what to wear, who is beautiful and who is not, what to think, how to act, what to value and what not to value, how to live, and so much more. Because we instantly digest a visual, the argument is hard to see, as reality is shaped by the repetition of themes in images, especially once a stereotype becomes the norm.

While Collins goes on to discuss the creation of the "other" in relationship to what is presented as the norm, we can glean additional insight in an article published in 2019, where Ellen E. Jones describes the impact of the "mammy" in American culture:

> Maybe the most important thing to know about mammy, though, is that she never actually existed. As evidenced in the research of historians including Cheryl Thurber and Patricia Turner, while the care of white children in the antebellum US South was sometimes entrusted to enslaved people, these "house slaves" were typically light-skinned teenage girls (conditions for enslaved black women were, in any case, so harsh that 90 per cent died before their 50th birthday). Given the poor diet available to slaves, they were also highly unlikely to have been either fat or jolly. All this, according to the psychologist Chanequa Walker-Barnes, "affirms that Mammy was a largely mythical figure with little basis in the lived experiences of black women."[32]

She also writes that "the mammy was a creation of white supremacy" and was needed to absolve whites of the guilt of slavery by apearing to love and nurture white children.[33] In 1981, Andy Warhol included the mammy in his myths series, Jones points out, right alongside "Santa, Uncle Sam, and Mickey Mouse." It was only in 2020 that the well-known Aunt Jemima image was dropped from bottles of syrup and boxes of pancake mix, however.[34]

While images of Black women have obviously been used to define and subjugate them, "Rhonda Goodman, a Stanford doctoral student in art and art history and a Geballe Dissertation Prize Fellow at the Humanities Center, has studied the little-known artwork for messages that reveal the social and

---

31. Collins, *Black Feminist Thought*, 69.
32. Jones, "From Mammy."
33. Jones, "From Mammy."
34. Kesslen, "Aunt Jemima."

political attitudes of the time. She focused her research on the way artists portrayed slave auctions, in particular."[35] What Goodman discovered is that in 1853 Eyre Crow created sympathy for African Americans by drawing "In the Richmond Slave Market," which was subsequently published in the *Illustrated London News* in 1856 and then reprinted in several papers. He then painted "Slaves Waiting for Sale in Virginia," an oil painting displayed at the Royal Academy in 1861. By analyzing the emotions present in the African Americans portrayed, one sees how the visual rhetoric of the piece humanizes and inspires an emotional connection to the subjects who, in turn, became an iconic representation of slaves in America. Goodman's work shows an interesting alternative view of depictions of Black women as slaves because they became a part of abolitionist rhetoric in the nineteenth century.

Clearly, racism and misogyny make good partners in art that seeks to demean Black women, but visual culture has long been a double-edged sword for women, sometimes undermining equality and sometimes arguing for equality, as we can see in the example of the visual representation of the slaves being sold at an auction. In the last decade or so, scholars have researched the pervasiveness of white culture and how it makes racism invisible at times. Despite the many efforts of the entertainment industry to represent diversity, when I view women in books like Robert Cumming's *Art: A Visual History* and E. H. Gombrich's *The Story of Art*, I see a history of mostly white people: white people as Greek gods, white people as Jesus and Mary, white people as famous Greek philosophers, white people who are dressed finely in a display of money and goods, white people winning wars, and white people riding valiant horses.

We also have a culture where sexism and the exploitation of women is often the norm. When I turn on the TV, I see overly sexualized women in skin-tight clothing and heavy makeup, but I also see highly skilled and educated women, such as in the popular series *Virgin River* with the nurse, Melinda Monroe (played by Alexandra Breckenridge), and the powerful mayor, Hope McCrea (played by Annette O'Toole). The women who play these characters don't rely on displays of skin or emphasis on their sexuality, yet both are undeniably attractive.

If I were to only focus on the shows I watch, I would begin to feel hopeful about the portrayal of women, but I see something else reflected in the way students dress on campus, with low-cute shirts and naked buns hanging out the back of cropped shorts—and I know I'm being naïve. I couldn't get through the first episode of *Game of Thrones* because it comes too close to

---

35. Haven, "How Antebellum."

pornography. And that is just one example of many. Too many TV series try to capitalize on getting as close to porn as possible.

Add to that a healthy dose of violence and you get the comedian Kathy Griffin, who mistakenly assumed it to be ordinary enough to allow her to display Trump's severed head as a "joke." Even commercials are becoming more and more crass, with my latest disdain directed toward one that had a woman's vagina singing, one that had a disembodied finger picking a nose, and one that featured a woman taking off her bra and pulling it through her sleeve.

The treachery of visual culture in the twenty-first century is that too much of it misleads women into thinking sexuality is power. Feminists who celebrate the "slut walk" and who object to "slut shaming" are clueless about how demeaning it is to choose to be objectified and to be noticed for physical, not intellectual, features. Fortunately, the "Guerrilla Girls" pointed out the hypocrisy of art in the 1980s with the now-famous poster of a naked woman with a guerilla head that reads, "Do women have to be naked to get into the Met. Meseum?" in large letters. In smaller text, the poster reads, "Less than 5% of the artists in the Modern Art section are women, but 85% of the nudes are female."[36] So again, the irony of feminists taking opposite sides is evident. Yet the discord is also good. One group corrects the excesses of the other.

While I could probably write a hundred pages on how women are portrayed now and in the past, I will leave you with a few questions I ask myself when analyzing a visual image. These have been borrowed from composition textbooks, websites, and most recently, from *Everyone's an Author*.[37]

1. Who is the main figure?
2. How are key images arranged?
3. What is the relationship between the main figure and the background?
4. What is excluded from the main figure or background?
5. What use of color, contrasts of light and shade, or repeated figures are present? How do these details create a message for the viewer?
6. What first draws your attention?
7. Is the focal point centered or offset? Does this emphasize something in the message?
8. How does the focus or lack of focus contribute to the message?

36. Guerrilla Girls, "Do Women Have to Be Naked to Get into the Met. Museum?," quoted in Freedman, *Essential Feminist*, 392.

37. Lunsford et al., *Everyone's an Author*.

9. Do any background figures or lines draw your attention either to the focal point or away from it?
10. What story does the visual suggest?
11. Do certain objects or figures act as symbols or metaphors?
12. How do these elements support the visual's message or purpose?
13. Who has power in this visual? Who does not?
14. Who is included? Who is excluded?
15. Are there sexist, racist, etc. stereotypes portrayed here? Are these stereotypes promoted or challenged?
16. What can you learn by investigating the contexts: photographer, place, subjects, time, place of publication, audience reception/response, politics, ethics, religious connotations, and genre?

By analyzing the images the permeate our world, we can resist normalizing ideologies we object to, refute images that objectify or demean women, and create our own persuasive pieces to develop arguments we seek to support through a variety of means. Finally, by listening to those labeled as "anti-feminists," we can take reasoned critiques into account as we articulate our position in this rather complicated conversation, and we can scrutinize those who act or speak out of malice to fight for values in line with our faith.

Key takeaways:

- Not all anti-feminists would define themselves as such. Some earn the moniker after offering a thoughtful critique of feminism or a particular feminist.
- Some anti-feminists support men in various ways and face criticism for it.
- Some define women who do not support the right to an abortion as anti-feminist, although this definition is too focused on one issue when feminists take all sorts of positions on a wide range of issues.
- A thoughtful analysis of images can often reveal the persuasive powers they have. An exploration of contexts for an image can show how they may have affected their original audience.

# 7

# Making Decisions about the Future

*Defining Yourself, Choosing a Program, Entering the Profession*

The Battlefield: Your mind and your potential future career as an educator.

The Opponents: Those who wish to educate you but with limits on what you can choose to believe as a Christian and in response to that education versus those who allow free room for education and for belief.

The Opponents: Those who wish to only hire and provide tenure for faculty who hold similar political, religious, and social beliefs versus those who wish to preserve room for thoughtful and respectful differences.

*Behold, I will do a new thing, / Now it shall spring forth; / Shall you not know it? / I will even make a road in the wilderness / And rivers in the desert.—Isaiah 43:19, NKJV*

I dwell in the Sonoran Desert, just north of the Mexican border. I like this translation of Isaiah because it says "desert" and not "wasteland." The desert is anything but a wasteland. It is brimming with life, and we have the San Pedro River not too far from us. We have coyotes who sing their eerie songs in the deep of night; javelinas who are the same gray as the sky at dusk and who traipse through our fields and our neighborhoods; road runners who look frail but can kill snakes; and lizards, jackrabbits, and the beautiful quail we are so known for in plentiful supply. Hawks soar over my backyard, screaming into the wind. There are snakes, yes, and slow-moving tarantulas that come out at dusk. There are the birds that nest in the trees, and Sierra Vista is called the "hummingbird capital of the world." Between the bees, the bats, and the hummingbirds, our hummingbird feeders need regular attention. Surrounded by mountains which are broken up by rivers and streams and covered in trees, the life of the desert is anything but a dry wasteland.

So it is with women's studies. What may appear to be a missing history is just one that lies undiscovered. When we research women's histories and writings, we make rivers in the desert. Sitting in archives and in the hearts and memories of people are stories that just have not been told. These stories interrupt master narratives and stereotypes formed by scholars who were simply writing about what they knew at the time. For example, Pentecostals are characterized as poor, uneducated, and backwards. But our first bishop, J. H. King, was anything but those things. He traveled the world and was educated. He does not fit into the small box built by those who do not know his story. Women preachers are characterized as secretly wishing to be like men, as trying to take away a man's place—a man's opportunity for leadership. But women preachers do not seek those things. The truth does not match the narrative. So when I find men and women digging into the past, I am overwhelmed by a sense of profound joy. What will they uncover? What streams will flow in a desert where before there were none? What stereotypes will fall?

But do you have to be a feminist to engage in the search? And by the way, why would a Christian woman claim to be a feminist? The rhetorical tools of the stereotypical feminist are anger, denigration, condescension, self-righteousness, self-pity, contention, and hatefulness, all in the pursuit of either equality or, in some cases, superiority. Many secular and formerly Christian theologians openly hate God and disregard Christ's life and example because if God is a spirit and there is no male or female, they know for certain Christ occupied a male body while on earth. To worship or to be saved by someone who is male is an affront. Part of the feminist stereotype is a need for separation from men or from a society that is perceived as irredeemably flawed. In fact, Alice Walker's idea of "womanism" was different precisely for her love of community. On the other hand, feminist scholars wield knowledge as a means of critiquing hegemonic social structures that keep certain groups at a disadvantage economically, politically, socially, or spiritually. Without feminists, would we be able to dismantle the types of patriarchy that held women down for so long?

Furthermore, if you do claim to be a feminist, then what kind are you? There's no single definition of feminism, nor are many of the theories simple once you begin to really explore them. Second-wave feminists were the first to bring in beliefs antithetical to Christian beliefs and actions on a national stage. Second- and third-wave feminists made feminism political in a very different way than first-wave feminists did. And the numbers of conservatives identifying with any wave are few and far between these days—outside of the university. Usually these are women, such as with Christians for Biblical Equality, who clearly define their connection to both Christianity and to feminism but who firmly root their identities in Christ, not in a social movement. Many feminist theologians are perceived as a threat to conservative, traditional Christian beliefs as well, so it is important to do this. So why identify with a group that has no singular definition?

In "What is Feminism?" Rosalind Delmar points out that feminists are fragmented in practice and belief but developing a "feminist consciousness" is part of what separates a feminist from someone who is not. She also writes that "it is by no means absurd to suggest that you don't have to be a feminist to support women's rights to equal treatment, and that not all those supportive of women's demands are feminists."[1] Is feminism a social movement? It is a philosophy? Is it a set of political beliefs? Or is it like a religion, much like some venerate the idol of science these days? Those who claim to be "woke" are suspiciously similar in tone to converts who find themselves in a new way of thinking they are not willing to question.

The answer, in short, is that a person can define her position just like everyone else claiming to be a feminist. For me, a feminist does not accept inequality in social, religious, economic, or political structures. She (or he) does not remain silent when she sees inequality. So for someone willing to take action and to have a voice, a feminist is a person of strong beliefs and strong actions. She puts her ideas into practice. However, for a Christian, she does so by lining up her goals with the Bible. Guided by the Holy Spirit, she works in tangent to bring about positive change. She also works with her community—both men and women—which seeks to right the wrongs that are in a particular institution or part of culture.

From my perspective, if a feminist sees a law that needs to change, she (or he) fights to change it. If she sees a policy in the workplace or in church that needs to change, she fights to change it. If she sees there is inequality in political structures—which are in every workplace, every church, and of

---

1. Delmar, "What is Feminism?," 9.

course, our local, state, and federal governments—she fights to change it. So a feminist is a term that connotes action backed by strong belief. That's why I can comfortably claim to be a feminist when it suits my purposes to do so. Not because I agree with everyone (because, as you have seen, both feminists and their theories are full of contradictions), but because I am not willing to accept inequality and I am not afraid to speak, act, and try to change structures within my realm of influence. However, I do not often call myself a feminist. In my opinion, my identity is rooted in being a Christian. Feminism, noble as it may sound in the idealistic definition I have provided, is subordinate to my faith. In other words, I will follow Christ first. All other ideas must be measured in light of him.

Whether you are a Christian or not, you might consider the anti-feminist Christina Hoff Sommers's definition of feminism. She "concludes her book with a call for a revitalized right-feminism, which she calls 'freedom feminism.'"[2]

> [Freedom feminism is feminism that] stands for the moral, social, and legal equality of the sexes—and the freedom of women to employ their equal status to pursue happiness in their own distinctive ways. Freedom feminism is not at war with femininity or masculinity, it does not seek to bring down capitalism, and it does not view men and women as warring tribes. Conspiracy theories about universal patriarchal oppression are nowhere in its founding documents . . . Put simply, freedom feminism affirms for women what it affirms for everyone: dignity, fairness, and liberty.[3]

The rhetorical tools of a Christian feminist are vastly different than the stereotypical secular feminist. Instead of separation, there is a love of community. The church is a source of hope and support and is a way to contribute to others through service in the church and beyond its walls. Instead of anger, there is humility. Proverbs 16:32 says, "He who is slow to anger is better than the mighty, / And he who rules his spirit than he who takes a city" (NKJV). Instead of denigration, there is the idea that you are to put others ahead of you. Philippians 2:3 says, "Do nothing out of selfish ambition or vain conceit. Rather, in humility value others above yourselves" (NIV). Instead of condescension, there is the desire to rebuild in the context of love. First Thessalonians 5:11 says, "Therefore encourage one another and build each other up, just as in fact you are doing" (NIV). Instead of self-righteousness, there is a recognition that we all fall short and are flawed.

2. Gonzalez, "Freedom Feminism."
3. Gonzalez, "Freedom Feminism."

Proverbs 11:2 says, "When pride comes, then comes disgrace, / but with humility comes wisdom" (NIV). Instead of self-pity, faith. Instead of contention, the desire to seek and to obtain peace. Instead of hatefulness, there is the idea of loving a neighbor—even if that neighbor needs to change to stop limiting or hurting others.

Whereas the stereotypical feminist is vulgar, the ideal Christian feminist is always respectful in all she says and all she does. Whereas the stereotypical feminist sometimes relies on cursing and hatefulness as she vents her feelings to the world, the ideal Christian feminist draws on the Bible and on a solid education to establish clear points, and she shows respect for her audience with kind words and wise, knowledgeable language. Whereas the stereotypical feminist demands that others adopt her beliefs without question, the ideal Christian feminist allows others to see all sides and make informed choices. A Christian feminist is not threatened by the fact that others disagree and have strong arguments. After all, control and bullying are not effective tools. Psalm 119:51 says, "The proud have held me in great derision, / Yet I do not turn aside from your law" (NKJV). The Christian knows where to find the truth. Moreover and most importantly, she is not emotionally dependent upon the approval of those who do not walk in the way of truth. These are the things I aspire to; these are the things I imagine Christian feminists should be. Are they all true in practice? Of course not. But it doesn't mean that these should not be goals for Christian men and women who also believe in equality and wish to advocate for it.

So now let me ask, what if you want to know more? There are many things left out of this book. Feminism as a teaching methodology is one. The Vanderbilt Center for Teaching and Learning provides an excellent guide for that. Basically, it is a philosophy of teaching that values the ideas that knowledge is socially constructed and personal experience is a legitimate way of knowing (as opposed to other methods, such as the scientific method). It teaches us to recognize the power structures in place and how they affect us, to understand that identity is not simple (intersectionality comes into play here), and to value community through classroom activities that reflect these principles. Basically, it is a point of view translated into various options for practice.[4] Of course, there is a large body of research tied to feminist pedagogy. But what if you are not yet a teacher? What if you are a student who wants to engage in women's studies? Where should you do that? Which program is the best fit?

Ask yourself these questions: What knowledge am I seeking? Am I looking to round out a bachelor's degree program with a few courses? Am

---

4. "Guide to Feminist Pedagogy."

I hoping for a master's program that will set me up to be a better working professional, say, in the field of social work or in business? Do I want to earn a doctorate and teach in a women's and gender studies program? Do I want to learn about theology and women? The law and women? Literature and women? History and women? Many times you will major in history, literature, or law and then take a course or two that focuses on women and that area of study. Other times, you may wish to take many more courses and there are programs for that too.

Then ask yourself: Do I need to take a course to get the knowledge I want? Maybe you just want to read some of the books I've listed in one of the appendixes to this book. Maybe you just want a course or two in order to broaden your perspective. Maybe you could take one of many of the free, online college courses widely available for your own benefit and knowledge (since these don't count for actual college credit). Maybe you just want to listen to some Ted Talks. At the bachelor's degree level, you are really free to enjoy taking courses as you wish—or not. However, if you are hoping to earn a master's degree or a doctoral degree, there are some things to consider.

For those who are interested in women's history and issues associated with equality, there are several avenues to consider for further exploration. For one, there has been a surge in women's and gender studies programs at all levels—from bachelor's to doctoral. However, review the course descriptions and faculty carefully. Do you want an entire course in sexuality or gender studies? What about one in feminist pedagogies? Is the program limited to one department with a few faculty teaching courses in it? Or is it interdisciplinary? Some of the strongest programs draw on courses in women's history from the history department, in women and religion from the religion department, and so on. Others are strong because all faculty are experts in women's and gender studies (although this is also interdisciplinary). Some college faculty will not allow you to express or retain beliefs that run contrary to theirs on certain issues. Make sure your beliefs line up before you even consider applying to a program if it's one of those taught by a few professors in a women's and gender studies program that stands alone and is not interdisciplinary. An interdisciplinary program spreads out who is involved and how. It is a very different experience than a program taught by a few faculty with doctorates in women's and gender studies. It might be that you need to focus on women's studies by piecing courses together at a Christian institution instead of enrolling in a program at a secular institution. There are many courses in women's history, women's rhetoric, women and religion, women and politics, and so on that are taught at Christian institutions as well as secular. There are Christian universities that offer majors in women and religion or in women's studies if you want to earn a degree at one of those institutions. It is worth considering all options.

If you are going to apply for a master's or a doctoral program, you need to know who the professors are before you even start filling out the application. To get to know what a faculty member truly thinks and believes and what beliefs will be supported within a program—since many programs are not transparent about these things—read what he or she has written. Read that person's latest journal article, latest book, or latest blog. Just having a conversation is not good enough. People represent themselves wonderfully in informal situations but not so wonderfully if they feel your views threaten a dearly held belief. So make yourself as completely and as fully aware of who the faculty members are before signing up for a course or applying for a program. You are checking to see if you fit. If you don't, keep looking. And keep this in mind: You wouldn't vote for a political candidate who does not represent what you believe, would you? If you are a Christian, you wouldn't attend a church that supports beliefs contrary to your own, would you? The university is very much like these other institutions. So be careful. To clarify, it is perfectly okay to take courses from those who hold different beliefs. I did, and I flourished. However, some faculty will not allow you to retain certain beliefs about marriage, sexuality, gender, and family, so know these things before you go into a program. Again, when considering a program for the master's level and above, it is vitally important to know who is teaching. Can you contact alumni to get their opinions about the program and its faculty? Who have they helped and in what way? In my doctoral program at the University of Arizona, I carefully researched the faculty and made a visit to the campus to meet them. I had my ups and downs, but I was able to do the work I wanted to do. The courses there were perfect for what I wanted to do with my career in teaching at the college level. I took courses in writing program administration, histories of rhetoric, pedagogy, visual rhetoric, and service learning. These courses are no longer part of the curriculum at the University of Arizona, but they were perfect for what I wanted to do at the time I was part of the program. My professors were supportive and they were leaders in the field. Students warned me away from some professors and advocated for others. Overall, I chose wisely.

When researching a department and its faculty, take the temperature. Don't be fooled. Not every faculty member likes all of the other faculty members. So do they still treat each other and the students professionally? Can they overlook petty disputes to work for students? Again, what do the alumni say?

Also, keep in mind that every semester spent in a doctoral program beyond the five years allotted is often at the student's own expense. More than that, instead of earning money as a new assistant professor, you have to live on the meager earnings of a graduate assistant another year. You lose another year of credit towards a pension, another year of knowing where you will live, and another year stuck in the same place instead of getting started on a new life elsewhere. You lose another year of excellent medical benefits and a year that could count toward your tenure. The stress of an unplanned year added to a doctoral program is something to strongly consider. So if the alumni tell you a particular professor cost them an additional year in the program, see if that story is repeated and be aware.

One final bit of advice for this section is that if you are entering a doctoral program and you hope to be a professor yourself, the faculty will be the ones writing letters on your behalf. Your job interview begins on day one of your doctoral program. Don't ever forget that. And don't forget that once you earn the degree you want, if you start applying for jobs as an assistant professor, you need to do a whole new type of research.

So what happens when you complete a doctoral degree and look for a job? I spent five years as an assistant professor of English at Longwood University in Farmville, Virginia. My husband was laid off due to cuts in defense spending, and we came back to Arizona a few years ago. I've been teaching full-time at the local community college since then. However, let me take you back to the year I was searching for a job and completing a dissertation—then defending it in an oral exam and revising it—raising a three-year-old and an eleven-year-old, trying to keep my marriage going, attempting to keep a house (somewhat) clean and stocked with food, and doing all of these things while living on peanuts. I was tired. I was stressed. I was busy from before dawn until the end of the day and often in the middle of the night. If you are a parent, you know. So I was not doing my homework as I should have been when looking for a full-time position. I did enjoy the years I spent as an assistant professor, but it came with a few lessons.

Here are a few things I learned the hard way.

You are going to live in a new town. Does it have the resources and activities you need and value? The nearest mall from Farmville took an hour to drive to. This is fine, except I grew up in Oklahoma City and then spent five years in Tucson. I was used to having a way to buy shoes, clothing, and other items without having to sacrifice an entire day getting there and back. Also, the medical care in Farmville was the worst I've ever experienced anywhere—even worse than the current small town where I reside. This is a problem when you have two kids and, of course, anytime an emergency arises. On the other hand, we could be on the beach in about three hours if we headed east. Busch Gardens was a couple hours away. If we went two or three hours north, we would be on the DC Mall with all of the amazing museums. A couple hours west were the mountains where my daughter went snowboarding with her high school all winter for about $50 a trip. Speaking of my daughter, she's in love with horses. She completed a bachelor's in equine science last year and is almost done with a master's in equestrian studies right now. In Farmville, there was no shortage of horses, as you can well imagine. We found the best trainer for her—she had a down-to-earth kind of wisdom and years of experience, and she was kind to everyone. Farmville itself had a yearly arts and crafts festival, outdoor movies on Main Street during the summer, a couple of wonderful parks, a brand new YMCA and pool, and some really beautiful scenery.

If you have kids or if you plan to, what are the schools like? I relied on the realtor's glowing recommendation. Imagine my surprise when I learned the middle school my daughter would be attending wasn't even accredited at the time. I was told by some to consider sending my children to the local private school. It was $14,000 a year in tuition. After paying tuition for two kids, my salary would be cut to less than half. Tuition, as you know, comes out after taxes. Needless to say I did not have a spare $28,000 a year; my kids would not be going to private school. The public schools provided some challenges for both. However, they both found a place in the schools after a rocky start. It all worked out. It wasn't great, but we survived a mix of racial tensions (Farmville chose to close its schools for five years in the '50s rather than desegregate), a few mediocre teachers, an abundance of school fights which required a full-time security officer to be on duty at all times at the high school, and all of the other stuff that goes with public schooling.

Are you going to rent or buy? If I had done even one minute of research on the housing in Farmville, I would have learned there were houses sitting on the market for years. Not months. *Years.* After a year or two, my husband and I wanted to move closer to his job because the commute was terrible. But since we couldn't sell, we couldn't move. Worse, when we were forced to leave Farmville five years later after he was laid off from his job, we still couldn't sell. The house went into a deed in lieu of foreclosure after a year sitting on the market. We lost all of our investment in it. We were denied a new mortgage for several years. On the other hand, we had the best neighbors we have ever had. We celebrated a potluck Thanksgiving and the Fourth of July together, and Jerry and I hosted our own "big dork" New Year's Eve party where we played board games and had a potluck meal, and everyone just walked home when they got tired. No need to wait for midnight. Boy, do we miss the community we had there!

Where will you go to church? The church I picked was chosen because it was an Assemblies of God congregation. I had no idea the townspeople were determined to ostracize the university people. I spent three years in that church. I made every effort and sometimes embarrassed myself reaching out. I never made a single friend. After that, I moved on to Calvary Chapel. It was a good move for me, but I should have done my homework long before then. Yet Calvary Chapel was the best church I ever attended. The people there treated me like family and stayed in touch long after I left.

Okay, so that's real-life stuff. Of course, you will research the university and its program before you apply. You will reference them in your cover letter. You'll clearly demonstrate you are applying specifically to that university and want to contribute to that specific department. You will talk to everyone you know to get advice on the program and its people. It really is a small world. People know people. Listen to others when you are warned away from a particular place. It may save you some heartache.

What other advice do I have for you? Well, think about these things:

Is everyone on the hiring committee tenured? How many people in the department are there and how many are tenured? If you look at old catalogs, they sometimes list the faculty. What's the turnover like? Are there always new faculty every year? Why? This is important because it says a lot about an institution when the tenure-track faculty don't stay. Is it growing? Are people retiring? Or do people come, stay a year, and go? People don't take a job at a university and then move on for no reason. Sure, the reasons might be complicated. But if there is a lot of turnover, there are probably a lot of problems. Also, if people aren't tenured there's a problem. Maybe it's because of departmental politics. No one on my hiring committee was tenured. The head of the hiring committee—the only other professional in my field with a degree in rhetoric and composition—left the year I started. While I didn't know her well enough to state the reasons she moved on, I can say that turnover was a huge problem. When you are looking for a job, you are looking for a group that has people who have been there for many years. A few new faces are fine. However, you want to see that people are staying because that means they are being paid fairly and are being treated well by the institution and in the department. If you don't see that, my advice is to keep looking.

Who will you be working with? Since these are the people who will decide if *you* get tenure, you need to know. Just as you read the work of your professors when considering a master's or doctoral program, read the work of your potential future colleagues. Granted there will be at least one person in your new department who will give you advice once you are hired. But do your best before that time. You can do all you can to get to know the people in advance, but once you get into a department, remember you now have another, five-year-long interview that starts on day one. What fun. So watch what you say and how you say it. Make every effort to keep the criticism (of the department, a colleague giving you trouble, the institution, your pay/benefits, etc.) to yourself and to be kind to everyone. One other note: When you go on the campus visit, you will most likely have lunch and dinner with faculty. Take note of who shows up. It is more important to know who didn't. You can sometimes figure out who is the department's bad apple that way.

Do they offer access to the faculty handbook? If not, ask for a copy. What are the tenure requirements? Whatever they are, take them seriously, even if they seem simple to achieve. If they are easy to achieve and only a few people are tenured, then ask why people keep leaving. You should probably not ask that question directly, but see if you can find out by using other channels, such as members of your dissertation committee who might know some of the faculty or even know people from your field who worked there and then left.

What will the working conditions be like? At Longwood, we taught four courses in the fall and four in the spring. We had the lowest pay in the region according to the salary studies the faculty kept doing in hopes that things might change, but we were not allowed to take on teaching online for extra income. As a mother of two, I wanted to drop my children off at school, so I requested that I not teach classes at 8 a.m. Being a parent of young kids is a temporary privilege. I wasn't asking for a lifelong accommodation, but there was some tension between those who had kids and those who didn't anytime these things came up. Thankfully, despite some vocal whiners, they worked around my schedule and approved days off so I could do field trips and other special events with my kids.

What will your retirement look like? You may have thirty years to go, but planning from day one is important, especially if your salary is low. The state contributed 5 percent of my salary into a pension plan until the recession in 2008 or 2009. They then decided I would contribute the 5 percent and they would contribute nothing. So after taxes, I got a pay cut. But I also needed to open an account with TIAA Cref since the pension would be small. This is what happens when the pay is small and your contributions are small. So I put small amounts into that account as well. When I left Longwood after five years, I had about $12,000 in my pension fund. Longwood did not match it. At my current institution, I am well paid. I will have a great pension when I retire, and my institution matches my contributions, which are in the neighborhood of 11 percent. I had more in my pension in a short time here than I did in five years working for Longwood. My TIAA Cref account is now well funded. No, I'm not ready to retire now, but one day this will matter immensely. Make sure it matters to you before you take a job somewhere. Gets lots of advice for retirement planning. Hire a professional if you can. Make a good plan to ensure a strong future for yourself.

Maybe this should have been the first question, but what are the students like? Are they there to learn? Is respectful communication between students and faculty the norm? How are student complaints handled? Someone somewhere will complain about you for some reason. Don't think that just because you've been teaching a couple of years with no problems you are magically immune. So find out what happens. Talk to faculty when you go on the campus visit. Ask a direct question of the chair during your interview alone with him or her. Also, are the students open to working with faculty on presentations, publications, and internships? What is the culture? For example, at Longwood the students either lived on campus or close by in town in apartments owned by the university. The students were heavily involved in every event, so getting student participation was never an issue. The issue was how to handle everyone who showed up because you wanted to be prepared! At Cochise College, there are no dorms on the Sierra Vista campus. Many of our students experience deep poverty and many stresses. Some are just out of prison. Some have kids they are trying to support on a job at the local grocery store. Some have learning disabilities that have prevented them from being admitted to a university. Some have been out of school for a decade or more. Students from the local high schools have varying levels of literacy and our developmental reading and English courses are full. We systematically embed reading instruction in all courses. As a Hispanic Serving Institution, some have problems, since English is a second language. The opportunities here to work with students are quite different. They are desperate for a better life, not for a better social event. At both institutions, the students were wonderful, but their needs are vastly different. So what is important to you? The rescue missions I perform with the community college students? Or would you rather work with students who have all the basics and want to focus on other things, like presentations and scholarships? Both types of students make for a fulfilling career, but you need to know what to expect before you accept a position somewhere.

When you do a campus visit, have questions to ask. You want to interview the people you'll be working with just as much as they want to interview you. If you are on a campus visit, you are probably one of their top three choices. You made it past the interview; now they want to see you in the environment. Don't be afraid to ask about things such as the following: How long does it take to get a new course approved? What are the goals of this department? How do you see me using my work to improve things here or what do you hope I will contribute to this department? For me, I would also check out the library and ask about certain databases I like to use. I have no access to some through the community college, so I have to rely on the University of Arizona to get to materials I need. If you are a professor, you will most likely be doing research. So ask the questions you need to ask.

To conclude, this book was a pleasure to write, and I sincerely hope it is a useful tool for you. I hope you use it as a starting place for more research. Every theory in the appendix has a plethora of texts you can read to start really engaging with just about any aspect of feminism you choose to study more deeply. I hope I have inspired you to want to know more or to at least reflect on the way feminist ideas have revealed something interesting about our culture and about your life. Consider using this book as a starting place for making your own list of readings or adding key events to a timeline for yourself. You can add the theories I did not include or add quotes from feminists who have defined each theory to shine light on its ideologies as well as contradictions and places of overlap between theories. I hope you write on every page of this book, adding questions, responses, summaries, connections, and anything you had to look up—definitions, references to people/places/events, references to philosophies or theories, and so on. Finally, I hope you write about why you are or are not a feminist. Define that term, reflect on it, quote from those you've read, and challenge the rest of us to think harder about this. The battles for equality have changed and will continue to evolve, and we must work together to find a better future.

Ultimately, as Christians our most important calling is to follow Christ. I think this verse sums things up perfectly: "Righteousness will go before Him, / And shall make His footsteps our pathway" (Psalm 85:13 NKJV). In all things you do, think, or believe, submit them to the guidance of the Holy Spirit. As Christians, listen the voice of our heavenly Father. There is no question beyond his reach and no conundrum beyond his wisdom; truth is found in the living entity of Christ. While so much of contemporary academic scholarship attempts to drive us away from the teachings of the Bible, the darkness is never darkness to him: "In Your light we see light" (Ps 36:9 NKJV).

# Appendix A

### THE WAVES OF FEMINIST HISTORY

The first wave of feminism includes the seventeenth to nineteenth centuries with roots in earlier times that stretch back to the Old Testament.

The second wave was roughly around the 1960s and '70s.

The third wave started sometime in the 1980s or '90s and went into the early twenty-first century.

Some say we are now in the postfeminist wave; others say we are in the fourth wave. The fourth wave is said to have begun in 2012.[1]

The main concerns of first-wave feminism were as follows:

Women were not allowed to speak in public.

Women were not allowed to speak in public, much less to "mixed" audiences of men and women. Women who violated this social more were referred to as "promiscuous" and often faced physical abuse by individuals or by a crowd. There is a plethora of historical documentation to support this assertion.

A woman had no legal existence.

Coverture laws meant that once a woman became a wife, she became a dependent. According to the Harvard Business School website, coverture laws

---

1. "History of Feminism."

"stipulated that a married woman did not have a separate legal existence from her husband."

### A woman was property, not a person.

A woman did not have a right to her own earnings if she found a way to earn money. "A married woman or *feme covert* was a dependent, like an underage child or slave, and could not own property in her own name or control her own earnings, except under very specific circumstances."[2]

### A mother had no right to her children.

A woman's right to her own children was not entrusted to her. "When a husband died, his wife could not be the guardian to their under-age children."[3] Divorce often did not give women custody, even in cases of abuse and alcoholism.

### Women had limited rights.

On the other hand, "widows did have the right of 'dower,' a right to property they brought into the marriage as well as to life usage of one-third of their husband's estate," and "though a married woman was not able to sue or sign contracts on her own, her husband often did have to obtain her consent before he sold any property his wife inherited."[4]

### Women had no access to an equal education or to equal opportunities (except in rare cases).

At this time, a woman's highest calling was to be a wife. Imagine removing all possibility of a career and only getting access to the lowest levels of education or only to ornamental courses (painting, needlework, music, etc.). So once married, you had achieved all you could achieve. A woman did not have the right to obtain an education equal to that offered to men. It would not be until after the Civil War that universities began opening to women more and more.

2. "Women and the Law."
3. "Women and the Law."
4. "Women and the Law."

### Women had no access to decent work opportunities.

The only work available to unmarried, divorced, or widowed women required them to perform manual labor (cleaning, laundry, etc.) for little money, forcing them into poverty along with their children—that is, if they retained custody of them.

### Women had no right to vote or to have political representation.

Most associate first-wave feminism with a concern for the right to vote, which is known as suffragism. Indeed, this was a major concern. If you don't have a vote, you don't matter to politicians vying for power. It was like that then; it is like that now.

### By the end of the nineteenth century, women in America had rights to the following:

- Have legal representation. Many coverture laws were abolished.
- Speak in public to "mixed" audiences.
- Obtain an education equal to that offered to men.
- Vote in some states. The federal right to vote came in 1920.
- Publish texts under their own names without feeling they must use pseudonyms.
- For African American women, have freedom from slavery.

Second-wave feminism, which occurred roughly in the 1960s and '70s, focused on different things. Echoing Seneca Falls, the National Organization of Women (NOW) wrote a Bill of Rights in 1967 which included demands to do the following:[5]

1. Pass the Equal Rights Amendment.
2. Give women equal employment opportunities.
3. Protect women's jobs after childbirth.
4. Let working parents deduct childcare expenses from their taxes.
5. Establish public childcare facilities.

---

5. Tong and Botts, *Feminist Thought*, 23–24.

6. Give women the right to obtain an equal education.
7. Reform welfare programs to help women who needed job training, housing, and family allowances.
8. Stop limiting women's contraceptive choices.

In addition, the goals of second-wave feminists were as follows:

1. Sought to add women to history within the university by forming their own journals, conferences, and eventually, academic programs. This concerns in the work of third-wave and, if you choose to use the term, fourth-wave feminists. The pursuit of recovering the histories and contributions of women continues. Also, for about the last decade or so, you can earn a master's or a doctorate in women's studies.
2. Criticized a sexist, patriarchal mindset and sought to challenge it within whatever context it existed.
3. Opened the doors to divergent views on sexuality, reproduction, and women's roles. Some promoted incest and embracing lesbianism to avoid men. Some embraced pornography and prostitution; others did not. Some valued a woman's ability to bear children; others wished for an alternative. Some considered gender to be "fluid."
4. Fought for equality in the workplace.
5. Wanted their jobs protected while on maternity leave. This echoes the goals of NOW.
6. Wanted access to birth control. Abortion was legalized in 1973.
7. Wanted to pass the Equal Rights Amendment but ended up with the Civil Rights Act and Title VII instead.
8. Wanted to redefine the gender category "woman" and to abolish the category in favor of women's freedom to define themselves as they chose.
9. Wanted to redefine God to fit their new emphasis on equality. This means many things. For some it meant creating a whole new god complete with a female counterpart. For others, it meant getting rid of anything that disrupted their politics. For others, it meant a new interpretation of Scripture. For yet others, it meant contextualizing Scripture so that the requirement voiced by Paul for women to learn in silence became time-bound. They also wanted to restructure Christian thought and practice. This was continued from first-wave feminists who, intentionally or not, did something similar—although not in the

language of the university, as the highly educated second-wave feminists did.
10. Sought political representation, such as through Kennedy's Commission on Women. They formed political groups—in particular, the National Organization of Women (NOW).

Second-wave feminists also realized that feminism had largely been focused on the needs of white, middle-class women. A bridge into third-wave feminism was the Combahee River Collective statement published in 1977. Third-wave feminists added a focus on race, class, and sexuality. Three important things came up in this statement:

1. A critique of capitalism because it is "patriarchal."
2. A critique of feminists (like Betty Friedan) who have ignored the goals of women who are not white, middle class, and educated.
3. A realization that oppression comes from many different angles (which goes with the theory of intersectionality, defined best in 1989 by Crenshaw).[6]

Issues addressed in second- and third-wave feminism include the following:

## Sexist structures in the workplace.

Women who were sexually harassed had little or no recourse. Pay for the same job was lower for women than it was for men. There was prejudice against women with children or who were of childbearing age since they would need time off work.

## Internal struggles to be the ideal woman who stays home to raise kids versus a desire to obtain an education or to work outside the home.

Women faced pressure to measure success by how well they took care of their husbands and families. Societal pressure included forcing women to choose between a family and a career.

---

6. "Women and the Law."

The absence of women from history, academic journals, and academic conferences.

While women could participate in all of these academic pursuits, they were expected to study men in history, not women. The academic journals and conferences focused on men's histories, not women's.

The emergence of women claiming a sexual orientation that did not fit in with heteronormative society.

Women faced additional pressures to conform to the ideals articulated by American society in the 1940s and 1950s. Second-wave feminists were concerned with sexual freedom and third-wave feminists were concerned with gender identity and how sexuality is shaped by society.

The idea that one's biology determines one's destiny.[7]

With gender understood as a "social construction," the possibilities for women are greater if one does not limit the possibilities for personhood because of biology.

The lack of civil rights.

By treating women as members of one group, they drew on the language of the civil rights movement to fight for change. This was evident in the abolitionist struggles of the nineteenth century and in the fight against racism in the twentieth century. More recently, civil rights for the LGBTQIA are of concern.

The lack of access to contraceptives.

For some minority groups, women faced sterilization in an attempt to "help" them. For others, religious belief barred them from using contraceptives. This resulted in families with more kids than they could financially support.

---

7. "Radical Feminism.".

### Recognition of overlapping, intertwined contexts that created struggles for women, particularly women who were not white or middle class.

Kimberlé Crenshaw's articulation of intersectionality provided a way to talk about these issues. Part of this is a rejection of the broad category of woman.

### Recognition of the role standpoint theory plays in understanding the struggles within a particular context.

Patricia Hill Collins helps define how a person from inside a particular community understands and experiences struggles in a way that one from outside cannot understand.

### Seeing sexism within museums, textbooks, scholarship, visual media, and other contexts.

Third-wave feminists helped point out discrepancies between standards for women and men.

### Divergent theories and a lack of unity.

A plethora of often-contradictory theories has characterized feminism and made it difficult to work as a group toward a common goal.

### Technology and its relationship to women.

Moving into an understanding of how technology has affected women and their identities and what that means in terms of new types of challenges is another aspect of third-wave feminism. What role does technology play in the subordination of different women? In the liberation of these women?

### A recognition that women from different counties face different forms of oppression.

Transnational feminism emerged in the third wave but seems to have gained a lot of attention in the twenty-first century. Feminists concerned with a particular problem in a particular context bond together to solve that problem and then move on. Transnational feminism is not defined by divergent theories as second- and third-wave feminism are, but it is defined by divergent actions in response to problems.

### Increasing participation in government.

Women have gained political power by the vote, but also by holding positions in government at state and federal levels.

### A recognition of abuse.

Women have seen the relationship between sex and abuse throughout history, but in the twentieth century and most certainly in the twenty-first century, discussions have been frank and clear. In religious contexts, abuse is sometimes sanctioned in the name of "submission" in marriage, and women become limited in their ability to escape physical, sexual, emotional, or psychological abuse. Women outside of the U.S. may suffer socially or culturally sanctioned abuse. For example, one of the most well-known forms of abuse is that of African women whose genitalia are mutilated as a means of controlling them.

### A belief in embracing pornography, prostitution as an acceptable profession, and sexual freedom in all its forms.[8]

Some groups of second-wave feminists found freedom in these concepts. In the twenty-first century, the realities of sex trafficking have turned most away from a romanticized notion that prostitution is an acceptable profession. The "slut walk" has encouraged women to dress as provocatively as they wish (and was formed in response to "victim blaming"), and the realms of sexual freedom have widened to include all forms of sexuality outside of pedophilia and bestiality. Protests against "blaming the victim" are part of a rhetorical strategy used to defend a woman's right to dress provocatively, and celebrities have been publicly shamed for suggesting otherwise.

---

8. Tong and Botts, *Feminist Thought*, 51; 268.

Freedom from religion.

Many twenty- and twenty-first-century feminists have turned away from religion, believing it perpetuates a patriarchal system. However, feminist theologians are helping to make the connections between liberation and feminism clear, especially in the twenty-first century.

Feminist theologians point out the Bible cannot be read or applied without criticism.

Methods for understanding and interpreting the Bible have been used to argue for freedom and equality within Christianity.

For feminist theologians, the idea of submission does not equate to subordination.

Citing physical, sexual, and emotional abuse within the home, feminist theologians have problematized the concept of submission so that it is no longer a cover for abuse within the home or church.

## CURRENT ISSUES IN FOURTH-WAVE OR POSTFEMINISM

Continued discrimination in the workplace, particularly in terms of unequal wages, is a key concern.

While many pin this on various factors, on the whole, women still earn less than men.

Sexual harassment and the refusal to acknowledge it remains a problem.

The #MeToo Movement was born out of finally winning some battles in this area. Rape and other types of harassment were made public and several prominent men were brought to justice.

### Political activism is used as a tool for change.

The 2017 Women's March in DC and various cities, the Black Lives Matter Movement, the MeToo Movement—all are part of many U.S.-based political groups or activities. The celebration of women, such as in LadyFests, creates a chance for women to celebrate political views, art, and solidarity. Activism is also focused on international contexts, which goes along with the ideas of transnational feminism.

### The media is used to construct desired ideals in a society.

This is both a problem and a solution. While images of women continue to be part of the oppression of women, the media is used to portray women in desired ways. Film, music, TV, news shows, TED Talks, live theater, art, websites, and many other mediums are used to offer female characters or showcase successful women who match the ideal characteristics of feminists: education, intelligence, strength, shrewdness, bravery, and so on. These mediums are also used to portray relationships that are not heteronormative.

### An enduring concern for the environment.

As an outgrowth of second and third-wave feminism, feminists in the twenty-first century are still very much concerned about the environment. Ecofeminism captures these views, but the views are not contained within that ideology.

### Capitalism is the enemy.

Lindsey German explains the main tenets of twenty-first-century feminism:

1. Capitalism is a form of oppression.
2. Women's oppression is a product of a class society.
3. Women are exploited at work and have the "double burden of family and childcare."
4. Instead of leaving behind traditional family roles, now they are expected to do work and take care of the home.
5. The "glass ceiling" is there for privileged women to break, but the majority of women cannot.

6. Working-class women do not profit from a capitalist system the way middle- and upper-class women do.
7. Women are still sex objects in many contexts.
8. Objectification leads to abuse.
9. Controlling your body allows control over your life.
10. Capitalism requires some members to sacrifice family time to achieve success.
11. Genuine liberation comes with socialism.
12. We have to fight for our beliefs.[9]

## Publication is a means of communication, but so is social media.

Women can choose how and where to share their views in countless academic and non-academic forums.

## Participating in a variety of marches and other events that highlight women's issues are ways to create some solidarity.

All kinds of opportunities in the United States and internationally exist for women to come together for marches, concerts, or other events. For example, the London Feminist Film Festival is focused on films related to feminist themes. In the UK, the Women's Equality Party formed in 2015.

---

9. German, "21st Century Feminism."

# Appendix B

*Selected Key Terms*

### ANDROCENTRISM

"Male centeredness, which is the value set of our dominant culture based on male norms."[1]

### BODY POLITICS

Refers to the struggle against violence and to politics surrounding a woman's body.[2]

### COLONIALISM

According to the *Stanford Encyclopedia of Philosophy*, "colonialism is a practice of domination, which involves the subjugation of one people to another." Additionally, "the practice of colonialism usually involved the transfer of population to a new territory, where the arrivals lived as permanent settlers while maintaining political allegiance to their country of origin." Postcolonial theory, defined by Edward Said, who drew on Michel Foucault, focuses on the "relationship between knowledge and power." Controlling knowledge can constitute part of domination, such as of a culture or a group of people.[3]

---

1. Humm, *Dictionary of Feminist Theory*, 9.
2. Humm, *Dictionary of Feminist Theory*, 27.
3. "Colonialism."

Decolonial theory is much the same as Postcolonial theory except it focuses on Latin Americans and their experiences. It focuses on how to "recover" and articulate Latin Americans' own knowledge in their own terms, taking this away from the control of a colonizing power.[4]

## CONSCIENTIZATION

A term borrowed from Paulo Friere which originally referred to how students learn but which feminists use to describe awareness they are discriminated against.[5]

## DUALISM

Anything that is "institutionalized in patriarchy," such as "culture and nature" or "public and private," is rejected by feminists who long for more "integrated relationships."[6]

## ESSENTIALISM

"The theory that any entity such as an individual, group, object, or concept has innate and universal qualities."[7] This directly challenges those who believe reality is socially constructed and that men and women, for example, are not biologically determined to have certain abilities or certain predispositions. It's reductive and limits one's agency.

## HIDDEN CURRICULUM

The idea that social and cultural constructs underlie traditional education.[8]

## INTERSECTIONALITY

"Black legal scholar Kimberlé Crenshaw coined the term 'intersectionality' in her insightful 1989 essay, 'Demarginalizing the Intersection of Race and

 4. "Post-colonial Theory."
 5. Humm, *Dictionary of Feminist Theory*, 45.
 6. Humm, *Dictionary of Feminist Theory*, 71.
 7. "Essentialism."
 8. Humm, *Dictionary of Feminist Theory*, 121.

Sex: A Black Feminist Critique of Antidiscrimination Doctrine, Feminist Theory and Antiracist Politics."[9]

> The term intersectionality was coined by civil rights activist and professor Kimberlé Crenshaw and can be defined as "the interconnected nature of social categorizations such as race, class, and gender as they apply to a given individual or group, regarded as creating overlapping and interdependent systems of discrimination or disadvantage." By adding the idea of intersectionality to feminism, the movement becomes truly inclusive, and allows women of all races, economic standings, religions, identities and orientations for their voices to be heard.[10]

## KYRIARCHY

"The term kyriarchy was coined by Elisabeth Schussler Fiorenza in her 2001 book, *Wisdom Ways: Introducing Feminist Biblical Interpretation*. In the glossary, she defines kyriarchy as: 'a neologism . . . derived from the Greek words for "lord" or "master" (*kyrios*) and "to rule or dominate" (*archein*) which seeks to redefine the analytic category of patriarchy in terms of multiplicative intersecting structures of domination . . . Kyriarchy is best theorized as a complex pyramidal system of intersecting multiplicative social structures of superordination and subordination, of ruling and oppression.' In other words, the kyriarchy is the social system that keeps all intersecting oppressions in place."[11]

## MUJERISTA

Refers to theologians from Central and South American countries but who now live in the U.S.[12] According to the Oxford Encyclopedia of the Bible and Gender Studies, "Mujerista criticism is the practice of analyzing, interpreting, and evaluating biblical texts from the perspective of Latinas' religious faith and the role it plays in their daily life experiences, in lo cotidiano ('everyday life'). This critical approach, also known as mujerista biblical

---

9. Smith, "Black Feminism."
10. Hawk, "Intersectional Feminism."
11. Ferguson, "Kyriarchy 101."
12. Clifford, *Introducing Feminist Theology*, 26.

interpretation, is grounded in Latinas' struggle for survival and their conviction that reading the Bible must contribute to their liberation."[13]

## MUTED GROUP THEORY

> MGT originated within the discipline of anthropology. The husband and wife anthropological team of Edwin and Shirley Ardener coined the term "Muted Group Theory" in 1975. Edwin Ardener, seeking an explanation for why women's perspectives and voices were absent from anthropological studies, realized that women's voices are "often more 'inarticulate' than men, and thus pose special technical problems for the inquirer." He argued that women are at a disadvantage in expressing matters of concern unless their views are presented in a form acceptable to men or to "women brought up in the male idiom." Edwin adopted the term "muted" over the word "inarticulate" to counter some feminists' misunderstanding that he was referring to a biological condition."[14]

Shirley Ardener noticed women often ended up in a set of parentheses when referred to in a text. In 1981, Cheris Kramarae tied this to communication theory. There are three main tenets:

1. Dominant and sub-dominant groups experience life differently. Dominant groups control terms.
2. The sub-dominant group is less respected and their contributions less acceptable.
3. "Normalizing and centering all points of reference within the dominant experience, while the voices of non-dominant individuals and groups are minimized, stigmatized, or muted, can be described as cultural imperialism."[15]

---

13. Guardiola-Saenz, "Mujerista Criticism."
14. Barkman, "Muted Group Theory."
15. Barkman, "Muted Group Theory."

## PATRIARCHY

"A system of male authority which oppresses women through its social, political, and economic institutions."[16]

## SOCIAL CONSTRUCTIONISM

Reality is constructed through language and social interaction. "The social constructionist perspective contends that individuals and their differences are created or constructed through social processes (e.g., political, religious, and economic) rather than an innate quality within the individual. Furthermore, the categorization of individuals into groups explains more about how society functions than about individuals."[17]

## STANDPOINT THEORY

> A feminist theoretical perspective that argues that knowledge stems from social position. The perspective denies that traditional science is objective and suggests that research and theory have ignored and marginalized women and feminist ways of thinking. The theory emerged from the Marxist argument that people from an oppressed class have special access to knowledge that is not available to those from a privileged class. In the 1970s feminist writers inspired by that Marxist insight began to examine how inequalities between men and women influence knowledge production. Their work is related to epistemology, the branch of philosophy that examines the nature and origins of knowledge, and stresses that knowledge is always socially situated. In societies stratified by gender and other categories, such as race and class, one's social positions shape what one can know.[18]

Key theorists: Sandra Harding, Dorothy Smith, Patricia Hill Collins

## SUBALTERN

An inferior person. "In the twentieth and twenty-first centuries, under the influence of Marxism, nationalism, postcolonialist theory, and feminism,

---

16. Humm, *Dictionary of Feminist Theory*, 200.
17. "Social Constructionism."
18. Borland, "Standpoint Theory."

subaltern has come to be used broadly to represent subordination in social, political, religious, and economic hierarchies." Spivak theorized this in the context of the university.[19]

## THE "OTHER"

Simone de Beauvoir termed this in 1955 in *The Second Sex* to "explain how, in patriarchal culture, woman is set up as the negative, the inessential, the abnormal to the male."[20]

---

19. "Subaltern."
20. Humm, *Dictionary of Feminist Theory*, 197.

# Appendix C

*Selected feminist theories and brief explanations are provided below.*

### ABOLITIONIST FEMINISM

- In the nineteenth century, some believed that "women's oppression and emancipation" was "parallel" to that of "Black liberation from slavery."[1]

### ANARCHIST FEMINISM OR ANARCHA FEMINISM

- The term "anarchy" points to a rejection of an overarching government in favor of one that is "community based."[2]
- The family with the father as the head is also rejected. All power structures that convey authoritarianism are rejected, not just patriarchy.

### ASIAN AMERICAN FEMINISM

- Allies itself with "postcolonialist critiques of Western imperialism."[3]

1. Humm, *Dictionary of Feminist Theory*, 1.
2. "Basic Introduction."
3. Tong and Botts, *Feminist Thought*, 121.

- They are the "other" in American society—defined as "interstitial," or not white and not Black.[4] There was a shift where Asian Americans were defined as white in the US, changing their position in society. "The space between the social enactment of identity and its idealization reveals the structures that consolidate social power in its multiple manifestations."[5]

## BLACK AND WOMANIST FEMINISMS

- "Womanist" is defined by Alice Walker in a book she published in 1983 called *In Our Mother's Gardens*. She wrote that "womanist is to feminist as purple is to lavender." The term comes from "womanish" and celebrates a woman who loves other women, sexually or not; who "appreciates and prefers women's culture"; who wants to be a part of a community and not separate; and who is a "universalist" by believing we are all part of the human race, no matter our color.[6]
- The Combahee River Collective Statement of 1977 brought the exclusion of African American women and other minorities to the forefront.
- Drawing on Crenshaw's definition of intersectionality, Black feminists take it further. Patricia Hill Collins argues in "The Contours of an Afrocentric Feminist Epistemology" that "while a Black woman's standpoint and its accompanying epistemology stem from Black women's consciousness of race and gender oppression, they are not simply the result of combining Afrocentric and female values—standpoints are rooted in real material conditions structured by social class."[7]
- Pervasive problems with segregation, discrimination, poverty, education, housing, racism, and sexism, along with the characterization of Black women as laborers, form the central concerns of Black feminists.
- Black feminists formed organizations to centralize and to work together. In 1968,

    > Black women from the Student Non-Violent Coordinating Committee formed the Third World Women's Alliance. In 1973,

---

4. Tong and Botts, *Feminist Thought*, 122.
5. Tong and Botts, *Feminist Thought*, 123.
6. Tong and Botts, *Feminist Thought*, 123.
7. Collins, *Afrocentric Feminist Epistemology*.

a group of notable Black feminists, including Florynce Kennedy, Alice Walker, and Barbara Smith, formed the National Black Feminist Organization. In 1974, Barbara Smith joined with a group of other Black lesbian feminists to found the Boston-based Combahee River Collective as a self-consciously radical alternative to the NBFO. The Combahee River Collective was named to commemorate the successful Underground Railroad Combahee River Raid of 1863, planned and led by Harriet Tubman, which freed 750 slaves.[8]

- Concern with the sterilization of Black women, Latin American women, and Native American women that stemmed from Margaret Sanger's emphasis on eugenics—which resulted in campaigns to exterminate these races through sterilization—are a key component of these feminists' challenges. Some startling statistics: "In 1974, an Alabama court found that between 100,000 and 150,000 poor Black teenagers were sterilized each year in Alabama.... A 1970s study showed that 25 percent of Native American women had been sterilized, and that Black and Latina married women had been sterilized in much greater proportions than married women in the population at large. By 1968, one-third of women of childbearing age in Puerto Rico—still a US colony—had been permanently sterilized."[9]

- In the first wave of feminism, the focus was on the "deconstruction of stereotypical notions of womanhood."[10]

- Difference is a strength.

- "Oppression operates simultaneously along a variety of avenues."[11]

- White women are perceived as indifferent to the needs of Black women.

- According to Patricia Hill Collins, in the US African American women's oppression comes through three things: economics, politics, and "controlling" images.[12]

- According to Tong and Botts, epistemology, or the way we construct and validate knowledge, should be "concrete, subjective, and partial" as opposed to "abstract, objective, and impartial." Dialogue validates "knowledge claims." Knowledge is fluid and does not constitute the

8. Smith, "Black Feminism."
9. Smith, "Black Feminism."
10. Smith, "Black Feminism."
11. Tong and Botts, *Feminist Thought*, 111.
12. Patricia Hill Collins, quoted in Tong and Botts, *Feminist Thought*, 116.

norm for everyone. Each person's contribution to the community should be "cherished." A person is personally accountable for his or her own "knowledge claims."[13]

## CARE-FOCUSED FEMINISM

- These feminists ignore the long-standing view that "women have any particular essence"—or essential characteristics—and focus on valuing work in the home as opposed to work outside of it.[14]
- A focus on emotion, even a positive one as caretakers, aligns women with stereotypical roles.

## CHRISTIAN FEMINISM

- This consists of three main categories: "those that challenge the theological view of women and the androcentricity of traditional theology, those that challenge the theological laws that bar women from ordination," and "those that evaluate the church as an institution and aim to upgrade the professional status of women in the church."[15]

## CULTURAL OR "DIFFERENCE" FEMINISM

- They "rejected the notion that men and women are intrinsically the same and advocated celebrating the qualities they associated with women, such as their greater concern for affective relationships and their nurturing preoccupation with others. Inherent in its message was a critique of mainstream feminism's attempt to enter traditionally male spheres. This was seen as denigrating women's natural inclinations by attempting to make women more like men."[16]

---

13. Tong and Botts, *Feminist Thought*, 117.
14. "Radical Feminism."
15. Humm, *Dictionary of Feminist Theory*, 36–37.
16. "Second Wave of Feminism."

## DECOLONIAL FEMINISM

- By objecting to identity politics which reduce all women to one category, these feminists turned to "diversity feminism" and intersectionality.
- These feminists focus on the relationship between the "colonizer" and the "colonized." Because capitalist structures are used to exploit women, they critique them.
- These feminists take into account the "coloniality of gender," language, and "hybridity, multiplicity, and mestizaje."[17]

## ECOFEMINISM

- Emerging in 1974, feminism is united with concern for the earth, for the protection of children from abuse, and for the protection of animals.[18] It "argues that patriarchal oppression destroys Nature in the name of profit and progress."[19]

## EXISTENTIALIST FEMINISM

- "A philosophical theory which argues that individuals are free and responsible agents able to transcend their social roles and determine their own development."[20]

## I-FEMINISM

- Also known as individualist feminists, members of this group promote "'self-ownership,' which referred to the moral jurisdiction every human being has over his or her own body and over the products of his or her own labor. This approach not only embraced private property

---

17. "Radical Feminism."
18. "Feminism versus Feminisms."
19. Humm, *Dictionary of Feminist Theory*, 73.
20. Humm, *Dictionary of Feminist Theory*, 83.

and natural rights, but also involved the refusal to impose virtue, or social purity, on peaceful individuals."
- They seek to solve problems without help from the government.
- "Class" is not based on biology but on politics and economics, and is therefore fluid.[21]

## INDIGENOUS FEMINISM

- As the colonized, these feminists focus on issues of colonialism and have the desire to not be included in dominant society but to be valued as they are. They focus on creating alliances that "directly address differences." They want recognition that their ways of knowing are different and they emphasize "sovereignty."[22]

## LATIN AMERICAN/LATINA/CHICANA FEMINISM

- Focuses on a critique of inequality in the Chicano movement.[23] Archetypes must be rewritten.[24]
- Focuses on intersectionality, especially racism and homophobia.[25]
- Has a sense of alterity or "otherness."[26]
- Desire for freedom from colonists' thinking.

## LIBERAL FEMINISM

According to the *Stanford Encyclopedia of Philosophy*, liberal feminists are characterized by these beliefs:

- Freedom means "living a life of one's own choosing."

---

21. McElroy, "Individualist."
22. Tong and Botts, *Feminist Thought*, 125.
23. Tong and Botts, *Feminist Thought*, 118.
24. Tong and Botts, *Feminist Thought*, 119.
25. Tong and Botts, *Feminist Thought*, 119.
26. Tong and Botts, *Feminist Thought*, 120.

- Freedom means "political autonomy" or the ability to "co-author" the "conditions under which one lives."
- All women should be "free of violence and the threat of violence."
- All women should be "free of the limits set by patriarchal paternalistic and moralistic laws;" these include laws that prohibit women from taking certain jobs, laws against prostitution, laws against abortion, restrictions on pornography, and discrimination against non-heterosexual relationships.
- The "gender system," or the "patriarchal nature of inherited traditions and institutions," must be investigated so remedies can be sought.
- Women should not have to face discrimination based on stereotypes, poverty, race, ethnicity, culture, or sex—including at work, where it is often assumed that no one there has caretaking responsibilities.
- Women should not be exploited in relationships that require them to give more than they receive.
- "Martha Nussbaum proposes an account of the good life that has 'at its heart, a profoundly liberal idea . . . the idea of the citizen as a free and dignified human being, a maker of choices.'"
- Female children should be raised free of sexist stereotypes, educated to pursue careers and economic independence, and taught sex education.
- Women should be equally represented in politics and political power should be used to achieve feminist goals.
- Classical-liberal or libertarian feminists believe the state is what brings oppression and that laws should prevent "coercive interference" and even be made to favor women.
- Equity feminists seek equality for all in the laws of the state.
- Cultural libertarian feminists look at all institutions (education, church, state, etc.) and how they limit women.[27]
- Finally, in the *Introduction to Communication* course with Lumen Learning, liberal feminism is linked with NOW, or the National Organization of Women

---

27. "Liberal Feminism."

## MARXIST AND SOCIALIST FEMINISMS

- "Marxist feminists question how a capitalist system supports a division of labor that privileges men and devalues women."
- "Extending Marxist feminist thought, Socialist Feminists believe that women's unpaid labor in the home is one of the fundamental causes of sexism and oppression of women. Moreover, patriarchy, the system of sex oppression is connected with other forms of oppression, such as race and class."[28]

## POSTFEMINISM

- Goals for equality have already been achieved, so there is no longer a need for feminists.[29]

## POSTMODERN FEMINISM

- A break from a "single philosophy or explanation of culture."[30]
- Postmodernism is "a late 20th-century movement characterized by broad skepticism, subjectivism, or relativism; a general suspicion of reason; and an acute sensitivity to the role of ideology in asserting and maintaining political and economic power."[31]

## POSTSTRUCTURAL FEMINISM

- Poststructural feminism is heavily influenced by Cixous, Irigaray, and Kristeva and focuses on "how language and meaning-systems structure experience." These theorists are criticized for using one category

---

28. "Feminism versus Feminisms."
29. "Feminism versus Feminisms."
30. Humm, *Dictionary of Feminist Theory*, 215.
31. "Postmodernism" (*Britannica*).

of "woman": white and middle class. They heavily focus on language and semiotics.[32]

In "Poststructural Feminism in Education," Elizabeth Adams St. Pierre argues that poststructuralism is a response to humanism. The "themes" of humanism include the following:

1. Language is transparent.
2. The self is "stable" and "coherent."
3. Reason and philosophy can "provide an objective, reliable, and universal foundation of knowledge."
4. If reason is applied, the knowledge that results will be true.
5. Reason can overcome conflicts between "truth, knowledge, and power."
6. "Freedom consists of obedience to laws that conform to the necessary results of the right use of reason"[33]

Poststructuralism's response to the idea that words simply reflect the world around them without allowing for a plurality of meanings draws on semiotics to demonstrate that words do not have an intrinsic meaning but are often defined in relationship to other words in language. Meaning is arbitrary. Deconstructionism is part of this and separates the word from its single meaning to expose systems of hierarchy. Meanings shift.[34]

Discourse is not analyzed for its essential meanings. Rather, poststructuralism asks the following questions: How does discourse function? Where is it to be found? How does it get produced and regulated? What are its social effects? How does it exist?" These questions are used to explore the role of language in the establishment of power, control, knowledge, and institutions as well as its relationship to the state and the nature of intellectuals.[35]

Reason is affected by history and by the situation. Common sense is not an infallible truth-finding tool. "Reason is always situated, local, and specific, formed by values, passions, and desires."[36] Reason is not an objective tool. Feminists critique reason because women have been deemed irrational in some instances.

"Power, resistance, and freedom" are not equally distributed but can be fought for. Power is built out of relations between people and exercised from

---

32. "Radical Feminism."
33. St. Pierre, "Poststructural Feminism," 480.
34. St. Pierre, "Poststructural Feminism," 483–85.
35. St. Pierre, "Poststructural Feminism," 485.
36. St. Pierre, "Poststructural Feminism," 487.

multiple points in society. This means power can be reclaimed at a personal, institutional, or governmental level.[37]

Theorists such as Derrida, Foucault, Saussure, and Descartes, among others, are important for understanding this area of feminism, which is an investigation of power: who has it, how it is exercised, how it is created, and how it is maintained.

## POWER FEMINISM

- Emerged in the 1990s and encourages women not to be victims, but also engages in victim-blaming.[38]

## PSYCHOANALYTIC FEMINISM

- Psychoanalytic feminism is defined as the following:

  A theory of oppression, which asserts that men have an inherent psychological need to subjugate women. The root of men's compulsion to dominate women and women's minimal resistance to subjugation lies deep within the human psyche. This branch of feminism seeks to gain insight into how our psychic lives develop in order to better understand and change women's oppression. The pattern of oppression is also integrated into society, thus creating and sustaining patriarchy. Through the application of psychoanalytic techniques to studying differences between women and men as well as the ways in which gender is constructed, it is possible to reorganize socialization patterns at the early stages of human life. Societal change, or a 'cure,' can be developed through discovering the source of domination in men's psyche and subordination in women's, which largely resides unrecognized in individuals' unconscious.[39]

---

37. St. Pierre, "Poststructural Feminism," 490–91.
38. "Feminism versus Feminisms."
39. Wolff, "Psychoanalytic Feminism."

## RADICAL FEMINISM

- Focuses on oppression in a systematic way.
- "Consciousness raising," "rap groups," and the "personal is political" are associated with these feminists.[40]
- They see power as a system of "domination" and "subordination," closely tied to heterosexual sex.
- These women embrace intersectionality and the rejection of a "fixed gender identity."
- They investigate ways that "power and privilege continue to hold women back."[41]
- "In contrast to the pragmatic approach taken by liberal feminism, radical feminism aimed to reshape society and restructure its institutions, which they saw as inherently patriarchal. Providing the core theory for modern feminism, radicals argued that women's subservient role in society was too closely woven into the social fabric to be unraveled without a revolutionary revamping of society itself. They strove to supplant hierarchical and traditional power relationships they saw as reflecting a male bias, and they sought to develop nonhierarchical and antiauthoritarian approaches to politics and organization."[42]

## REVALORIST FEMINISM

- Revalorist feminists are "dedicated to uncovering women's history through writings, art, and traditional activities such as sewing. Once uncovered, they can be incorporated into educational curriculum, used as a basis for reevaluating existing theoretical and methodological perspectives, and receive a more positive or accepted place in society. Their approach is to move women's positions, ideas, and contributions from the margin to the center."[43]

---

40. "Feminism versus Feminisms."
41. "Radical Feminism."
42. "Second Wave of Feminism."
43. "Feminism Versus Feminisms."

## SEPARATIST

- These feminists believe the system can't be fixed, so they advocate for "woman-centered communities." Lesbian separatist feminists advocate for choosing lesbianism to remain separate from men.[44]

## SEX-POSITIVE FEMINISM

- Ideas about sex are socially constructed. Queer and alternative sexualities should be addressed positively.[45]

## SPIRITUAL FEMINISM

- Also known as myth feminism, it embraces the spiritual nature of women, Native American spirituality, Wicca or witchcraft, and the "goddess within."[46]

## THIRD-WAVE AND QUEER FEMINISM

- Lesbian feminists fight for equal rights in marriage and adoption, in the workplace, and in areas of health.[47]
- Terms like "homonormativity" (the normalization of homosexual relationships), "homonationalism" (the identification of certain groups as homophobic), and "identity politics" (which focus on how members of a group can coalesce around common goals) are tied to queer feminism.[48]

---

44. "Feminism Versus Feminisms."
45. "Third Wave."
46. Humm, *Dictionary of Feminist Theory*, 274-5.
47. "Third Wave."
48. "Third Wave."

## THIRD-WORLD FEMINISM

- "Western feminist discourses classify 'third world women' as 'powerless,' 'exploited,' 'backward,' 'illiterate,' and 'sexually harassed,' which is problematic because they are considering 'third world women' as a homogenous and unitary group having similar interests, oppressions, histories and struggles."[49]
- "Intersectionality; gender relations considering colonization, race, ethnicity, class, and localization and contextualization of the concepts like 'reproduction, marriage, family, patriarchy, sexual division of labor' are the major tenets of third world feminist theories."

## TRANSNATIONAL FEMINISM

- "Transnational feminists examine issues from a global perspective while considering how they intersect with our lived experiences in the United States." They "focus on intersections across nationality (including race and ethnicity), sex, gender, and class within the context of modern day imperialism and colonialism." Their focus is on how the domination and subjugation of Black and Brown people means a "loss of culture, language, and heritage" as opposed to a focus on how to circumvent "gender roles" to escape oppression. Liberation comes from within a community or nation; it is not "bestowed" by those in power.[50]
- "Transnational feminism is a body of theory and activism that highlights the connections between sexism, racism, classism, and imperialism."[51]

## TRANSFEMINISM/TRANS FEMINISM

- These feminists focus on transgender perspectives on feminism and embrace "sex-positive feminism, postmodern/poststructuralist feminism, queer theory and intersectionality."

---

49. "Main Tenets."
50. Valoy, "Transnational Feminism."
51. Valoy, "Transnational Feminism."

- This group also points out the challenges associated with the following perspectives: "heterosexism (where heterosexuals are viewed as more legitimate than homosexuals), monosexism (where people who are exclusively attracted to members of a single sex are viewed as more legitimate than bisexuals/pansexuals), masculine-centrism (where masculine gender expression is viewed as more legitimate than feminine gender expression)."[52]
- Instead of focusing on patriarchy as the oppressor, they focus on a gender binary as the oppressor.
- Terms like "cissexual," "cisgender," and "cis privilege" are associated with this movement. "Cis" means the same, so for those who identify as the sex they were born with, these terms address the privileges exercised by those who follow the norm.[53]

## WOMEN OF COLOR FEMINISMS IN THE UNITED STATES

- The emphasis is not on gender, but on "multiple and interlocking systems of oppression" such as race, homophobia, and class oppression. Crenshaw's term "intersectionality" is a unifying focus.[54]
- African American women in the 1970s and '80s felt they had more in common with third-world women than with white American women.
- Concerns include "universal health care, school desegregation," and "police brutality."[55]
- The term "women of color" is problematic. It implies that white women are the norm and those of other races can be lumped into one category.

---

52. Serano, "Trans Feminism."
53. Serano, "Trans Feminism."
54. Tong and Botts, *Feminist Thought*, 107.
55. Tong and Botts, *Feminist Thought*, 108.

## MEN'S MOVEMENTS

### Pro-Feminist Men

- "The ability to express emotions, to seek nurturing relationships, and to fight against cultural sexism are all concerns of Pro-Feminist Men. The organization NOMAS (National Organization for Men Against Sexism) represents this group of men."[56]

### Promise Keepers

- A Christian group that encourages men to be "servant leaders" in the home.[57]

---

56. "Feminism Versus Feminisms."
57. "Feminism Versus Feminisms."

# Appendix D

## SELECTED TEXTS BY FEMINISTS

What follows is a list of selected feminists from each wave. Those who identify as Christian are italicized. Those who are not italicized either do not identify as Christian, or I was unable to tell from their biographies whether they are Christian.

Left off the list are novelists, poets, magazine writers and editors, artists, and most of the women preachers. Not every text written from a feminist perspective is something that qualifies as a "theory" (which is usually backed by a scholar who holds a doctoral degree). However, these texts were powerful shaping forces for women's rights, as they reached the public in other ways, not just through direct argument. They created places for others to identify with them through storytelling or religious expressions and experiences, and enacted change where a direct argument could not have. Currently, fiction, poetry, memoir, art, film, and music are all ways feminists express themselves.

The list that follows does not include the many women who were feminists but did not write anything of note. Some women practice and speak for feminism but never produce a speech, article, or book that articulates their ideas about feminism. In addition, there are many feminist academic journals, magazines, online publications/websites, and more.

*Christine De Pizan. The Book of the City of Ladies.* Translated by Earl Jeffrey Richards. New York: Persea Books, 1982. Originally published in 1405.

*Margaret Fell. Women's Speaking Justified and Other Pamphlets.* Edited by Jane Donawerth and Rebecca M. Lush. Tempe, Arizona: Arizona Center for Medieval and Renaissance Studies, 2018. Originally published in 1666.

*Sor Juana Inés de la Cruz.* "The Poet's Answer to the Most Illustrious Sister Filotea De La Cruz." In *The Answer: Including Sor Filotea's Letter and New Selected Poems.* New York: Feminist Press at the City University of New York, 2009. Originally published in 1691.

*Mary Astell. A Serious Proposal to the Ladies.* Edited by Patricia Springborg. Ormskirk: Broadview, 2002. Originally published in 1694.

*Abigail Adams.* Letters to John Adams: "Remember the Ladies," "Man is a Dangerous Creature," and "Absolute Power over Wives." 1775–76. Available online through the Massachusetts Historical Society: https://www.masshist.org/digitaladams/archive/doc?id=L17760713aa&bc=%2Fdigitaladams%2Farchive%2Fbrowse%2Fletters_1774_1777.php.

*Judith Sargent Murray.* "On the Equality of the Sexes." In *Selected Writings of Judith Sargent Murray.* Edited by Sharon M. Harris. New York: Oxford University Press, 1995. Originally published in 1790.

*Mary Wollstonecraft. A Vindication of the Rights of Woman: With Strictures on Political and Moral Subjects.* London: Printed for J. Johnson, 1792.

———. *Thoughts on the Education of Daughters, with Reflections on Female Conduct in the More Important Duties of Life.* London: Printed for J. Johnson, 1787.

*Hannah More. Strictures on the Modern System of Female Education: With a View of the Principles and Conduct Prevalent among Women of Rank and Fortune.* Volume 2. Cambridge Library Collection—Education. Cambridge: Cambridge University Press, 2010. Originally published in 1799.

*Sarah Moore Grimké. Letters on the Equality of the Sexes and Other Essays.* Edited by Elizabeth Ann Bartlett. New Haven: Yale University Press, 1988. Originally published in 1837. See especially Letters III, IV, and XIV.

*Margaret Fuller. Woman in the Nineteenth Century.* New York: Greeley & McElrath, 1845.

*Elizabeth Cady Stanton.* "Address of Mrs. Elizabeth Cady Stanton, Delivered at Seneca Falls and Rochester, N.Y., July 19th and August 2, 1848." New York: R.J. Johnston, 1870. See "The Declaration of Sentiments."

*Lucretia Mott.* "Discourse on Woman." Iowa State University: Archives of Women's Political Communication. This speech was delivered on December 17, 1849. Available here: https://awpc.cattcenter.iastate.edu/2017/03/21/discourse-on-women-dec-17-1849/.

*Elizabeth Cady Stanton. Solitude of Self.* Washington: Government Printing Office, 1915. Originally published in 1892. Available here: https://www.loc.gov/item/93838358/.

*Angelina Grimké Weld.* "Address at Pennsylvania Hall." This speech was delivered in 1838. Available here: https://www.pbs.org/wgbh/aia/part4/4h2939t.html.

*Maria W. Stewart.* "Lecture Delivered at the Franklin Hall." In *Available Means: An Anthology of Women's Rhetorics.* Edited by Joy Ritchie and Kate Ronald. 110–13. Pittsburgh: University of Pittsburg Press, 2002. This speech was delivered in Boston in 1832.

———. "Religion and the Pure Principles of Morality, the Sure Foundation on Which We Must Build." In *Words of Fire: An Anthology of African-American Feminist Thought*. Edited by Beverly Guy-Shetfall. 26–29. New York: New Press, 1995. Originally published in 1831.

Sojourner Truth. "Speech at the Women's Rights Convention, Akron, Ohio." In *Available Means: An Anthology of Women's Rhetorics*. Edited by Joy Ritchie and Kate Ronald. 144–46. Pittsburgh: University of Pittsburg Press, 2002. This speech was delivered in 1851.

———. *The Narrative of Sojourner Truth: A Northern Slave, Emancipated from Servitude by the State of New York in 1828*. Edited by Olive Gilbert. Boston: printed by the author, 1850.

Catherine Booth. *Female Ministry, or, Woman's Right to Preach the Gospel*. London: Morgan and Chase, 1859.

Phoebe Palmer. *The Promise of the Father*. Eugene, OR: Wipf and Stock, 2015. Originally published in 1859.

———. *Tongue of Fire on the Daughters of the Lord, or, Questions in Relation to the Duty of the Christian Church in Regard to the Privileges of Her Female Membership*. N.p.: W.C. Palmer, 1869.

Lucy Stone. *The Woman's Journal*. A periodical founded by Stone and first published in 1870.

———. "The Progress of Fifty Years." In *The Congress of Women: Held in the Woman's Building, World's Columbian Exposition*. Edited by Mary Kavanaugh Oldham. 58–61. Chicago: Monarch, 1894. Lucy Stone gave this speech at the 1893 Chicago World's Fair.

Julia A. J. Foote. "Women in the Gospel." In *Words of Fire: An Anthology of African-American Feminist Thought*. Edited by Beverly Guy-Shetfall. 52–54. New York: New Press, 1995.

———. *A Brand Plucked from the Fire*. Cleveland: W. F. Schneider, 1879.

Frances Willard. *Woman and Temperance*. Chicago: Woman's Temperance Publishing Association, 1884.

———. *Woman in the Pulpit*. Boston: D. Lothrop Company, 1888.

Harriet Taylor Mill. *The Complete Works of Harriet Taylor Mill*. Edited by Jo Ellen Jacobs and Paula Harms Payne. Bloomington, IN: Indiana University Press, 1998. See "The Enfranchisement of Women," 1851.

John Stuart Mill. *The Subjection of Women*. London: Longmans, Green, Reader, and Dyer, 1869.

Anna Julia Cooper. *A Voice From the South*. Xenia, OH: Aldine, 1892.

———. "The Status of Women in America." In *Words of Fire: An Anthology of African-American Feminist Thought*. Edited by Beverly Guy-Shetfall. 44–50. New York: New Press, 1995. Originally published in 1892.

Ida B. Wells-Barnett. "Lynch Law in All Its Phases." In *Available Means: An Anthology of Women's Rhetorics*. Edited by Joy Ritchie and Kate Ronald. 189–201. Pittsburgh: University of Pittsburg Press, 2002. Originally published in 1893.

Susan B. Anthony. "The United States of America v. Susan B. Anthony." In *Available Means: An Anthology of Women's Rhetorics*. Edited by Joy Ritchie and Kate Ronald. 152–56. Pittsburgh: University of Pittsburg Press, 2002. Originally published in 1873.

Alice Paul. "The Equal Rights Amendment." 1923. Available here: https://dp.la/primary-source-sets/the-equal-rights-amendment.

Rebecca Harding Davis. *Life in the Iron Mills*. 1861. Available here: https://www.gutenberg.org/files/876/876-h/876-h.htm

Fanny Fern (Sarah Payson Willis Parson). *American Working Class Literature: An Anthology*. New York: Oxford University Press, 2007. Originally published in 1868. See "The Working Girls of New York."

Charlotte Perkins Gilman. *Women and Economics, a Study of the Economic Relation between Men and Women as a Factor in Social Evolution*. London: G. P. Putnam's Sons, 1906.

———. *The Man-Made World: Our Androcentric Culture*. New York: Charlton Company, 1911.

Emma Goldman. "The Tragedy of Woman's Emancipation." In *The Essential Feminist Reader*. Edited by Estelle B. Freedman. 168–74. New York: The Modern Library, 2007. Originally published in 1906.

Olive Schreiner. *Woman and Labor*. Toronto: T. Frowde, 1911.

Margaret Sanger. *Woman and the New Race*. In *The Essential Feminist Reader*. Edited by Estelle B. Freedman. 211–16. New York: The Modern Library, 2007. Originally published in 1920.

Virginia Woolf. *A Room of One's Own*. New York: Harcourt and Brace, 1929.

———. *Shakespeare's Sister*. Foreword by Kate Mosse. Great Speeches of the 20th Century. London: The Guardian, 2007. Originally published in 1929.

———. "Professions for Women." In *Available Means: An Anthology of Women's Rhetorics*. Edited by Joy Ritchie and Kate Ronald. 242–46. Pittsburgh: University of Pittsburg Press, 2002. Originally published in 1942.

Alice Dunbar Nelson. "The Negro Woman and the Ballot." In *Words of Fire: An Anthology of African-American Feminist Thought*. Edited by Beverly Guy-Shetfall. 86–88. New York: New Press, 1995. Originally published in 1927.

Mary Ritter Beard. *Woman as Force in History: A Study in Traditions and Realities*. New York: The MacMillan Company, 1946.

Simone de Beauvoir. *The Second Sex*. In *The Essential Feminist Reader*. Edited by Estelle B. Freedman. 251–62. New York: The Modern Library, 2007. Originally published in 1949.

Betty Friedan. *The Feminine Mystique*. In *The Essential Feminist Reader*. Edited by Estelle B. Freedman. 269–82. New York: The Modern Library, 2007. Originally published in 1963.

Mary Daly. *The Church and the Second Sex*. New York: Harper and Row, 1968.

Frances Beale. "Double Jeopardy: To Be Black and Female." In *Words of Fire: An Anthology of African-American Feminist Thought*. Edited by Beverly Guy-Shetfall. 146–56. New York: New Press, 1995. Originally published in 1970.

Linda La Rue. "The Black Movement and Women's Liberation." In *Words of Fire: An Anthology of African-American Feminist Thought*, edited by Beverly Guy-Shetfall. 164–74. New York: New Press, 1995. Originally published in 1970.

Pauli Murray. "The Liberation of Black Women." In *Words of Fire: An Anthology of African-American Feminist Thought*, edited by Beverly Guy-Shetfall. 186–98. New York: New Press, 1995. Originally published in 1970.

———. "Testimony, House Committee on Education and Labor." In *The Essential Feminist Reader*. Edited by Estelle B. Freedman. 283–87. New York: The Modern Library, 2007. Originally published in 1970.

Angela Davis. "Reflections on the Black Woman's Role in the Community of Slaves." In *Words of Fire: An Anthology of African-American Feminist Thought*. Edited by Beverly Guy-Shetfall. 200–218. New York: New Press, 1995. Originally published in 1970.

Mary Ann Weathers. "An Argument for Black Women's Liberation as a Revolutionary Force." In *Words of Fire: An Anthology of African-American Feminist Thought*. Edited by Beverly Guy-Shetfall. 158–62. New York: New Press, 1995. Originally published in 1970.

Shulamith Firestone. *The Dialectic of Sex: The Case for Feminist Revolution*. New York: Bantam Books, 1971.

Margaret Walker Alexander. "Black Women in Academia." In *Words of Fire: An Anthology of African-American Feminist Thought*. Edited by Beverly Guy-Shetfall. 454–60. New York: New Press, 1995. Originally published in 1972.

Sally Miller Gearheart. *Loving Women/Loving Men: Gay Liberation and the Church*. San Francisco: Glide Books, 1974.

Hélène Cixous. "The Laugh of the Medusa." In *The Essential Feminist Reader*. Edited by Estelle B. Freedman. 318–24. New York: The Modern Library, 2007. Originally published in 1976.

Combahee River Collective. "A Black Feminist Statement." In *Words of Fire: An Anthology of African-American Feminist Thought*. Edited by Beverly Guy-Shetfall. 232–40. New York: New Press, 1995. Originally published in 1977.

Audre Lorde. "The Master's Tools Will Never Dismantle the Master's House." In *The Essential Feminist Reader*. Edited by Estelle B. Freedman. 331–35. New York: The Modern Library, 2007. Originally published in 1979.

Michele Wallace. *Black Macho and the Myth of the Superwoman*. New York: Warner Books, 1980.

Phyllis Trible. *God and the Rhetoric of Sexuality*. Philadelphia: Fortress, 1978.

———. *Texts of Terror: Literary-Feminist Readings of Biblical Narratives*. Philadelphia: Fortress, 1984.

Jacquelyn Grant. "Black Theology and the Black Woman." In *Words of Fire: An Anthology of African-American Feminist Thought*. Edited by Beverly Guy-Shetfall. 320–36. New York: New Press, 1995. Originally published in 1979.

Starhawk (Miriam Simos). *The Spiral Dance: A Rebirth of the Ancient Religion of the Great Goddess*. San Francisco: Harper and Row, 1979.

Merle Woo. "Letter to Ma." In *Available Means: An Anthology of Women's Rhetorics*. Edited by Joy Ritchie and Kate Ronald. 307–14. Pittsburgh: University of Pittsburg Press, 2002. Originally published in 1980.

Cheryl Clarke. "Lesbianism: An Act of Resistance." In *Cheryl Clark Papers*. The New York Public Library Archives and Manuscripts. 1981. http://archives.nypl.org/scm/30060.

Alarcón, Norma. "Chicana's Feminist Literature: A Re-vision through Malintzin/or Malintzin: Putting Flesh Back on the Object." In *This Bridge Called My Back: Writings by Radical Women of Color*, 2nd ed. Edited by Cherríe Moraga and Gloria Anzaldúa. 182–90. New York: Kitchen Table Women of Color, 1983.

Barbara Smith. "Some Home Truths on the Black Feminist Movement." In *Words of Fire: An Anthology of African-American Feminist Thought*. Edited by Beverly Guy-Shetfall. 254–68. New York: New Press, 1995. Originally published in 1983.

Alice Walker. "In Search of Our Mother's Gardens." In *Available Means: An Anthology of Women's Rhetorics*. Edited by Joy Ritchie and Kate Ronald. 315–23. Pittsburgh: University of Pittsburg Press, 2002. Originally published in 1983.

Rosemary Radford Reuther. *Sexism and God-Talk: Toward a Feminist Theology*. Boston: Beacon, 1983.

Adrienne Rich. "When We Dead Awaken: Writing as Re-Vision." In *Available Means: An Anthology of Women's Rhetorics*. Edited by Joy Ritchie and Kate Ronald. 268–82. Pittsburgh: University of Pittsburg Press, 2002. Originally published in 1971.

bell hooks (Gloria Jean Watkins). "Homeplace (A Site of Resistance)." In *Available Means: An Anthology of Women's Rhetorics*. Edited by Joy Ritchie and Kate Ronald. 383–90. Pittsburgh: University of Pittsburg Press, 2002. Originally published in 1984.

Donna Haraway. "A Cyborg Manifesto: Science, Technology, and Socialist-Feminism in the Late Twentieth Century." In *Simians, Cyborgs, and Women: The Reinvention of Nature*. 149–81. New York: Routledge, 1991. Originally published in 1985.

Beth E. Richie. "Battered Black Women: A Challenge for the Black Community." In *Words of Fire: An Anthology of African-American Feminist Thought*. Edited by Beverly Guy-Shetfall. 398–404. New York: New Press, 1995. Originally published in 1985.

Paula Gunn Allen. "Grandmother of the Sun: Ritual Gynocracy in Native America." In *Available Means: An Anthology of Women's Rhetorics*. Edited by Joy Ritchie and Kate Ronald. 341–55. Pittsburgh: University of Pittsburg Press, 2002. Originally published in 1986.

Gloria Anzaldúa. "La Conciencia de la Mestiza: Toward a New Consciousness." In *The Essential Feminist Reader*. Edited by Estelle B. Freedman. 385–90. New York: The Modern Library, 2007. Originally published in 1987.

———. "How to Tame a Wild Tongue." In *Available Means: An Anthology of Women's Rhetorics*. Edited by Joy Ritchie and Kate Ronald. 357–65. Pittsburgh: University of Pittsburg Press, 2002. Originally published in 1987.

Gloria Joseph. "Black Feminist Pedagogy and Schooling in Capitalist White America." In *Words of Fire: An Anthology of African-American Feminist Thought*. Edited by Beverly Guy-Shetfall. 462–72. New York: New Press, 1995. Originally published in 1988.

Deborah K. King. "Multiple Jeopardy, Multiple Consciousness: The Context of a Black Feminist Ideology." In *Words of Fire: An Anthology of African-American Feminist Thought*. Edited by Beverly Guy-Shetfall. 294–318. New York: New Press, 1995. Originally published in 1988.

Trinh T. Minh-Ha. *Woman, Native, Other: Writing Postcoloniality and Feminism*. Bloomington: Indiana University Press, 1989.

Uma Narayan. "The Project of Feminist Epistemology: Perspectives from a Non-Western Feminist." In *Gender/Body/Knowledge: Feminist Reconstructions of Being and Knowing*. Edited by Alison M. Jaggar and Susan Bordo. 256–69. New Brunswick, NJ: Rutgers University Press, 1989.

Sonia Ann Johnson. *Wildfire: Igniting the She-Volution*. Albuquerque, New Mexico: Wildfire Books, 1989.

———. *SisterWitch Conspiracy.* CreateSpace, 2010.
Guerrilla Girls. "When Sexism and Racism Are No Longer Fashionable." In *The Essential Feminist Reader.* Edited by Estelle B. Freedman. 385. New York: The Modern Library, 2007. Originally published in 1989.
———. "Do Women Have to Be Naked to Get into the Met. Museum?" In *The Essential Feminist Reader.* Edited by Estelle B. Freedman. 385. New York: The Modern Library, 2007. Originally published in 1989.
Patricia Hill Collins. *Black Feminist Thought: Knowledge, Consciousness, and the Politics of Empowerment.* Boston: Unwin Hyman, 1990.
———. "The Social Construction of Black Feminist Thought." In *Words of Fire: An Anthology of African-American Feminist Thought.* Edited by Beverly Guy-Shetfall. 338–58. New York: New Press, 1995. Originally published in 1989.
Chandra Talpade Mohanty. "Under Western Eyes: Feminist Scholarship and Colonial Discourses." *Boundary* 2.12/13 (1984) 333–58.
Cherrie Moraga. "From a Long Line of Vendidas: Chicanas and Feminism." In F*eminist Studies/Critical Studies.* Edited by Teresa de Lauretis. London: Palgrave Macmillan, 1986.
Judith Butler. *Gender Trouble: Feminism and the Subversion of Identity.* New York: Routledge, 2006. Originally published in 1990. See "Identity, Sex, and the Metaphysics of Substance."
Kimberlé Crenshaw. "Mapping the Margins: Intersectionality, Identity Politics, and Violence against Women of Color." *Stanford Law Review* 43.6 (1991) 1241–99.
Kathleen Hanna and Bikini Kill. "Riot Grrrl Manifesto." In *The Essential Feminist Reader.* Edited by Estelle B. Freedman. 394–96. New York: The Modern Library, 2007. Originally published in 1992.
Rebecca Walker. "Becoming the Third Wave." In *The Essential Feminist Reader.* Edited by Estelle B. Freedman. 397–401. New York: The Modern Library, 2007. Originally published in 1992.
Elizabeth Schlüsser Fiorenza. *But She Said: Feminist Practices of Biblical Interpretation.* Boston: Beacon, 1992.
Sandra Harding. "Subjectivity, Experience, and Knowledge: An Epistemology from/for Rainbow Coalition Politics." *Development and Change* 23 (1992) 175–93.
Cheris Kramarae, Ann Russo, and Paula A. Tredichler. *Amazons, Bluestockings, and Crones: A Feminist Dictionary.* London: Pandora, 1992.
Susan Bordo. *Are Mothers Persons? Reproductive Rights and the Politics of Subject-ivity.* Oakland: University of California Press, 2003. Originally published in 1993.
*Delores Williams. Sisters in the Wilderness: The Challenge of Womanist God-Talk.* Maryknoll, NY: Orbis, 1993.
Rosemary Hennessy. "Queer Visibility in Commodity Culture." *Cultural Critique* 29 (1994) 31–76.
Gertrude Mongella, Winona LaDuke, Palesa Beverley Ditsie, and Gro Haarlem. "United Nations, Fourth World Conference on Women, Speeches." In *The Essential Feminist Reader.* Edited by Estelle B. Freedman. 402–14. New York: The Modern Library, 2007. These speeches were given in 1995.
Minnie Bruce Pratt. "Gender Quiz." In *Available Means: An Anthology of Women's Rhetorics.* Edited by Joy Ritchie and Kate Ronald. 425–34. Pittsburgh: University of Pittsburg Press, 2002. Originally published in 1995.

Chela Sandoval. "Feminist Forms of Agency and Oppositional Consciousness: US Third World Feminist Criticism." In *Provoking Agents: Gender and Agency in Theory and Practice*. Edited by Judith Kegan Gardiner. 208—226. [Champaigne, IL?]: University of Illinois Press, 1995.

Sofia Villenas. "The Colonizer/Colonized Chicana Ethnographer: Identity, Marginalization, and Co-optation in the Field." *Harvard Educational Review* 66.4 (1996) 711-32.

Ruth Bader Ginsburg. *United States v. Virginia et al.* In *Available Means: An Anthology of Women's Rhetorics*. Edited by Joy Ritchie and Kate Ronald. 472–77. Pittsburgh: University of Pittsburg Press, 2002. Originally published in 1996.

Ofelia Schutte. "Cultural Alterity: Cross-Cultural Communication and Feminist Theory in North-South Contexts." *Hypatia* 13.2 (1998) 53–72.

Gloria Steinem. "Supremacy Crimes." In *Available Means: An Anthology of Women's Rhetorics*. Edited by Joy Ritchie and Kate Ronald. 491–94. Pittsburgh: University of Pittsburg Press, 2002. Originally published in 1999.

Naomi Kline. *No Logo: Taking Aim at the Brand Bullies*. Toronto: Knopf, 2000.

Cherrie Moraga. "From a Long Line of Vendidas: Chicanas and Feminism." In *Feminist Studies/Critical Studies*. Edited by Teresa de Lauretis. London: Palgrave Macmillan, 1986.

Peggy McIntosh. "White Privilege: Unpacking the Invisible Knapsack." In *Understanding Prejudice and Discrimination*. Edited by Scott Plous. 191–96. New York: McGraw-Hill, 2003.

Chao-Ju Chen. "The Difference that Differences Make: Asian Feminism and the Politics of Difference." *Asian Journal of Women's Studies* 13.3 (2007) 7–36.

Luana Ross. "From the 'F' Word to Indigenous/Feminisms." *Wicazo Sa Review* 24 (2009) 39–52.

Virginie Despentes and Stephanie Benson. *King Kong Theory*. New York: Feminist Press, 2010.

Leslie Bow. *Partly Colored: Asian Americans and Racial Anomaly in the Segregated South*. New York: New York University Press, 2010.

Kate Bornstein and S. Bear Bergman. *Gender Outlaws: The Next Generation*. Berkeley, California: Seal, 2010.

Cordelia Fine. *Delusions of Gender: How Our Minds, Society, and Neurosexism Create Difference*. New York: W.W. Norton, 2010.

Sylvia Walby. *The Future of Feminism*. Cambridge: Polity, 2011.

Caitlin Moran. *How to be a Woman*. New York: Harper Perennial, 2011.

Maile Arvin, Eve Tuck, and Angie Morrill. "Decolonizing Feminism: Challenging Connections between Settler Colonialism and Heteropatriarchy." *Feminist Formations* 25.1 (2013) 8–34.

Tristan Taormino. *The Feminist Porn Book: The Politics of Producing Pleasure*. New York: The Feminist, 2013.

Melissa V. Harris-Perry. *Sister Citizen: Shame, Stereotypes, and Black Women in America*. New Haven: Yale University Press, 2013.

Cheryl Sandberg. *Lean In: Women, Work, and the Will to Lead*. New York: Alfred A. Knopf, 2013.

Malala Yousafzai. *I Am Malala: The Girl Who Stood Up for Education and Was Shot by the Taliban*. New York: Little, Brown, and Company, 2013.

Jill Lepore. *The Secret History of Wonder Woman*. New York: Knopf, 2014.

Rebecca Solnit. *Men Explain Things to Me*. Chicago: Haymarket, 2014.

Leslie Jameson. *The Empathy Exams*. Minneapolis: Graywolf, 2014.

Roxanne Gay. "Confessions of a Bad Feminist." https://www.ted.com/talks/roxane_gay_confessions_of_a_bad_feminist?language=en. This TED talk was given in 2015.

Emma Watson. "HeForShe." https://www.youtube.com/watch?v=oE28bb11GQs. This speech was given at the program launch of HeForShe at the World Economic Forum in 2015.

Kate Harding. *Asking for It: The Alarming Rise of Rape Culture—And What We Can Do About It*. Boston: De Capo Lifelong, 2015.

Alison Dahl Crossley. "Facebook Feminism: Social Media, Blogs, and New Technologies of Contemporary U.S. Feminism." *Mobilization: An International Quarterly* 20.2 (2015) 253–68.

Alexandra Brodsky and Rachel Kaudur Nalebuff, eds. *The Feminist Utopia Project: 57 Visions of a Wildly Better Future*. New York: The Feminist, 2015.

Sady Doyle. *Trainwreck: The Women We Love to Hate, Mock, and Fear . . . and Why*. Brooklyn: Melville House, 2016.

Janet Mock. *The Trans List*. Directed by Timothy Greenfield-Sanders. 2016.

Rebecca Traister. *All the Single Ladies: Unmarried Women and the Rise of an Independent Nation*. New York: Simon and Schuster, 2016.

Chimamanda Ngozi Adichie. "We Should All be Feminists." https://www.ted.com/talks/chimamanda_ngozi_adichie_we_should_all_be_feminists?language=en. This TED talk was given in 2017.

# Appendix E

## *Timeline*

### SELECTED OLD TESTAMENT WOMEN[1]

Deborah, Judges 4–5; Hebrews 11:32–34: "Prophetess, warrior and only female judge of ancient Israel, wife of Lapidoth."
Esther, Esther 8: "The queen who saved her people from destruction."
Jael, Judges 4:17–22; 5:6; 24–27: "Killed Sisera, an enemy captain, as he slept by driving a tent pin through his head with a maul."
Jephthah's unnamed daughter, Judges 12: Sacrificed to God.

### SELECTED NEW TESTAMENT WOMEN[2]

Anna, Luke 2:26–28: "daughter of Phanuel, widow in the temple who recognized the infant Christ as the Messiah."
Elisabeth, Luke 1:5–80: "a descendent of Aaron, wife of Zacharias, mother of John the Baptist in her old age."
Joanna, Luke 8:1–3; 23:55; 24:10: "healed by Christ of evil spirits; one of the group of women who fed and cared for Christ and the apostles, also one of the women who saw the empty tomb."
Lydia, Acts 16:12–15, 40; Philippians 1:1–10: "a successful businesswoman, the first convert in her family who brought the rest to conversion."
Mary Magdalene, Matthew 27:56, 61; 28:1; Mark 15:40, 47; 16:1–19; Luke 8:2; 24:10; John 19: 25; 20:1–18: "freed of seven devils by Jesus, she became a devoted follower and caretaker. She was at the cross, at the tomb and the first to see the risen Christ."
Syntyche, Philippians 4:2: "one of the active members of the early church at Philippi."

---

1. Hunter, "Women of the Bible."
2. Hunter, "Women of the Bible."

## MYSTICS

Hrotsvit von Gandersheim (932–1002): Christianity's first known playwright; wrote *Dulcitius*[3]
Hildegard of Bingen (1098–1179): first wrote of her visions in 1141[4]
Julian of Norwich's (1343–?): *Revelations of Divine Love* published in 1395
Margery Kempe (1373–1438): dictated *The Book of Margery Kempe* to scribes in 1430, recording the story of her life and journeys
Joan of Arc (1412–1431): burned at the stake in 1431
Catherine of Genoa (1447–1510): had her first mystical experience in 1473
Bridget (Birgitta) of Sweden (1303–1373): wrote *Revelations*
Clare of Assisi (1194– ?): wrote *Testament*

## (MOSTLY) AMERICAN FEMINIST HISTORY TIMELINE

1637: Anne Hutchinson arrived in Boston, Massachusetts in 1634. She was exiled by the Puritans for preaching/teaching the Bible in 1637.

1656: The Puritans had Mary Fisher and Ann Austin's books burned in Boston. Mary and Ann were "met with physical humiliation, punishment, and deportation" to Barbados.[5]

1660: Mary Dyer was a Quaker who was executed in Boston by the Puritans in 1660 for trying to convert them.

1666: British Quaker Margaret Fell Fox published "Women's Speaking Justified, Proved, and Allowed by Scriptures."

1740s and '50s: The First Great Awakening revivals occured in the US, shaking the foundations of authority in the church because uneducated men and women could preach. Women spoke publicly to mixed audiences in religious gatherings.

1769: The colonies adopted the English practice of not allowing women to have property in their own names or to keep their own wages.

1777: All states (at the time) took away women's right to vote.

1776: Abigail Adams sent her "remember the ladies" letter to her husband.

1790–1840: The Second Great Awakening Revivals occurred in the US. These revivals again undermined the authority of men and the

---

3. "Women in the Medieval Church."
4. "Christian History Timeline."
5. Lindley, "*You Have Stept*," 10.

patriarchal structure of the church. Credibility was found in inspiration rather than education.

1792: Mary Wollstonecraft published *A Vindication of the Rights of Woman with Strictures on Political and Moral Subjects.*

1830: *Godey's Lady's Book* was first published.

1839–1880s: The coverture laws were repealed.

1839: Mississippi allowed women to own property in their own names—with permission from their husbands.

1848: Jane Hunt's tea party, which included Elizabeth Cady Stanton, Lucretia Mott, Martha Wright, and Elizabeth Cady Stanton, was held and the idea of the Seneca Falls Convention was born.

1848: Elizabeth Cady Stanton (aided by the Quaker Mary Mclintock and two of her daughters) wrote the "Declaration of Sentiments and Resolutions" and the Seneca Falls Convention was held in New York in July.

1849: Elizabeth Blackwell graduated from college as the first female medical doctor in the US.

1850: Lucy Stone organized the first woman's rights convention in Worcester, Massachusetts.

1851: Sojourner Truth gave her "Ain't I a Woman?" speech in Akron, Ohio at the Women's Rights Convention.

1866: The Fourteenth Amendment defined voters and citizens as male.

1869: Arabella Mansfield became the first woman licensed to practice law in Iowa.

1869: Ada H. Kepley was the first woman in the US to graduate from law school.

1869: Wyoming passed a law allowing women to vote.

1869: Susan B. Anthony and Elizabeth Cady Stanton founded the National Woman Suffrage Association.

1872: Victoria Claflin Woodhull was nominated for president of the US by the National Radical Reformers.

1872: Female federal workers were guaranteed equal pay.

1872: Susan B. Anthony voted illegally.

1873: The Supreme Court ruled that a married woman could be denied the right to practice law by the state.

1887: Susanna Medora Salter was the first woman elected mayor (Kansas).

1892: Anna Julia Cooper wrote the first book-length Black feminist book, *A Voice From the South*.

1892: The term "feminism" was first used at the First International Women's Conference in Paris and referred to equality and advocacy.

1893: Ida B. Wells-Barnett organized the Alpha Suffrage Club in Chicago.

1896: Ida B. Wells-Barnett helped organize the National Association of Colored Women's Clubs.

1909: Ida B. Wells-Barnett helped found the National Association for the Advancement of Colored People (the NAACP).

1916: Margaret Sanger opened a birth control clinic in Brooklyn.

1917: Jeanette Rankin of Montana was sworn in as the first woman elected to Congress in the House of Representatives.

1920: Federal legislation allowed women to vote in the US.

1932: Amelia Earhart was the first woman to fly nonstop across the Atlantic.

1932: Hattie Wyatt Caraway was the first woman elected to the Senate (Arkansas).

1932: The National Recovery Act resulted in massive job losses for women since more than one family member could not hold a federal job.

1933: Frances Perkins became the first female cabinet member, serving as Secretary of Labor during the Roosevelt administration.

1935: The National Council of Negro Women was formed.

1938: Virginia Woolf formed the Outsiders Society in *Three Guineas*.

1942: Virginia Woolf gave the speech "Professions for Women."

1952: Simone de Beauvoir published *The Second Sex*.

1953: Jerrie Cobb underwent astronaut testing.

1955: Rosa Parks refused to give up her seat to a white man on a bus in Alabama.

1960: The first commercially produced birth control pill became available.

1961: Eleanor Roosevelt chaired Kennedy's Commission on the Status of Women.

1963: The Equal Pay Act was passed by Kennedy.

1963: Betty Friedan published *The Feminine Mystique*.

1964: The Civil Rights Act was passed under the Johnson administration.

1964: The Equal Employment Opportunity Commission was created.

1965: The Supreme Court ruled that married couples could use contraception.

1966: The National Organization for Women (NOW) was founded, and Betty Friedan was its first president.

1967 or 1968: Affirmative Action for women (a focus on hiring candidates because they are female).

1967: The International Alliance of Women was held in London.

1968: The Equal Employment and Opportunity Commission removed sex-based job descriptions from advertisements.

1969: The Chicana feminist movement was born.

1970: The North American Indian Women's Association (NAIWA) was formed.

1970: Kate Millet coined the phrase "the personal is political" in *Sexual Politics*; Maggie Humm attributes it to Carol Hanisch.[6]

1970: San Diego State University was the first university to offer courses in women's studies.

1970: Governor Ronald Reagan signed a law establishing "no fault" divorce.

1970: The Radicalesbians group is formed by the Lavendar Menace.[7]

1971: Reed v. Reed ruled that administrators of estates could not discriminate between the sexes.

1972: Title IX was passes under President Nixon.

1973: Roe v. Wade allowed for women to get an abortion.

1973: Billie Jean King won an exhibition match in tennis.

1973: The Comisión Femenil Mexicana Nacional was formed.

1973: The National Black Feminist Organization held its first meeting in New York.

1974: The Supreme Court made it illegal to force pregnant women to take maternity leave.

---

6. Humm, *Dictionary of Feminist Theory*, 204.
7. Humm, *Dictionary of Feminist Theory*, 235.

1974: Congress protected women from housing discrimination.

1974: Michelle Wallace founded the National Black Feminist Organization.

1974: The Combahee River Collective was formed.

1974: The Women's Educational Equity Act was enacted.

1974, Equal Credit Opportunity Act was passed.

1975: Military academies had to admit women.

1975: The Supreme Court ruled that women could not be denied the right to serve on juries.

1975 or so: Women of All Red Nations (WARN) was formed.

1978: The Pregnancy Discrimination Act was passed.

1978: The first marital rape case with two people still living together was tried.

1979: Audre Lorde published "The Master's Tools Will Never Dismantle the Master's House."

1979: Jacquelyn Grant published "Black Theology and the Black Woman."

1980: The World Conference of the United Nations Decade for Women: Equality, Development and Peace was held in Copenhagen.

1981: The Supreme Court overturned the law that man controlled the property owned with his wife.

1981: The Supreme Court ruled that not requiring women to sign up for selective service was constitutional.

1981: Sandra Day O'Conner was sworn in as the first female justice on the Supreme Court.

1983: Alice Walker defined "womanism" in "In Search of Our Mother's Gardens."

1983: Sally Ride was the first American woman in space.

1984: Geraldine Ferraro became the first woman to run for vice president.

1984: The Supreme Court ruled that clubs could not deny women membership.

1986: The Supreme Court ruled that a workplace could be held responsible for sex discrimination.

1989: The Supreme Court ruled that the state had a right to deny funding for abortions and could prohibit hospitals from performing abortions.

1989: Kimberlé Crenshaw coined the term "intersectionality" in her essay "Demarginalizing the Intersection of Race and Sex: A Black Feminist Critique of Antidiscrimination Doctrine, Feminist Theory and Antiracist Politics."

1992: The Supreme Court ruled that minors could be required to get permission from parents for an abortion and that a waiting period for women seeking abortion could be imposed.

1993, Janet Reno became the first female attorney general in the US during the Clinton administration.

1993: Marital rape became illegal in all fifty states.

1997: Madeleine Albright was sworn in as the first female Secretary of State during the Clinton administration.

1994: The Violence Against Women Act was passed under Clinton.

1995: The Fourth World Conference on Women was held in Beijing.

1997: The Third Wave Foundation was formed.

2003: The Partial-Birth Abortion Ban Act was passed.

2006: Tarana Burke founded the Me Too Movement

2007: Democrat Nancy Pelosi became the first female Speaker of the House.

2008: Sarah Palin, the governor of Alaska, was the first Republican woman to run for vice president.

2009: Michelle Obama founded the Let Girls Learn Initiative, now the Girls Opportunity Alliance.

2009: The Lilly Ledbetter Fair Pay Restoration Act was passed.

2012: Patrisse Cullors co-founded the Black Lives Matter Movement.

2013: The US allowed women to serve in combat positions.

2016: Democrat Hillary Clinton became the first woman to be the nominee for president.

# Appendix F

## FEMINISM AS A LENS FOR ANALYSIS

When drawing on feminist writings or theories, be sure you fully understand the authority of the writer or speaker. Some feminists have a position that gives them a certain amount of credibility. For example, we would not care much about Abigail Adams if she had not been married to the president and if her letters had not been preserved and studied. However, she was mostly uneducated and struggled with basic literacy. Other feminists have a bachelor's degree or less education but are known for their political activism. Some hold PhDs. However, someone with a PhD in political science speaking on biblical matters does not have the authority someone with a PhD in theology has. Many people exaggerate their level of expertise and importance when they are trying to persuade an audience. So the first thing to do is to put the author of the information you wish to use into context. Understand that even if the information corroborates the views you have, the authority of the speaker does not increase simply because you agree with him or her.

Next, put the text into its proper context. When was it written? Where was it published originally? Who was the target audience? By putting a text into context (historical, political, social, etc.) you can learn much more about the message. It is a mistake to take a message written in 1963 and criticize it because it does not meet the expectations of a contemporary audience. Put it into context and recognize its power (or lack thereof) within that context. That being said, many feminist scholars are recovering the work of women who had little or no real influence in their time. While it is valuable work, a scholar should contextualize the piece properly and be careful about making overstatements regarding its efficacy in its time.

Next, make sure any quoted or paraphrased material you use from a text is represented as accurately as possible. Be sure to read the whole text (if at all possible—I say this knowing Betty Friedan's famous book is over 500 pages in length), or at least the entire chapter. Use secondary sources that you evaluate carefully in conjunction with quoted or paraphrased material by feminists. Use sources that you get through scholarly databases. If you use Google, you need to verify the currency, accuracy, and purpose of the website. Don't be afraid to discard questionable sources. Research each author. Is the author a student? Don't use that source then, at least not in college-level work, or make it clear you are using something written by a non-expert. I recently read a post by someone claiming to have studied theology all his life. Does that make him an expert? No, not even a little bit. So know who it is you are listening to before you present that person's work as an authoritative source in your paper.

Vet your sources carefully. Use books or e-books you collect from your college or university library. Use encyclopedias that have editors and fact-checking. Be wary of newspaper articles that present a very short narrative with little information. Magazines have easily identifiable target audiences. Is that article appropriate for your research? Blogs, websites, tweets, Facebook posts—all of these must be fact-checked if you consider using them at all. The quality of your sources represents who you are as a student. Are you the student who read three newspaper articles and wrote a paper? Or are you the student who read three scholarly articles—around twenty pages each—and then drew on information that reflects depth, insight, and accuracy and that was reviewed by experts in that field of study (this is what "peer-reviewed" means). As a teacher, I always check out the list of references first. That's how I know if the student is serious or just hoping for a C.

Finally, get some help. Good writing and research are a result of getting a good reader or two. The best case is to have your instructor read your work. You may not have the opportunity as you draft, however. Consider forming a group with other students. They are encountering similar information and you can help each other by looking at content, coherence, logic, and quality (not by editing). When your argument is thin, is not supported adequately with sources, or simply does not make sense, your fellow students can point this out before it reaches an instructor's eyes. The next best thing is to use the writing center. Many tutors have good advice for creating a structured, well-researched, properly documented paper for college classes. As a last resort, you can ask your mom/dad/grandma/grandpa/neighbor/friend/roommate to look over your work.

# FEMINISM AS A LENS FOR LITERARY CRITICISM

According to Purdue OWL, "feminist criticism is concerned with "the ways in which literature (and other cultural productions) reinforce or undermine the economic, political, social, and psychological oppression of women."[1] Notice this perspective assumes that these factors do oppress women. So the focus is not on how women have successfully occupied positions of power—many do and have in Western history—but on the forces that present challenges to women in a particular culture because they are women. Intersectionality reveals and names overlapping areas—such as race, religion, gender, social class, economic class, and so on—that play a role in the oppression of women. These challenges are shaped by a patriarchal or misogynistic society to varying degrees.

Any analysis of a text begins with defining the rhetorical situation and contextualization. As discussed earlier, who is the author? The targeted audience? As Ede and Lunsford would say, who is the audience addressed and who is the audience invoked? (Those are two different things: An audience for a writer is a work of the imagination. The audience addressed is not necessarily the one that is invoked. We can't control who reads our texts or responds to them. Authors have very little control over their work once printed.) Was this text influential in its time? If not, why not? If so, why so? Is it a "recovered" text drawn from archival research that became influential after its time? Where was this first published? When was it written? To further contextualize the text, what master narratives (overarching stories) defined that historical period? For example, we know that African Americans were oppressed as slaves in the nineteenth century, but we also have Anna Julia Cooper, "born to a slave mother and her master," who "published the first book-length feminist text, *A Voice From the South*."[2] This smaller, specific narrative is more significant in light of the overarching historical facts we know about prejudice, slavery, and racism.

Also, what are the moral and ethical codes that seem to dominate a particular historical period? As I demonstrated with Christian women, particularly preachers and speakers in the nineteenth century, mastering the language of Christianity was required to have real influence on their audience, since the doctrines in place had real effects on the behavior of Americans in that time. We have seen a change in the latter twentieth century and early years of the twenty-first century, as our society can now be defined as "post-Christian." What are the political contexts that

---

1. "Feminist Criticism."
2. Guy-Sheftall, *Words of Fire*, 43.

are significant? As we can see from the first chapter of this book, many of the problems first-wave feminists faced had to be resolved through political action. What is the genre, or type, of text you are analyzing? Does it follow the conventions of that genre or change them? Is this significant? A feminist critic might look at a text using one or more of these perspectives in order to analyze it:

- "Women are oppressed by patriarchy economically, politically, socially, and psychologically; patriarchal ideology is the primary means by which women are oppressed."[3] Again, intersectionality could be a useful tool for you to use to determine what a particular woman might perceive as oppressive and what sorts of challenges (race, economics, religion, age, etc.) overlap as you analyze a text.

- "In every domain where patriarchy reigns, woman is other: she is marginalized, defined only by her difference from male norms and values."[4] As a scholar, I would first ask: Is this true? To what extent? What sort of effects does the way a woman is defined have on that woman? Then I would analyze the text to see if this is in play and to what extent. In *Beginning Theory*, Peter Barry states that feminist critics "challenge representations of women as 'Other,' as 'lack,' as part of 'nature.'"[5]

- "All of Western (Anglo-European) civilization is deeply rooted in patriarchal ideology, for example, in the Biblical portrayal of Eve as the origin of sin and death in the world."[6] This is important, but not as important as the work of feminist theologians who provide ways to understand and contextualize Scripture. The statement here can be defined as a "master narrative"—an oversimplification of Western history. The truth is that history is often complex and contradictory and breaks down when individual stories in its fabric are examined. So if you take this perspective as an analytical lens for a text, keep in mind that what you find might be considerably more complex.

- "While biology determines our sex (male or female), culture determines our gender (scales of masculine and feminine)."[7] Barry frames it in terms of raising the "question of whether men and women are 'essentially' different because of biology or are socially constructed as

3. "Feminist Criticism."
4. "Feminist Criticism."
5. Barry, *Beginning Theory*, 134.
6. "Feminist Criticism."
7. "Feminist Criticism."

different."[8] In other words, how do we define what is "male" and what is "female" and how does that shape the text we are analyzing?

- "All feminist activity, including feminist theory and literary criticism, has as its ultimate goal to change the world by prompting gender equality."[9] Does the text you are analyzing demonstrate this idealistic goal? Whereas Barry writes that feminist critics "make clear the ideological base of supposedly 'neutral' or 'mainstream' literary interpretation,"[10] are you able to see how taking a feminist lens is ultimately taking a biased position as you interpret the text? It's okay to do so, but you should own it.

- "Gender issues play a part in every aspect of human production and experience, including the production and experience of literature, whether we are consciously aware of these issues or not."[11] Perhaps this is true, but I would ask, to what extent? Barry adds that feminist critics see "reading as a political act."[12] How is your interpretation a political act?

Questions for analysis might include:

- How are the relationships between men and women portrayed?
- What are the power relationships between men and women (or characters assuming male/female roles)?
- How are male and female roles defined?
- What constitutes masculinity and femininity?
- How do characters/authors/speakers embody these traits?
- Do characters/authors/speakers take on traits from opposite genders? How so? How does this change others' reactions to them?
- What does the work reveal about the operations (economically, politically, socially, or psychologically) of patriarchy?
- What does the work imply about the possibilities of sisterhood as a mode of resisting patriarchy?
- What does the work say about women's creativity?

---

8. Barry, *Beginning Theory*, 134.
9. "Feminist Criticism."
10. Barry, *Beginning Theory*, 134.
11. "Feminist Criticism."
12. Barry, *Beginning Theory*, 134.

- What does the history of the work's reception by the public and by critics tell us about the operation of patriarchy?
- What role does the work play in terms of women's literary history and literary tradition?
- What is the overarching conflict in the text? Between men and women? Women and a spiritual world or entity? Women and society? Women and their own, internalized limitations (women vs. self)?

To conclude, it is clear that "feminist literary criticism of today is the direct product of the 'woman's movement' of the 1960s," and that movement always recognized the power of how women were portrayed in texts.[13] Beginning in the 1980s—in whird-wave feminism—feminist literary criticism became more "eclectic" by incorporating theories I have touched on in this book, such as structuralism, Marxism, and linguistics.[14] Since then, feminist literary critics have developed more contemporary theories about power and language as well. To conduct an analysis using feminism as a lens means you need to carefully describe and define your lens as well as provide an analysis. It could be an enormously constructive and useful way of discovering exactly how you connect with feminist theories. Additionally, it might be more productive for understanding the texts that define feminist perspectives than just reading through essays in an anthology of feminist readings.

---

13. Barry, *Beginning Theory*, 121.
14. Barry, *Beginning Theory*, 123.

# Appendix G

One of the best ways to expand our knowledge about women is to do archival research. What is archival research? It is simply research where you collect primary sources, analyze and contextualize them, and use them to answer guiding research questions. Laura Schmidt of the Society of American Archivists provides a useful guide for archival research. She begins by defining ways that archives are different than libraries (although the library can have archival materials and the archives can have the types of media a library has). Besides offering limited access to their materials, what they have is different:

> Archives can hold both published and unpublished materials, and those materials can be in any format. Some examples are manuscripts, letters, photographs, moving image and sound materials, artwork, books, diaries, artifacts, and the digital equivalents of all of these things. Materials in an archives are often unique, specialized, or rare objects, meaning very few of them exist in the world, or they are the only ones of their kind. [1]

Primary sources can be found in archives—online or in communities, special library collections, museums, and also in personal collections. Primary sources can be created. Oral histories, interviews, photographs, films, and travel narratives are all examples of primary sources. Let's make a list of types of primary sources:

- Newspapers
- Diaries
- Photographs

---

1. Schmidt, "Using Archives."

- Films
- Objects: clothing, housewares, furniture
- Art
- Music
- Letters
- Government publications
- Autobiographies or memoirs
- Sermons
- Pamphlets
- Travel narratives
- Books
- An organization's records
- Magazines
- Newsletters
- Maps
- Political cartoons
- Advertisements
- Speeches
- Magazines
- Laws and regulations

The Mina Rees Library suggests you establish the scope of your research (Is this for a short paper? A website? A dissertation?) and budget your time carefully, since doing archival research often takes much more time.[2] Also, if you are new to archival research, schedule some time with a librarian to help form a plan so you can do your research strategically.[3]

Before you go to an archive, establish a set of research questions to help limit and focus your research. For example, when writing my dissertation, I wanted to know about women preachers from the International Pentecostal Holiness Denomination. I only wanted women who lived in Oklahoma (my home state). So my questions were:

2. "Archival Research."
3. "Archival Research."

1. Who was preaching in Oklahoma before it became a state (1907), in the early twentieth century, in the mid-twentieth century, and in the late twentieth/early twenty-first century?
2. What were their experiences like?
3. Where did they preach?
4. How did they establish their ethos, or authority and credibility?
5. What kinds of texts can I find? Letters? Photos? Autobiographies? Sermons? Denominational materials with mentions of women preachers?
6. What kinds of contexts do I need to research? Historical? Native American? Geographical? Social? Political? Certainly I must research the doctrines of the denomination, the people who established them, and how they changed as well as the history of Pentecostalism (since there are hundreds of denominations that use that title).
7. What challenges did these women face and from whom? Why were they challenged and on what basis? Who supported them?

Once you have established a set of research questions (although these can change at any time), you can do a search by visiting an archives, a special collections library, a museum, or an online archive. Many archives and museums have extensive online collections for you to explore. The Mina Rees Library Libguide suggests you always set up an appointment if visiting an archive.[4] Laura Schmidt lists the types of archives you might visit: "college and university archives," "corporate archives," "government archives," "historical societies," "museums," "religious archives," and "special collections."[5]

Schmidt also provides the following list of online materials, although some are only accessible through a database, such as WorldCat:

- Check Archive Finder at http://archives.chadwyck.com/home.do. This site contains listings from thousands of American and British archives (requires purchase or subscription).
- Check ArchiveGrid at http://beta.worldcat.org/archivegrid/. This database contains nearly a million collection descriptions from thousands of libraries, archives, and museums.
- Check ARCHIVESCANADA.ca at http://www.archives-canada.ca/. This gateway to archival resources from over

---

4. "Archival Research."
5. Schmidt, "Using Archives."

eight hundred repositories across Canada contains linked archival repository databases for each province.

- Check Archives Wiki at http://archiveswiki.historians.org/index.php/Main_Page. Sponsored by the American Historical Association, this page links to several archives from around the world and provides commentary about the archives from a researcher perspective.

- Browse the website of the Library of Congress at http://www.loc.gov/index.html. The Library of Congress is America's national library, and the world's largest.

- Visit the website of the National Archives and Records Administration (NARA) at http://www.archives.gov/. NARA oversees the preservation of United States federal government materials. There are two additional resources that can be accessed through NARA:

- AAD (Access to Archival Databases) at http://aad.archives.gov/aad/ is a search engine for some of NARA's holdings of electronic records.

- ARC (The Archival Research Catalog) at http://www.archives.gov/research/arc/ is an online catalog of NARA's nationwide holdings in the Washington, DC area, regional archives, and presidential libraries.

- Search the National Union Catalog of Manuscript Collections (NUCMC) at http://www.loc.gov/coll/nucmc/. NUCMC provides descriptions of manuscript and archival collections from a wide variety of American repositories. The information produced by NUCMC is shared with the WorldCat database (mentioned above).

- Explore the Smithsonian Institution Archives at http://siarchives.si.edu/. The Smithsonian Institution Archives is the record keeper of the Smithsonian—collecting, preserving, and making available the official records of the Smithsonian's 19 museums, nine research centers, and the National Zoo.[6]

Once at the archive or library, talk to people. Ask about historical centers and smaller archives. Reach out for help as much as you can. You never know who will have a lead on what you are looking for. As I began work on my dissertation, I reached out to the head of the archives in Oklahoma City, Dr. Harold Hunter. He pointed me toward many of the materials I ended up using and very generously provided a bibliography of about a hundred

6 Schmidt, "Using Archives."

books I needed to read to understand the history of Pentecostalism and how these women fit into it.

Schmidt suggests learning how to search a particular archives most effectively. She calls these various ways of searching "finding aids."[7]

While at the archive or library, be ready to collect images of things you can't take with you. A camera on your phone is good, but if they have a printer, bring a thumb drive (if you can't email the file from the printer) and scan and save what you want. The Mina Rees Library suggests keeping a research journal and carefully noting what you got and from where.[8] Schmidt suggests checking out the policies on laptops and the reproduction of materials before you go as well.[9] She also suggests finding out who holds the copyright to the materials you find. For example, you can't publish an unpublished poem without the consent of the copyright holder. This may be the archives or the poet. You can't publish a picture you find without the consent of the copyright holder either. So be sure to ask what the procedure is for getting permissions for using the materials you wish to use while at the archives.

Be ready to investigate surprises. Perhaps you thought all Oklahoma women preachers were white women from the lower economic and social classes, but then you discover exceptions to that stereotype. This is part of the pleasure of archival research. Collect, analyze, and enjoy!

Put your discoveries into context. Get several readers—experts—to review your drafts. I had Dr. Hunter as a guide and Dr. Vinson Synan served on my dissertation committee. His ability to check all the references to history and theology meant my work was accurate.

The Mina Rees Library libguide also suggests that you explore the significance of your topic. This can be done at any point in the process but is perhaps the most important piece of archival research. How does your research tell a brand new story? How does it interrupt oversimplified histories? How does your work add to our understanding of a culture, time period, or group of people?

Finally, Schmidt offers an extensive list of links to do research using the archives, but here are two you might consider:

- The Society of American Archivists Glossary of Archival and Records Terminology, http://www2.archivists.org/glossary. A very thorough resource outlining the terms and definitions used in the archival profession.

7. Schmidt, "Using Archives."
8. "Archival Research."
9. Schmidt, "Using Archives."

- "So You Want to be an Archivist: An Overview of the Archival Profession," http://www2.archivists.org/careers/beanarchivist. Information on what archivists do and a short video on "A Day in the Life of an Archivist."

As you embark on archival research, keep in mind that there are plenty of grants and funding opportunities for those doing research as graduate students or scholars. Be sure to investigate opportunities in your area of study when you are ready, keeping in mind that some may take up to a year to be awarded.

# Bibliography

"About Spelman College." Spelman College: A Choice to Change the World. https://www.spelman.edu/about-us.

"Agnes N. Ozman (1870–1937)." Apostolic Archives International Inc. https://www.apostolicarchives.com/articles/article/8795590/174072.htm.

Alexander, Estrelda Y., ed. *Black Fire Reader: A Documentary Resource on African-American Pentecostalism*. Eugene, OR: Cascade, 2013.

———. "Presidential Address 2010: When Liberation Becomes Survival." *Pneuma* 32 (2010) 337–53.

———. *The Women of Azusa Street*. Cleveland: Pilgrim, 2005.

Alexander, Kimberly Ervin, and James P. Bowers. *What Women Want: Pentecostal Women Ministers Speak for Themselves*. Eugene, OR: Wipf & Stock, 2018.

"Ann Lee: American Religious Leader." *Britannica*. https://www.britannica.com/biography/Ann-Lee.

"Antifeminism." Encyclopedia.com. https://www.encyclopedia.com/history/dictionaries-thesauruses-pictures-and-press-releases/antifeminism.

"The Anti-Suffrage Review April 1909." A History of the World. http://www.bbc.co.uk/ahistoryoftheworld/objects/lOYp3pGjRhWkouODfS17VQ.

Archer, Melissa, and Kenneth J. Archer. "Complementarianism and Egalitarianism—Whose Side are You Leaning On?" *Pneuma* 41 (2019) 66–90.

"Archival Research." Mina Rees Library. https://libguides.gc.cuny.edu/archivalresearch/research-process.

Ashcroft, Bill. *Post-Colonial Transformation*. Philadelphia: Routledge, 2001.

"Atavistic." Dictionary.com. https://www.dictionary.com/browse/atavistic?s=t.

Austin, Michael. *Reading the World: Ideas that Matter*, 4th ed. New York: W. W. Norton and Company, 2020.

Barkman, Linda Lee Smith. "Muted Group Theory: A Tool for Hearing Marginalized Voices." *Priscilla Papers* (October 2018). https://www.cbeinternational.org/resource/article/priscilla-papers-academic-journal/muted-group-theory-tool-hearing-marginalized.

Barry, Peter. *Beginning Theory: An Introduction to Literary and Cultural Theory*. New York: Manchester University Press, 1995.

"A Basic Introduction to Anarcha Feminism." Women's Solidarity Movement. http://www.wsm.ie/c/introduction-anarcha-feminism-anarchist.

Bernstein, Leandra. "More Pro-Life Groups Removed as Official Partners of the Women's March." *WJLA*, January 18, 2017. https://wjla.com/news/local/more-pro-life-groups-removed-as-partners-of-the-womens-march.

"The Bible." History.com. https://www.history.com/topics/religion/bible.

Bietenhard, Sophia, and Silvia Schroer. *Feminist Interpretation of the Bible.* New York: Bloomsbury, 2004.

Bizzell, Patricia, and Bruce Herzberg. "Sor Juana Ines de la Cruz." In *The Rhetorical Tradition: Readings from Classical Times to the Present*, 780–90. 2nd ed. Boston: Bedford St. Martin's, 2001.

———. *The Rhetorical Tradition: Readings from Classical Times to the Present.* 2nd ed. Boston: Bedford St. Martin's, 2001.

Borland, Elizabeth. "Standpoint Theory." *Brittanica.* https://www.britannica.com/topic/standpoint-theory.

Bowell, T. "Feminist Standpoint Theory." *Internet Encyclopedia of Philosophy.* https://www.iep.utm.edu/fem-stan/#H4.

Brekus, Catherine. *Strangers and Pilgrims: Female Preaching in America, 1740–1845.* Chapel Hill: The University of North Carolina Press, 1998.

Brilmyer, S. Pearl. "Darwinian Feminisms." In *Gender: Matter*, edited by Stacy Alaimo, 19–34. London: Macmillan Interdisciplinary Handbooks, 2017.

"CBE's Mission and Values." CBE International. https://www.cbeinternational.org/content/cbes-mission.

"Centuries of Citizenship: A Constitutional Timeline." National Constitution Center. https://constitutioncenter.org/timeline/html/cw08_12159.html.

"Christian History Timeline." Christian History Institute. https://christianhistoryinstitute.org/magazine/article/christian-history-timeline-four-vivid-centuries.

Claassans, Juliana L. "The Woman of Substance and Human Flourishing: Proverbs 31:10–31 and Martha Nussbaum's Capabilities Approach." *Journal of Feminist Studies in Religion* 32.1 (2016) 5–19.

Clabaugh, Gary K. "A History of Male Attitudes Towards Educating Women." *Educational Horizons*, Spring 2010, 164–78.

Clarke, Edward H. *Sex in Education: Or, a Fair Chance for Girls.* Boston: James R. Osgood and Company, 1873.

Clifford, Anne M. *Introducing Feminist Theology.* New York: Orbis, 2001.

Collins, Gail. *America's Women: 400 Years of Dolls, Drudges, Helpmates, and Heroines.* New York: Perennial, 2003.

Collins, Patricia Hill. "Toward an Afrocentric Feminist Epistemology." World Wide Web. 1990. http://www.woldww.net/classes/Principles_of_Inquiry/Collins-AfrocFemEpistemology+.htm.

"Colonialism." *Stanford Encyclopedia of Philosophy.* https://plato.stanford.edu/entries/colonialism/#PosColThe.

Combs, Stephen. "Freshman Comp: Often More About Politics than Sentences." The James G. Martin Center for Academic Renewal. https://www.jamesgmartin.center/2015/07/freshman-comp-often-more-about-politics-than-sentences.

"Community Colleges: The History of Community Colleges, the Junior College and the Research University. The Community College Mission," Education Encyclopedia. https://education.stateuniversity.com/pages/1873/Community-Colleges.html.

Cott, Nancy. *The Grounding of Modern Feminism*. London: Yale University Press, 1989.

Cox, Harvey. *Fire From Heaven: The Rise of Pentecostal Spirituality and the Reshaping of Religion in the Twenty-first Century*. Cambridge: Da Capo, 1995.

"Critical Thinking." *Stanford Encyclopedia of Philosophy*. https://plato.stanford.edu/entries/critical-thinking/#ProcThinCrit.

"Cyberfeminism." *Encyclopedia of New Media*. Sage. https://study.sagepub.com/sites/default/files/Ch17_Cyberfeminism.pdf.

Daly, Mary. *Beyond God the Father: Toward a Philosophy of Women's Liberation*. Boston: Beacon, 1973.

———. *The Church and the Second Sex*. Boston: Beacon, 1986.

———. "Document 12: Excerpts from Mary Daly, *Beyond God the Father: A Philosophy of Women's Liberation*." In *How Did Catholic Women Participate in the Rebirth of American Feminism?*, edited by Mary Henold, . Binghamton, NY: State University of New York at Binghamton, 2005. https://documents.alexanderstreet.com/d/1000681780.

Deasy, Jo Ann. "Women Leaders in Evangelical Congregations." In *Religious Leadership: A Reference Handbook*, edited by Sharon Henderson Callahan, 276–81. Los Angeles: Sage, 2013.

Delmar, Rosalind. "What is Feminism?" In *Theorizing Feminism: Parallel Trends in the Humanities and Social Sciences*, edited by Anne C. Herrmann, and Abigail J. Stewart, 5–28. 2nd ed. Boulder, CO: Westview, 2001.

Diamond, Anna. "Fighting for the Vote with Cartoons." *New York Times*, August 14, 2020. https://www.nytimes.com/2020/08/14/us/suffrage-cartoons.html.

Dotson, Kristie. "Inheriting Patricia Hill Collins's Black Feminist Epistemology." *Ethnic and Racial Studies* 38.13 (2015) 2322–28.

Downey, Maureen. "Is Higher Education Biased against Traditional Christians?" *Atlanta Journal-Constitution*, July 16, 2017. https://www.ajc.com/blog/get-schooled/higher-education-biased-against-traditional-christians/OvUZDRhTjVTpPIb3oa9ALN.

"Elisabeth Schüssler Fiorenza." Harvard Divinity School. https://hds.harvard.edu/people/elisabeth-sch%C3%BCssler-fiorenza.

"Eschatology." Dictionary.com. https://www.dictionary.com/browse/eschatology?s=t.

"Essentialism." *Open Education Sociology Dictionary*. https://sociologydictionary.org/essentialism/#definition_of_essentialism.

"Existentialism." *Oxford Languages Dictionary*. https://languages.oup.com/google-dictionary-en/.

"Existentialism." *Stanford Encyclopedia of Philosophy*. https://plato.stanford.edu/entries/existentialism.

Faulk, Odie B., and William D. Welge. *Oklahoma: A Rich Heritage*. Sun Valley, CA: American Historical, 2004.

Fell, Margaret. "Women's Speaking Justified, Proved, and Allowed by the Scriptures." In *The Rhetorical Tradition: Readings from Classical Times to the Present*, edited by Patricia Bizzell and Bruce Herzberg, 677–84. 2nd ed. Boston: Bedford/St. Martin's, 2001.

"Feminism versus Feminisms." *Introduction to Communication*. Lumen Learning. https://courses.lumenlearning.com/suny-introductiontocommunication/chapter/feminism-versus-feminisms.

"Feminist Criticism (1960's to Present)." Purdue OWL. https://owl.purdue.edu/owl/subject_specific_writing/writing_in_literature/literary_theory_and_schools_of_criticism/feminist_criticism.html#:~:text=Feminist%20criticism%20is%20concerned%20with.women%22%20(Tyson%2083).

"Feminist Philosophy." *Stanford Encyclopedia of Philosophy*. https://plato.stanford.edu/entries/feminist-philosophy/#:~:text=In%20the%20mid%2D1800s%20the.rights%20for%20women%20based%20on.

"Feminist Theology." Encyclopedia.com. https://www.encyclopedia.com/philosophy-and-religion/christianity/christianity-general/feminist-theology.

Ferguson, Sian. "Kyriarchy 101: We're Not Just Fighting the Patriarchy Anymore." *Everyday Feminism*, April 23, 2014. https://everydayfeminism.com/2014/04/kyriarchy-101.

Fiorenza, Elizabeth Schlusser. *But She Said: Feminist Practices of Biblical Interpretation*. Boston: Beacon, 1992.

Freedman, Estelle B. *The Essential Feminist Reader*. New York: The Modern Library, 2007.

Friedan, Betty. *The Feminine Mystique*. New York: W.W. Norton and Company, 1963. https://nationalhumanitiescenter.org/ows/seminars/tcentury/FeminineMystique.pdf.

German, Lindsey. "21st Century Feminism." *Socialist Review*, October 2009. http://socialistreview.org.uk/340/21st-century-feminism.

Gines, Kathryn. "Ruminations on Twenty-Five Years of Patricia Hill Collins's Black Feminist Thought: Knowledge, Consciousness and the Politics of Empowerment." *Ethnic and Racial Studies* 38.13 (2015) 2341–48.

Gjelten, Tom. "Christian Colleges that Oppose LGBT Rights Worried about Losing Funding." *NPR*, March 27, 2018. https://www.npr.org/2018/03/27/597390654/christian-colleges-that-oppose-lgbt-rights-worried-about-losing-funding-under-ti.

Gonzalez, Christian Alejandro. "The Freedom Feminist: Talking with Christina Hoff Sommers." *City Journal*, May 30, 2020. https://www.city-journal.org/talking-with-christina-hoff-sommers.

Grady, Constance. "The Waves of Feminism, and Why People Keep Fighting over Them, Explained." *Vox*, July 20, 2018. https://www.vox.com/2018/3/20/16955588/feminism-waves-explained-first-second-third-fourth.

Granberg-Michaelson, Wes. "Think Christianity Is Dying? No. Christianity Is Shifting Dramatically." *Washington Post*, May 20, 2015. https://www.washingtonpost.com/news/acts-of-faith/wp/2015/05/20/think-christianity-is-dying-no-christianity-is-shifting-dramatically/.

Greves, Abigail. "Daughter of Courage: Reading Judges 11 with a Feminist Pentecostal Hermeneutic." *Journal of Pentecostal Theology* 25 (2016) 151–67.

Grewal, Inderpal, and Caren Kaplan. *An Introduction to Women's Studies: Gender in a Transnational World*. 2nd ed. Boston: McGraw-Hill, 2006.

Grimaldi, William A. "The Auditor's Role in Aristotelian Rhetoric." In *Oral and Written Communication: Historical Approaches*, edited by Richard Leo Enos, 65–81. Newbury Park, CA: Sage, 1990.

Guardiola-Saenz, Leticia. "Mujerista Criticism." *The Oxford Encyclopedia of the Bible and Gender Studies*. Oxford University Press, 2014. https://www-oxfordreference-com. ezproxy1.library.arizona.edu/view/10.1093/acref:obso/9780199836994.001.0001/ acref-9780199836994-e-27.

"A Guide to Feminist Pedagogy." Vanderbilt Center for Teaching. https://my.vanderbilt.edu/femped/habits-of-hand/a-few-examples/.

Gunter, Catharine, and Nancy E. Hicks, eds. "Our Wreath of Rosebuds." *Cherokee Rosebuds*, August 2, 1854. https://gateway.okhistory.org/ark:/67531/metadc99289/m1/1/zoom/?resolution=4&lat=2874&lon=1675.

"Gutenberg Bible." *Britannica*. https://www.britannica.com/topic/Gutenberg-Bible.

Guy-Sheftall, Beverly. *Words of Fire: An Anthology of African-American Feminist Thought*. New York: The New, 1995.

Haraway, Donna. *A Cyborg Manifesto*. Minneapolis: University of Minnesota Press, 2016.

———. "Situated Knowledges: The Science Question in Feminism and the Privilege of Partial Perspective." *Feminist Studies* 14.3 (1988) 575–99.

Hartocollis, Anemona, and Yamiche Alcindor. "Women's March Highlights as Huge Crowd Protests Trump: 'We're Not Going Away.'" *New York Times*, January 21, 2017. https://www.nytimes.com/2017/01/21/us/womens-march.html.

Harvey, Josephine. "RNC Speaker Endorses Absurd, Sexist Voting System Right before Taking Stage." *AOL*, August 26, 2020. https://www.aol.com/article/news/2020/08/26/rnc-speaker-endorses-absurd-sexist-voting-system-right-before-taking-stage/24600137/?fbclid=IwAR1uMEQ3quv3Qk793p9ox_X239U5NqJLxy2Pv6uvyG3Cw_DQnD3Go3Vf3Xc.

Haven, Cynthia. "How Antebellum Artists Used Their Work to Protest Slavery." *Stanford News*, February 13, 2009. https://news.stanford.edu/news/2009/february18/artists-slavery-protests-021809.html.

Hawk, Taylor. "What is 'Intersectional Feminism'?" Denison University. https://denison.edu/academics/womens-gender-studies/feature/67969.

Hemmer, Nicole. "Anti-Feminist Women Have a Long History in The United States." United States Study Center. https://www.ussc.edu.au/analysis/anti-feminist-women-have-a-long-history-in-the-united-states.

"Hermeneutics." Dictionary.com. https://www.dictionary.com/browse/hermeneutic?s=t.

Hicks, Stephen. "Why Postmodernists Train—Not Educate—Activists." The Atlas Society. https://www.atlassociety.org/post/why-postmodernists-train-not-educate-activists.

Hill Collins, Patricia. *Black Feminist Thought: Knowledge, Consciousness, and the Politics of Empowerment*. 10th ed. New York: Taylor and Francis, 2000.

"History of Feminism." *Britannica*. https://www.britannica.com/topic/feminism#ref216004.

Hull, Gretchen Gaebelein. "A Christian Response to Sexism: Biblical Feminism." https://www.cbeinternational.org/resource/article/priscilla-papers-academic-journal/biblical-feminism.

Humm, Maggie. *The Dictionary of Feminist Theory*. 2nd ed. Columbus: Ohio State University Press, 1995.

Hunt, Mary E. "The Life of 'Scholar-Activist' Rosemary Radford Ruether." *National Catholic Reporter*, October 14, 2014. https://www.ncronline.org/news/people/life-scholar-activist-rosemary-radford-ruether.

Hunter, Margaret. "Women of the Bible Timeline Part VI." *Amazing Bible Timeline* (blog), February 25, 2013. https://amazingbibletimeline.com/blog/women_of_the_bible_timeline_vi/.

Hyatt, Susan. "Spirit-Filled Women." In *The Holy Spirit: 100 Years of Pentecostal and Charismatic Renewal, 1901–2001*, edited by Vinson Synan, 233–64. Nashville: Thomas Nelson, 2001.

"In U.S., Decline of Christianity Continues at Rapid Pace." Pew Research Center. Last modified October 17, 2019. https://www.pewforum.org/2019/10/17/in-u-s-decline-of-christianity-continues-at-rapid-pace/.

Jaschik, Scott. "The Evolution of American Women's Studies." Inside Higher Ed. https://www.insidehighered.com/news/2009/03/27/evolution-american-womens-studies.

"Jemima Wilkinson: American Religious Leader." *Encyclopædia Britannica*. https://www.britannica.com/biography/Jemima-Wilkinson.

Jones, Ellen. "From Mammy to Ma: Hollywood's Favourite Racist Stereotype." BBC Culture. https://www.bbc.com/culture/article/20190530-rom-mammy-to-ma-hollywoods-favourite-racist-stereotype.

Journals of Gender, Women's, Feminist, and Sexuality Studies. National Women's Studies Association. https://www.nwsa.org/page/journals.

Kelley, Mary. *Learning to Stand and Speak: Women, Education, and Public Life in America's Republic.* Chapel Hill: The University of North Carolina Press, 2006.

Kelly, Bridget Turner. "Though More Women Are on College Campuses, Climbing the Professor Ladder Remains a Challenge." *Brookings* (blog), March 29, 2019. https://www.brookings.edu/blog/brown-center-chalkboard/2019/03/29/though-more-women-are-on-college-campuses-climbing-the-professor-ladder-remains-a-challenge/.

Kesslen, Ben. "Aunt Jemima Brand to Change Name, Remove Image That Quaker Says Is 'Based on a Racial Stereotype.'" *NBC News*, June 17, 2020. https://www.nbcnews.com/news/us-news/aunt-jemima-brand-will-change-name-remove-image-quaker-says-n1231260.

Kessler-Harris, Alice, and Nick Juravich. "Seeking Women's Rights: Colonial Period to the Civil War." *EdX Courses*. Columbia University. https://www.edx.org/course/seeking-womens-rights-colonial-period-to-the-civil.

King, Gilbert. "The Incredible Disappearing Evangelist." Smithsonian.com. https://www.smithsonianmag.com/history/the-incredible-disappearing-evangelist-572829/.

LaFrance, Adrienne. "The Weird Familiarity of 100-Year-Old Feminism Memes." *Atlantic*, October 26, 2016. https://www.theatlantic.com/technology/archive/2016/10/pepe-the-anti-suffrage-frog/505406/.

"Leadership and Members." Women's Service League. http://womensserviceleague.org/about/leadership-and-members.

Lee, Morgan. "John MacArthur No Stranger to Controversy." *Christianity Today*, October 23, 2019. https://www.christianitytoday.com/ct/2019/october-web-only/john-macarthur-beth-moore-controversy.html.

Lewis, Helen. "To Learn about the Far Right, Start with the 'Manosphere.'" *Atlantic*, August 7, 2019. https://www.theatlantic.com/international/archive/2019/08/anti-feminism-gateway-far-right/595642/.
"Liberal Feminism." *Stanford Encyclopedia of Philosophy*. https://plato.stanford.edu/entries/feminism-liberal/.
"Lilith." *New World Encyclopedia*. https://www.newworldencyclopedia.org/entry/lilith.
Lindley, Susan Hill. *"You Have Stept Out of Your Place": A History of Women and Religion in America*. Louisville, KY: Westminster John Knox, 1996.
"Livermore, Harriet (1788–1868)." Encylopedia.com. March 1, 2021. https://www.encyclopedia.com/women/encyclopedias-almanacs-transcripts-and-maps/livermore-harriet-1788-1868.
Lunsford, Andrea, et al., "Visual Analysis." In *Everyone's an Author*, 256–61. 3rd ed. London: W.W. Norton and Company, 2018.
MacHaffie, Barbara J. *Her Story: Women in Christian Tradition*. 2nd ed. Minneapolis: Fortress, 2006.
"Main Tenets of Third World Feminist Theories." Auwanthology. https://sites.google.com/site/anthologyauw/non-fiction/bonus-articles/main-tenets-of-third-world-feminist-theories.
"Mary Daly, Controversial Feminist Theologian." Thought.co. https://www.thoughtco.com/mary-daly-3529079#:~:text=In%20February%202001%2C%20Boston%20College.her%20professorship%20there%20in%202001.
"Mary Daly." Freedom from Religion Foundation. https://ffrf.org/news/day/dayitems/item/14879-mary-daly.
"Mary Daly." Liberation Theologies: Online Library and Reference Center. https://liberationtheology.org/people-organizations/mary-daly/.
"Mary Daly, Profile." LGBTQ Religious Archives Network. https://lgbtqreligiousarchives.org/profiles/mary-daly.
"Mary Daly, Quite Contrary." *Irish Times*, February 28, 2021. https://www.irishtimes.com/culture/mary-daly-quite-contrary-1.220486.
"Mary Wollstonecraft." Biography. https://www.biography.com/scholar/mary-wollstonecraft.
Masci, David, and Michael Lipka. "Where Christian Churches, Other Religions Stand on Gay Marriage." Pew Research Center. Last modified December 21, 2015. https://www.pewresearch.org/fact-tank/2015/12/21/where-christian-churches-stand-on-gay-marriage/.
May, James M. "Ethos and Ciceronian Oratory." In *Trials of Character: The Eloquence of Ciceronian Ethos*, 1–12. Chapel Hill and London: University of North Carolina Press, 1998.
McElroy, Wendy. "Individualist Feminism: The Lost Tradition." Independent Institute, August 1, 1998. https://www.independent.org/news/article.asp?id=16.
Mihesuah, Devon A. *Cultivating the Rosebuds: The Education of Women at the Cherokee National Female Seminary, 1851–1909*. Urbana: University of Illinois Press, 1998.
Mill, John Stuart. *The Subjection of Women*. The Gutenberg Project, 2008. https://www.gutenberg.org/files/27083/27083-h/27083-h.htm
Miller, Jonette O'Kelley. "Zilpha Elaw." *Charisma Magazine*. https://www.charismamag.com/site-archives/24-uncategorised/9614-zilpha-elaw.
Moraga, Cherríe, and Gloria Anzaldua, eds. *This Bridge Called My Back: Writings by Radical Women of Color*. Watertown, MA: Persephone, 1981.

Mowczko, Marg. "Women Church Leaders in the New Testament." *Marg Mowczko* (blog), July 28, 2010. https://margmowczko.com/new-testament-women-church-leaders/.

Murray, Judith Sargent. *On the Equality of the Sexes*. Penn Libraries, 1790. https://digital.library.upenn.edu/women/murray/equality/equality.html.

"National Association Opposed to Woman Suffrage." National Women's History Museum. http://www.crusadeforthevote.org/naows-opposition.

"Normal School." Brittanica.com. https://www.britannica.com/topic/normal-school.

Norton, Mary Beth. *Liberty's Daughters: The Revolutionary Experience of American Women 1750–1800*. Ithaca, NY: Cornell University Press, 1980.

"Ontology." *Oxford Languages Dictionary*. https://languages.oup.com/google-dictionary-en/.

Petchesky, Rosalind Pollack. "Fetal Images: The Power of Visual Culture in the Politics of Reproduction." In *Theorizing Feminism: Parallel Trends in the Humanities and Social Sciences*, edited by Anne C. Herrmann and Abigail J. Stewart, 416–42. 2nd ed. Boulder, CO: Westview, 2001.

"Phyllis Schlafly." Encyclopedia.com. https://www.encyclopedia.com/people/history/us-history-biographies/phyllis-schlafly.

"Post-colonial Theory." *Stanford Encyclopedia of Philosophy*. https://plato.stanford.edu/entries/colonialism/#PosColThe.

"Postmodernism." *Britannica*. https://www.britannica.com/topic/postmodernism-philosophy.

"Postmodernism." *Stanford Encyclopedia of Philosophy*. https://plato.stanford.edu/entries/postmodernism/.

"Radical Feminism." *Stanford Encyclopedia of Philosophy*. https://plato.stanford.edu/entries/feminist-philosophy/#:~:text=In%20the%20mid%2D1800s%20the.rights%20for%20women%20obased%20on.

Ritchie, Hilary. "Zilpha Elaw: Sanctifying Power." CBE International, March 5, 2014. https://www.cbeinternational.org/resource/article/mutuality-z-magazine/zilpha-elaw-sanctifying-power.

Ritchie, Joy, and Kate Ronald. *Available Means: An Anthology of Women's Rhetorics*. Pittsburg: University of Pittsburg Press, 2001.

Rogers, Mary F. *Contemporary Feminist Theory*. Boston: McGraw-Hill, 1998.

Roiphe, Katie. *The Morning After: Sex, Fear, and Feminism*. Amazon Synopsis. Boston: Back Bay, 1994.

"Rosemary Radford Ruether." Claremont School of Theology. https://cst.edu/academics/faculty/rosemary-radford-ruether/.

Ruelas, Abraham. *Women and the Landscape of American Higher Education: Wesleyan Holiness and Pentecostal Founders*. Eugene, OR: Pickwick, 2010.

Ruether, Rosemary Radford. *Sexism and God-Talk: Toward a Feminist Theology*. Boston: Beacon, 1993.

Russell, Letty M., and J. Shannon Clarkson, eds. *Dictionary of Feminist Theologies*. Louisville, KY: Westminster John Knox, 1996.

Schmidt, Laura. "Using Archives: A Guide to Effective Research." Society of American Archivists. https://www2.archivists.org/usingarchives.

"The Second Wave of Feminism." *Britannica*. https://www.britannica.com/topic/feminism/The-second-wave-of-feminism.

Seltzer, Madeleine, and Janis Tran. "The Power of Controlling Images." *Honors Journal*, November 7, 2018. University of Colorado. https://www.colorado.edu/honorsjournal/2018/11/07/power-controlling-images.

Serano, Julia. "Trans Feminism: There's no Conundrum about It." *Ms.*, April 18, 2012. https://msmagazine.com/2012/04/18/trans-feminism-theres-no-conundrum-about-it/.

Smith, Sharon. "Black Feminism and Intersectionality." *International Socialist Review* 91 (2016). https://isreview.org/issue/91/black-feminism-and-intersectionality.

"Social Constructionism." Open Education Sociology Dictionary. https://sociologydictionary.org/social-constructionism/#definition_of_social_constructionism.

Sommers, Christina Hoff. "Fact Checking 'Mrs. America.'" *Washington Examiner*, June 5, 2020. https://www.aei.org/articles/fact-checking-mrs-america/.

Stack, Peggy Fletcher. "40 Years after Her Mormon Excommunication, ERA Firebrand Sonia Johnson Salutes Today's 'Wonderful' Women, Says Men 'Bore Her.'" *Salt Lake Tribune*, January 18, 2019. https://www.sltrib.com/religion/2019/01/18/years-after-her-mormon/.

"Standpoint Theory." *Britannica*. https://www.britannica.com/topic/standpoint-theory.

Stanley, Susie C. *Holy Boldness: Women Preachers' Autobiographies and the Sanctified Self*. Knoxville: The University of Tennessee Press, 2002.

Steinhilber, Haley. "Harriet Livermore: 'A Stranger and Pilgrim.'" Brethren Historical Library and Archives. https://www.brethren.org/bhla/hiddengems/harriet-livermore-a-stranger-and-pilgrim/.

Stone, Lucy. "The Progress of Fifty Years." In *The Congress of Women: Held in the Woman's Building, World's Columbian Exposition, Chicago, U.S.A., 1893*, edited by Mary Kavanaugh Oldham, 58–61. Chicago: Monarch, 1894. https://digital.library.upenn.edu/women/eagle/congress/stone-lucy.html.

St. Pierre, Elizabeth Adams. "Poststructural Feminism in Education: An Overview." *Qualitative Studies in Education* 13.5 (2000) 477–515.

"Subaltern." Encyclopedia.com. https://www.encyclopedia.com/social-sciences-and-law/political-science-and-government/military-affairs-nonnaval/subaltern.

Suggs, M. Jack, et al. *Oxford Study Bible: Revised English Bible with the Apocrypha*. Oxford: Oxford University Press, 1992.

"Third Wave and Queer Feminist Movements." Unit V in *Introduction to Women Gender Sexuality Studies*. Lumen Learning. https://courses.lumenlearning.com/suny-introwgss/chapter/third-wave-and-queer-feminist-movements/.

"Third Wave of Feminism." *Britannica*. https://www.britannica.com/topic/feminism/The-third-wave-of-feminism.

"Thomas Jefferson." History.com. https://www.history.com/topics/us-presidents/thomas-jefferson.

"Thomas Jefferson and the Virginia Statute for Religious Freedom." Virginia Museum of History and Culture. https://www.virginiahistory.org/collections-and-resources/virginia-history-explorer/thomas-jefferson.

Tong, Rosemary, and Tina Fernandes Botts. *Feminist Thought: A Comprehensive Introduction*. 5th ed. New York: Westview, 2018.

"Transcript of the Trial of Anne Hutchinson, 1637." Bedford St. Martins. http://bcs.bedfordstmartins.com/WebPub/history/mckayunderstanding1e/0312668872/

Primary_Documents/US_History/Transcript%20of%20the%20Trial%20of%20 Anne%20Hutchinson.pdf.

"Ursuline." Brittanica.com. https://www.britannica.com/topic/Ursulines.

Valoy, Patricia. "Transnational Feminism: Why Feminist Activism Needs to Think Globally." Everyday Feminism. https://everydayfeminism.com/2015/01/why-we-need-transnational-feminism/.

Votaw, Clyde Weber. "Martyrs for the English Bible." *The Biblical World* 52.3 (1918) 296–99.

Warhol-Down, Robyn, et al., eds. *Women's Worlds: The McGraw-Hill Anthology of Women's Writing*. Boston: McGraw-Hill Education, 2008.

Welch, Kristen, and Abraham Ruelas. *The Role of Female Seminaries on the Road to Social Justice for Women*. Eugene, OR: Wipf & Stock, 2015.

———. *"Women with the Good News": The Rhetorical Heritage of Pentecostal Holiness Women Preachers*. Cleveland, TN: Centre for Pentecostal Theology, 2010.

Welch, Kristen. *Deep Roots: Defining the Sacred through the Voices of Pentecostal Holiness Women Preachers*. Kindle, 2013.

———. "The Female Seminary and the Rise of Social Justice for Women." *Annual Papers for the Society of Pentecostal Studies*, 2012. http://sps-usa.org/meetings/past-meetings.

———. "The Holy Spirit and Corderian Ethos." *Annual Papers for the Society for Pentecostal Studies*, 2008. http://sps-usa.org/meetings/past-meetings.

———. "Legacy as Techne in the Rhetorics of Women Preachers." *Annual Papers for the Society of Pentecostal Studies*, 2011. http://sps-usa.org/meetings/past-meetings.

———. "Post 1960's Pentecostalism and the Promise of a Future for Pentecostal Holiness Women Preachers." *Cyberjournal for Pentecostal-Charismatic Research* 16 (January 2007). n.p. http://www.pctii.org/cyberj/table.html.

———. "Preaching in the 'Open Air': The Ministries of Early Women Preachers in Oklahoma." *The Chronicles of Oklahoma* 88.3 (Fall 2010) 316–33.

———. "Rhetoric, Religion, and Authority: Pentecostal Holiness Women Preachers Speaking Truth." *Priscilla Papers*. 24.4 (Autumn 2010) 11–16.

"What Does Intersectional Feminism Really Mean?" International Women's Development Agency. https://iwda.org.au/what-does-intersectional-feminism-actually-mean/.

Williams, Delores S. *Sisters in the Wilderness: The Challenge of Womanist God-Talk*. New York: Orbis, 1993.

Wolff, Kristina. "Psychoanalytic Feminism." Abstract. Wiley Online Library. https://onlinelibrary.wiley.com/doi/abs/10.1002/9781405165518.wbeosp115#:~:text =Psychoanalytic%20feminism%20is%20a%20theory.deep%20within%20the%20 human%20psyche.

"Women and the Law." Women, Enterprise, and Society. https://www.library.hbs.edu/hc/wes/collections/women_law/.

"Women in Religion: Leader of the Shakers." History of American Women. https://www.womenhistoryblog.com/2008/12/ann-lee.html.

"Women in the Medieval Church." Christian History Institute. https://christianhistoryinstitute.org/magazine/article/women-in-medieval-church-a-gallery-of-christian-women-writers-of-the-medieval-world.

"Women's Christian Temperance Union." History.com. https://www.history.com/topics/womens-history/womans-christian-temperance-union.

"The Women's Rights Movement, 1848–1917." History, Art, and Archives. https://history.house.gov/Exhibitions-and-Publications/WIC/Historical-Essays/No-Lady/Womens-Rights/.

Woody, Thomas. *A History of Women's Education in the United States.* Volumes 1 and 2, New York: Octagon, 1966.

Wright, Lawrence. "Are Men Necessary?" Texas Monthly, February 1992. https://www.texasmonthly.com/articles/are-men-necessary/#:~:text=%E2%80%9CWhy%20have%20any%20men%20at.Only%20female%20offspring%20are%20produced.

"Your 2020 Feminist Events Calendar." Visible Women. https://www.stylist.co.uk/visible-women/feminist-events-suffrage-suffragette-centenary-london-manchester/184920.

Zikmund, Barbara Brown. "Women Leaders in Mainline Protestant Churches." In *Religious Leadership: A Handbook,* edited by Sharon Henderson Callahan, 287–96. Los Angeles: Sage, 2013.

www.ingramcontent.com/pod-product-compliance
Lightning Source LLC
Chambersburg PA
CBHW050845230426
43667CB00012B/2157